Prisoner of the Gestapo

Prisoner of the Gestapo

Tom Firth

Pen & Sword
MILITARY

First published in Great Britain in 2010 by
Pen & Sword Military
an imprint of
Pen & Sword Books Ltd
47 Church Street
Barnsley
South Yorkshire
S70 2AS

ISBN 978-1-84884-206-9

Typeset in 11pt Ehrhardt by
Mac Style, Beverley, E. Yorkshire

Printed and bound in the UK by CPI

Pen & Sword Books Ltd incorporates the imprints of Pen & Sword Aviation,
Pen & Sword Maritime, Pen & Sword Military, Wharncliffe Local History,
Pen and Sword Select, Pen and Sword Military Classics and Leo Cooper.

For a complete list of Pen & Sword titles please contact
PEN & SWORD BOOKS LIMITED
47 Church Street, Barnsley, South Yorkshire, S70 2AS, England
E-mail: enquiries@pen-and-sword.co.uk
Website: www.pen-and-sword.co.uk

Dedication

I would like to dedicate this book to the memory of the steadfast and staunch Polish people, many friends and especially those who so selflessly risked freedom and life, sheltering British prisoners of war. I feel this has been a much overlooked area and trust this book does in some measure remedy this.

Acknowledgements

My thanks to my wife Gillian for her unwavering support, Lorraine Wilson for processing the manuscript, and Henry Wilson of Pen & Sword Books, who steered the book through its final stages.

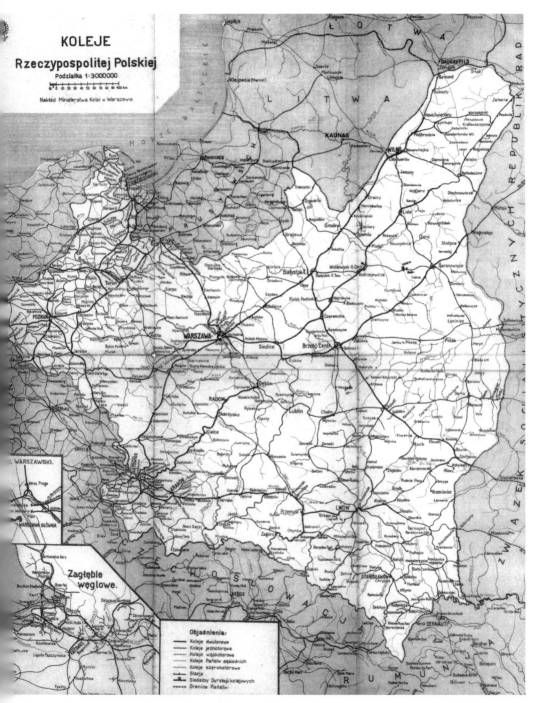

Map of Poland in the 1930s.

Chapter One

'Tomorrow morning you will be shot!'

These mind-numbing words, barked out in German, shook me to the core as I was hustled unceremoniously into Cell 152 in Montelupich Prison.

On that freezing afternoon in March 1942, clad in a single blanket, with crude wooden clogs on my bare feet, I felt I stood on the brink of a precipice – the end of my life in this world.

In that long hot summer of 1939 Europe stood on the brink, not that I concerned myself much about it, for as a sixteen and a half year old lad there were more immediate things to think about. We were in the last three weeks of the summer break and were all set for our departure to Eastern Poland. This holiday, which my old friend Jurek and I had planned for weeks, was finally coming to fruition. It was to be a boating holiday. My father had succumbed to my pleas to purchase an abandoned kayak which had been languishing in a boathouse by the Vistula, and when the deal was struck and the boat was ours, Jurek and I spend hours of devoted labour refurbishing it, giving it a lick of paint and even running up a sail on an old Singer sewing machine.

My father, whose import-export business required him to travel to England in August of 1939, was on the point of leaving Warsaw, where we had lived since 1930, taking with him my older brother George who, having finished school, was about to enter upon a new life in England and take up studies in naval architecture – or so he had hoped. My brother and I made an odd pair of 'foreigners' in our Polish school, George in his stoical manner managing to do rather better than I did. All in all we blended into our life at school painlessly, learned the language well and over the years made a number of firm and lasting friendships. How I envied George at that moment. However I realized that my turn would come, as I daydreamed the time away on many an occasion. I thought of joining the Army. Perhaps one of the Regiment of Guards – I had the height – or the Royal Tank Corps. It was definitely a toss-up between the two and I guess the tanks would have won because of my insatiable interest in anything that moved by internal combustion. George, in the meantime, armed with a letter of introduction personally written by no less than HM Ambassador to Poland, Sir William Howard Kennard, arrived at Samuel White Shipbuilders on the Isle of Wight to embark upon his new career straight away.

My parents were completely ill matched both in temperament as well as in their interests. Having met travelling on the Trans-Siberian railway during the

First World War, they were married in Vladivostock in 1917, only to be expelled when the communists in Russia gained control in the wake of the Revolution. They landed in Japan along with hundreds if not thousands of refugees fleeing from the new regime, and it was here, in Tokyo that I first saw the light of day, on 3 January 1922, reputedly the first European baby to grace the Imperial Japanese Hospital with its presence.

As though the flight to Japan was not enough for my parents to cope with, a severe earthquake which shook Tokyo prompted them to move to Yokohama where Father secured a job with the Pearl Insurance Company. However fate dealt a cruel hand when in 1923 a terrible earthquake devastated that city. Providentially, on the fateful day, my father was at home nursing a badly infected leg, having been stung by a jellyfish whilst swimming in the sea. At the same time my mother had decided to visit the town centre on some routine mission.

George and I in the meantime were being cared for by our amah in the 'servants annexe'. It collapsed like a pack of cards, trapping us as well as the amah and cook. The bungalow itself sustained relatively little damage however, Father, horrified at the sight that confronted him, made a desperate attempt at rescuing us from beneath the rubble, to no avail. Eventually, with the help of passers-by, we were all extricated, dazed and shocked, but otherwise none the worse for the experience. In the meantime, Mother, finding herself in the thick of the ruined city and picking her way through the wreckage, somehow found a rickshaw man willing to convey her along the roads which were still passable, full-tilt back home. Even then her journey was cut short and she made the rest of the way on foot.

Normal life in Yokohama was finished and all that remained for the family to do was leave the stricken city. Carrying only hand baggage we made our way to the harbour where amidst scenes of chaos and panic we were taken aboard a Dutch tanker. Having been picked up by one of the ship's lifeboats in the harbour we approached the tanker and, as the boat drew alongside, a crewman hurled me upwards into the arms of an unsuspecting and amazed sailor leaning over the rail. 'Never saw it coming,' were his words. We set sail as an international rescue operation began and in thick fog ran into a flotilla of US destroyers heading at full speed in the direction of Yokohama. According to our Captain Konning, it was a very close shave. We landed at Kobe, there to start a new life all over again. One wonders how my parents put up with all this. In Kobe we first lived in lodgings, then moved into a rented Japanese bungalow. Finally, when Father started work with the Rising Sun Petroleum Company, a larger, European-style house was rented in a 'European quarter' of Kobe. Later George and I attended an English Missionary school, the family having settled into a comfortable, pleasant and particularly cosmopolitan lifestyle. But in 1929 my parents made a decision which was to have a profound effect on the family.

In the autumn of that year, my father took four months leave during which we were to travel to Europe, first visiting Poland and then England, as neither of my parents had seen their own parents for many years. Of course, for us two boys this was to be the adventure of a lifetime. A short sea journey saw us at the port of Dairen on the mainland of China, from whence we travelled to Mukden, there to board the Trans-Siberian railway. Vastly fascinating, the train journey to Warsaw lasted over a week, with a brief break in Moscow. But our fascination was tempered by an overriding greyness and unhappiness that was the Russia of those days.

Chapter Two

After years of separation, the meeting with Mother's parents was an aptly moving occasion and during our sojourn in Warsaw we stayed in Grandmother Anna's spacious flat, in the centre of the city. Our time was taken up sightseeing, and visiting old friends and relations in a never-ending procession, but time soon slipped by and it was time to continue our journey to England, by train to Berlin and on to Hamburg. Hamburg was well known to my father as he had spent several years there before the first World War, and his sister Corinne had married a serving German officer. A further round of family gatherings and social visits ensued, ending in our departure to Southampton on board the German liner *City of St Louis*. (By a coincidence this ship of the Hamburg-America Line made news early in the Second World War by attempting to seek a safe haven for several hundred Jewish passengers who were fleeing from Nazi Germany. Tragically, and presumably for political reasons, none of the countries at which the ship called were prepared to accept the refugees with the result that the *City of St Louis* had to return to Germany).

From Southampton our journey ended in London where my father's parents and a sister awaited our arrival. A wonderful and memorable month was spent here in a small hotel with sightseeing trips being the order of the day: the Tower of London, Kew Gardens as well as all the important museums. It was all quite overwhelming and in fact was beginning to have a very unsettling effect on my mother. We moved on to Brighton where my grandparents had settled. Of course Brighton became an instant 'hit' as far as George and I were concerned, although it was well into autumn and many of the usual attractions had closed down. These were happy memories, though. However, it was at this time that my mother decided that she did not wish to return to Japan. Her insistence on this move must have come as a bombshell as far as Father was concerned, turning all their plans upside down, in addition to causing friction between my parents and the beginning of a rift which was never to be healed. Without doubt many hours of heated deliberation must have ensued, with the result that instead of Japan, we returned to Warsaw where we remained. A boarding school in England was considered for the two of us, but a lack of funds prevented that from happening. Instead, we were given intensive coaching lessons in the Polish language as well as other subjects in preparation for our entry to a suitable school in Warsaw. This was eventually accomplished, although not without a good deal of understanding on the part of the school authority.

In the meantime Father struggled with the problem of making a living in an entirely new and unfamiliar situation and the early years in Poland proved to be extremely difficult, causing further parental tensions. To add salt to the wound, Mother's father died shortly afterwards and her mother, who had been devoted to a children's home which she had established in the 1920s, set sail on a fundraising mission to the United States. She died in Chicago in 1932. At this point it is necessary to explain more of her involvement with the aforementioned children's home. Shortly after the 1917 Revolution in Russia, along with a handful of dedicated helpers, including a resident doctor, she set out to rescue Polish children who had become stranded in Soviet Russia, managing, in extremely hazardous conditions, to gather together about 800 children. Having done so she transported them to Vladivostok and then by sea to the safety of Japan. Their journey continued to the United States, where a number of children remained, being taken care of by relatives, and finally across the Atlantic, via France and Germany to Poland. It was in any sense an incredible feat. However they had remained in Japan for some considerable time, their sympathetic hosts providing them with proper shelter and assistance. During this sojourn, my grandmother had established a good relationship with the Japanese, which was to continue in later years. In consequence of this, a friendly rapport existed with the Japanese embassy in Warsaw, my mother also becoming drawn into this interesting association, which in the early war years proved to be unusually helpful to her.

For the first year of our life in Warsaw we lived in Grandmother Anna's flat. Upon her departure to America, however, it had to be given up and we moved into a smaller one in the next street. But as Father's business affairs improved, we were able to move to a pleasant suburb by the River Vistula.

In 1936, George and I visited Brighton where Father's sister Maude lived and in 1938 we paid an interesting visit to Hamburg where Aunt Corrine lived with her daughter Irene. But the time of peace was running out.

The summer of 1939 was yet another watershed in our lives. George's departure to England made me more restless and determined to finish school at the end of the next term, and follow in his footsteps. In August, my mother had planned to spend a short holiday in western Poland with an old family friend, whereas Jurek, my school chum and I were busily stowing our kayak into the luggage car of the train which was to take us to eastern Poland. In effect, our family had become completely split up and in the excitement of the moment, I could never have anticipated this state of affairs to remain so for ever. Somehow we never gave much thought to the impending war.

Chapter Three

Our rail journey lasted all night and on our arrival at Slonim in the early hours, we manhandled our kayak onto the station platform. Stowing our belongings into it we carried it across a meadow, setting it onto the waters of a narrow river. Our efforts had not been in vain, for our kayak looked good in its gleaming coat of white paint. We paddled upstream for about 2 miles until we reached the great lake at Albertyn. This was our destination, for Jurek's uncle Vacek and aunt Maria lived in the village nearby, and we were to stay with them for the remainder of our school holiday. Jurek knew the area well having visited it on several occasions. Albertyn was a sleepy village nestling on a gentle slope with a dirt road running through it, one end of which disappeared over the brow of the hill, the other end crossing the same railway line along which we had recently travelled. As insignificant as Albertyn was, it did have a flourishing wood mill which provided employment for most of its inhabitants. The mill stood no more than a third of a mile down the road on the other side of the railway track. Here too was our lake to which we repaired each morning carrying the kayak on our shoulders, ready for the day's sailing. These were truly idyllic and carefree moments, with the new school term seemingly light years away!

Then one day a letter from George arrived describing his impressions of London, how trenches were being dug in Hyde Park and anti-aircraft gun emplacements were being prepared, and yet as serious as the situation obviously was, I tried not to read too much into it. Maybe there wouldn't be a war after all. But every evening on his return from work at the mill, Vacek would sit down in grim silence and read the newspaper. 'Things seem to be getting worse by the day,' he would say thoughtfully. Hitler was ranting against the Poles again. 'Soviet Foreign Minister, Molotov, to fly to Berlin,' the Soviet Foreign Minister announced in the headlines.

One tranquil afternoon, having ended our day's sailing, Jurek and I sat on the edge of the lake idling away the time, when we heard the steady drone of an aircraft flying directly overhead. An aircraft in these parts was almost an unheard of occurrence, so we screwed our eyes upwards, barely able to see the plane heading on a westerly course at a great height. There was something strangely sinister about it, as though it was not meant to be seen. 'There he goes,' Jurek remarked casually. But he was right. It was indeed Molotov in that phantom plane and his meeting with Hitler in Berlin subsequently sealed Poland's fate for years to come.

Vacek became increasingly nervous as each news bulletin on the radio painted a blacker picture of the situation, and with it the stark realization that there was no hope for peace now. We were also told that the beginning of the new school term was being postponed for two weeks. On 1 September, Warsaw Radio broadcast news of the Nazi invasion of Poland. From that moment we remained glued to the set and suddenly I thought of my mother. She was in western Poland and would find herself right in the firing line! (Unbeknown to me, however, she had already returned to Warsaw.)

Our tranquil days on the lake were at an end and in the next few days trainloads of army conscripts rumbled through Albertyn on their way to the war which was raging in the west of Poland. It was a sad but stirring sight which had an unsettling effect on Jurek and myself. We both had serious thoughts of joining up, but Jurek's uncle Vacek and aunt Maria would not hear of it. On 3 September, the radio announced Britain's declaration of war on Germany and I was overcome by a wave of pride and excitement. The following day a telegram arrived requesting Jurek's immediate return to Warsaw. The message was from his scoutmaster and so, as a troop leader in the Scouts, Jurek had no option but to go. This left me in a confused state of mind, with both Vacek and Maria urging me to stay and wait to see what might happen. Further news broadcasts on Warsaw radio now barely concealed the gravity of the situation and when the steady encirclement of the city by the Germans commenced, all hope was abandoned. The Polish forces were unable to stop the relentless onslaught, especially the continuous and indiscriminate aerial bombardment, and presently all radio broadcasts came to an end. Suddenly, eight days after his departure, Jurek reappeared, exhausted and in a state of shock. He explained how all civic and military authorities had been ordered to leave the city almost on the day he had reached Warsaw, so that there was little else he could do but join in the mass exodus. The British embassy staff had left the premises on Nowy Swiat in a convoy of cars, taking the only escape route available to Romania, along with tens of thousands heading in that direction. Constantly harassed by the Luftwaffe, the British Military Attaché's wife, Mrs Shelley was seriously wounded. Jurek had managed to clamber on board the last train due to head east and away from the battle zone, and with all authority dissipated, it was left to the engine driver to decide what to do next! Crammed to capacity with civilians and service personnel, the train made slow and fitful progress as it came under attack from the dreaded Stuka dive-bombers, eventually grinding to a halt. Luckily, Jurek discovered an army truck which happened to be travelling in the general direction of Slonim, after which he was obliged to complete his journey to Albertyn on foot.

With the country now in a state of disintegration and with the cessation of radio broadcasts, we had to rely on fragmented news carried by passing refugees. Otherwise, Albertyn remained unaffected. But all that changed one day when a gathering of worried local inhabitants in the road outside prompted Jurek and I to join in. There were also six stalwart village policemen armed with rifles. There was subdued deliberation and conversation concerning the situation and much shaking of heads. The general mood was one of fear and apprehension.

In the meantime, on the far side of the railway track and well within our view, a volunteer group of aircraft spotters had perched themselves on top of a high stack of railway sleepers from whence they had kept up a daily vigil – enthusiastic, yet at the same time bored with the frustration of scanning the skies, up till now, at any rate, singularly devoid of enemy aircraft. Their perch afforded them a clear view of the countryside and a direct view up and down the railway line. By a mere chance, I turned around and, looking in the direction where the road disappeared over the brow of the hill, caught sight of an aircraft cutting across a gap in the trees, followed by many others in a silent and sinister procession, for the sound of their engines could not be heard. Practically choking with excitement, I managed to yell a warning. Fifteen aircraft were counted heading east, we guessed, to the large town of Baranowicze. Within a second Albertyn was charged with a high level of excitement. Stan, the burly Police Sergeant, rushed into the police station in order to telephone a warning to Baranowicze of the approaching raiders. It was a guess, but as good as any. Then I pondered: the enemy having completed their bombing raid would obviously head west and make a run for home using the railway line as a perfect visual guide. That being so, it meant that they would pass directly overhead. This was pure Biggles stuff! I tested my theory with Stan, whose face lit up in a broad grin. 'Dammit you could be right at that,' he said, warming to the idea with everyone else joining in agreement. Now was the time for action! Ordering all onlookers to take cover, he and his men straddled the road and faced the railway line with guns at the ready. Jurek and I begged him to let us use a couple of rifles but there were none to spare so, determined not to miss a thing, we stood right behind them. Faces peered nervously from behind curtains, cottages and fences as we waited. Apart from the occasional murmured voices, there was an eerie silence. A rough calculation suggested that if anything was to happen it would be in the next half hour. Minutes dragged by and still we waited. On top of their perch, our 'eyes', the plane spotters, were on full alert, eagerly searching the eastern skies through binoculars, as we impatiently awaited their signal. Imperceptibly, what with the waiting and the heat of the midday sun, the keen edge of concentration became somewhat blunted. Then suddenly there was a sound like thunder, the thunderous roar of engines, and there they were, right on top of us before anyone realized it, flying so low and so fast that it took one's breath away. As the first Dornier shot by skimming the telegraph poles lining the railway track, we had time to see the nose gunner, hunched in the plane's perspex nose dome, firing his machine gun in our direction. All hell broke loose. With sweat streaming down their faces, the six policemen fired at random at anything that moved. Then more machine-gun fire and a concerted broadside from our men as they got their act together, picking out a single aircraft at a time, and then another. 'Come on, let's get the swine!' shouted Stan. But, it was all over in a matter of seconds and as suddenly as they had appeared, so they had vanished. People emerged from their hiding places, excitedly discussing the event, and whilst Albertyn had thankfully come through it unscathed, I had the satisfaction of knowing that my theory had proved correct – Stan and his men had the proud claim to have actually left their mark on two of the aircraft. In the meanwhile, the spotters re-emerged from behind the pile of railway sleepers ruffled and bemused, having been completely taken by surprise by the low-flying raiders. Jurek, who had experienced far worse than this during his harrowing return to Albertyn, was convinced that the Germans would not let even this modest sign of resistance go by without retaliation, which could well mean a return visit by the raiders. His words were greeted with horror and dismay. There was nothing to be done now but wait and see. As minutes turned to hours, there was no sign of the enemy and everyone began to breathe more easily. Luck was on our side.

As fleeing refugees streamed through Albertyn, we learned that the Germans were now approaching the town of Wolkowysk, 35 miles to our west, but as an accurate assessment of the situation was impossible we had to take it for granted. This was disturbing news in itself and yet Poland's agony was far from over. A decision would have to be made immediately if we were to avoid falling into the hands of the Germans. Vacek and Maria saw no alternative but for Jurek and I to leave as soon as possible. We then studied a map and came to the conclusion that since Romania was too distant, the route north to Lithuania appeared to offer at least a fighting chance. To my intense annoyance I remembered that I did not have my passport with me since there had been no need for me to do so. Now there was nothing to be done about it but take our chances.

We set out early on the grey morning of 17 September with the first signs of autumn beginning to show. Even the heavens were sorrowing for Poland. Vacek and Maria had sacrificed their two bicycles in order to allow us to make our bid without them our chances would have been nil. Maria had prepared a small food parcel but we had nothing in the way of warm clothing at all. Consulting Jurek's ordnance map, we pressed on all that morning following footpaths, crossing fields and finding our way through forests. Speed was of the essence but the going was hard and slower than we had anticipated as there were no proper roads, and the odd stretches we had to follow were unmade and deeply rutted. All the while we hadn't come across a living soul save for a solitary peasant trying to coax along his steaming nag and cart. Later on we followed a wide sward which scythed its way across country and through forests for miles like an abandoned projected highway, which was in fact the Trakt Napoleonski, a creation of Napoleon's sappers enabling his armies to progress in reasonable comfort during their abortive Russian campaign. However, this relative luxury did not last for long and we were obliged to take to the impossibly difficult sandy paths again, eventually reaching signs of habitation and a reasonable footpath. To our surprise a cyclist approached pedalling for all he was worth. On drawing level with us he pulled up with a screech of brakes, breathless and shaking like a leaf.

'God! The Russians are coming in from the east and the Germans from the west. What is there to do?' he blurted and and without further ado took off again like a man possessed by the devil. For a moment we stood rooted to the spot wondering whether the man had taken leave of his senses, but with growing unease recalled hearing the distant rumble of artillery fire somewhere to our east earlier in the morning. It was brief but unmistakeable and we began to wonder if there was indeed credibility in the cyclist's outburst. With that depressing thought we pressed on along a path leading through a dense wood and, finally emerging from it, found ourselves standing on a high escarpment overlooking flat country stretching for miles in front of us. In the middle distance of this panorama, a highway ran at an angle as straight as a die. As we stood admiring the view we realized that the highway was in fact teeming with humanity. There must have been thousands of souls moving slowly in an easterly direction, but a closer look revealed an equal mass moving in the opposite direction, westward, resulting in chaos. Then on further observation we noted the presence of several stationary tanks on the road. As something of an amateur buff on tank recognition I was convinced they were Russian. We stood wondering what to do next and whether our chance of escape was now doomed to failure. Could we make it to the Lithuanian border before the Russians got there? In the end we decided to carry on until nightfall and Jurek, who was familiar with the area, said he knew of a good place where we could spend the night. Our immediate problem was that in order to get there we had to follow the highway for about a mile before turning off into the desired direction, a prospect which did not appeal to us at all, but we had no option. The descent from the escarpment was in itself an acrobatic feat which we managed without hurting ourselves or our bikes, and upon reaching the highway joined the thousands plodding steadily westward. There was no way in which the tanks could be avoided so we concluded the best thing to do was to try and get past them as quickly as possible. This was easier said than done. There was now no doubting their identity – their Russian crews appeared to be milling about brandishing revolvers in a belligerent fashion and were obviously in a state of tension. We forced our way through this bottleneck, suddenly to find ourselves in a vacuum and, too late, realized that approaching steadily from the opposite direction was a column of Polish troops, with us being 'pigs in the middle'. The Russian tanks had their guns trained on the approaching Poles and an obvious confrontation of the two forces seemed imminent. As the way ahead was completely barred we had no option but to wait and see what would happen. Several Russians, with revolvers drawn, then approached the Poles at the same time as a Polish sergeant stepped forward to meet his adversary. Genuinely thinking that the Russians were on their side, he expressed pleasure at their presence and how, with common effort, the Germans could be repelled. But his utterance was one of forlorn hope. One Russian's response was to point his revolver at the Sergeant and demand their surrender. Taken aback, the Sergeant began reasoning with the Russian and as other Russians approached the scene with sub-machine guns aimed at the Poles, the brave Sergeant erupted into a tirade accusing the Russians of treachery. 'You have betrayed us – you have stabbed us in the back and might just as well shoot us all, right now and be finished with it!'

'Listen, we are taking over your country, do you understand? Surrender immediately!' the Russian snarled.

We stood transfixed, listening to all this and realizing the position we were now in, for one shot aimed at the Russians could end in a massacre.

As the Russians closed in the Sergeant gave the order for his troops to drop their weapons, many with tears in their eyes as they obeyed his order. Weary with days of marching and utterly dispirited, this was the final straw. Poland was lost. What we had witnessed was the result of the secret agreement entered into by the Germans and the Russians to carve up Poland. But whereas the former had been unambiguous about its intentions, or relatively so, the Russians had kept quiet, and taken advantage of the situation. The devils were dancing with joy at their conquest!

Forcing our way through this tragic scenario we both felt desperately tired, dispirited and hungry. We turned off the main road as planned and entered a village where a band of men stood on the village green clutching an outsize red flag. As we passed them by they harangued us about the 'gallant Red Army'. Were they far away and had we seen them? They beamed excitedly. Our reply was curt, 'Haven't seen or heard of them.'

'Damned communists!' muttered Jurek.

Later we had the same experience in another village and responded in similar fashion, but with a growing revulsion towards the sort of people who would, it seemed, gladly trade their country to another. The natives of this eastern province of Poland of Byelorus, or White Russia, spoke a dialect I could barely comprehend. Many of them considered themselves to be more Russian than Polish, and resented living under Polish domination.

We were all in by the time we had reached our destination for the night, even the dusk failing to disguise the beauty and sheer tranquillity of the place. Leading the way through a wood, Jurek pointed to a faint light glimmering amongst the trees – it was a forest ranger's dwelling. We knocked on the door and entered. The forest ranger and his wife invited us to sit down and offered us a mug of milk each and some bread which we devoured hungrily. We sat around the large table with an oil lamp throwing deep shadows around the room, but the mood was sombre and little was said. What indeed could one say? We were all in a state of bemused shock. The ranger said that we were welcome to spend the night in the barn if we could find ourselves a space since others had got there before us. However, before turning, in we took a short walk to the edge of a lake and, kneeling down on the end of a wooden jetty, splashed ourselves with its cool clear water.

The ranger could not have spoken a truer word for once inside the barn we kept tripping over reclining bodies at every step in the total blackness, until a space was found high up in the hay loft. In spite of our exhaustion, sleep came fitfully and in our more lucid moments we discussed our next course of action in an undertone, so as not to disturb those asleep around us. All through the night until the early hours there was a relentless grinding of tanks and motorized vehicles moving along a distant road, ever deeper into Polish territory in an endless procession. At this point we could not see a ghost in hell's chance of effecting a border crossing into Lithuania, reasoning that the way things were going the Russians would have sealed it off by the time we got anywhere near it. There was no way of knowing, but in the event we decided on a return to Albertyn whilst we were still within striking distance of it.

Our return journey took a different route but now with every mile the picture worsened. Jubilant young communists careered up and down the roads by the truckload waving triumphant banners and chanting slogans. Tank after tank raced by carrying stolen bicycles, showering us with mud in their headlong rush, whilst elsewhere all the signs of looting were in progress. We were glad to turn off onto a road devoid of all the traffic save for a lone Polish policeman who approached sedately on his bicycle. As if from nowhere a mob suddenly appeared and, pouncing on top of him, dragged him off his bike, forcing him to his knees, and set about beating him, snatching his revolver from him. Yards separated us from this scene and momentarily we were trapped. Then one of the mob approached us demanding to know if we carried any firearms; having satisfied himself that we had none, he returned to the others by which time the poor policeman was heard to be pleading for his life. Later that morning we had to pass by a solitary Russian tank stationary by the roadside and surrounded by a crowd of admirers. Our presence seemed to attract their attention and we were beckoned to join them. They told us that the officer wanted to talk to us and with that we were shoved into the crowd to face the 'officer'. We were in no doubt that had it not been for the officer, things would have been different, but as it was they were on their best behaviour if rather arrogant and obviously wanting to impress the Russian with their allegiance. The 'officer', a tank commander, seemed reasonable enough and was obviously a very tired man. What worried us, however, was that our bikes in the meanwhile had been spirited away somewhere out of sight. A spokesman then demanded to see our identity cards, but the only ones we had were our seasonal railway dockets and these were passed around from hand to hand and carefully scrutinized, although we could tell that most of them were illiterate and hadn't the foggiest idea what they were looking at. The Russians were always inquisitive as to one's origin, background, parents' occupation, education and this kind of detail and the officer proved no exception to the rule. It was part of the system for officialdom to know everything about everyone. Eventually our bikes were returned to us, albeit we noted with considerable reluctance, and we were allowed on our way.

By nightfall we entered a forest with only two or three miles to go before reaching Albertyn and in the gathering darkness it was all I could do to keep up with Jurek's fleeting shadow, as we carried no lights to illuminate the way ahead. Then without warning we found ourselves charging headlong into a mob gathered in the middle of the road. Instantly surrounded, we were grabbed and jostled and questioned regarding our identity and destination. As we tried to explain, hostile voices started calling for our imprisonment, which turned into a chant: 'Lock them up, lock them up!' Others had a better idea demanding that we be handed over to the Red Army. Finally, when the baying abated, a lone voice called for our release saying that there was plenty of time for 'this sort of thing'. Amazingly, 'the voice' elicited several supporters, then suddenly, as though ignited, the two opposing factions became embroiled in a vicious slanging match with the two of us being ignored. Seizing this golden opportunity we edged away from the howling mob and, mounting our bikes, rode like fury into the blanket of darkness. Weaving our way in near pitch-blackness along a barely visible path, avoiding trees and jutting branches which appeared to reach out like evil tentacles, we emerged into a bright moonlit sky and only then felt safe enough to relax our headlong flight. How we managed to do so without a painful tumble I shall never know.

Chapter Four

Vacek and Maria's worries for our safety were allayed, but serious problems loomed large, for we were now faced with a situation no one had ever bargained for. The Soviet occupation of eastern Poland was in full swing, with endless columns of troops and horse-drawn supply wagons making their way through Albertyn. Amazingly they presented a sorry sight and in any terms looking like a rabble army in retreat instead of the much-vaunted 'glorious Red Army' which had in effect marched in without as much as firing a single shot. Even the local cock-a-hoop communists could hardly believe what they were seeing. Jurek and Vacek wept unashamedly at the thought of what was happening to their country. I pondered over my own position, for as a Briton, albeit with no passport to prove my national identity, to all intents I was no better than my good friends, maybe even worse, an enemy alien in the truest sense, as I could only draw the conclusion that as 'allies' of Germany, a state of hostility now existed between Soviet Russia and Britain. In the following days, as the Soviets tightened their grip on the population, so their propaganda increased accordingly. We were told that Poland had been liberated from the clutches of a fascist-bourgeois government and had everything to gain from the communist system, whose enemies had to be destroyed. This hate campaign became unrelenting and totally paranoid. The professional classes, the intelligentsia and the hated bourgeoisie became their prime targets for eradication, for no sooner had the military occupation been accomplished when the dreaded units of the NKVD (KGB) moved in to conduct their iniquitous arrests and mass deportations. It was the age-old Russian method of deporting countless thousands of 'unwanted' sections of the population in the most inhuman of conditions, in overcrowded cattle trucks by rail into the depths of Russia, there hopefully to be forgotten and with luck to perish.

The question remained whether to come out into the open and declare my identity as a British citizen, yet the stubborn fact remained that without my passport I could be in very deep trouble. However, unbeknown to me, diplomatic relations between Britain and Russia still existed, although even had I known, I doubt whether I would have known what to do without outside help. For a seventeen year old, that was a lot to contend with.

It took several months before the resumption of a postal service between the two zones of occupation, and as all mail was severely censored, messages had to be cautious and often circumspect. After many weeks of anxiety, wondering about my mother's safety, both of us received a letter assuring us that all in

Warsaw was well. We were advised to stay put, which meant, 'reading between the lines', that life in Warsaw must have been harrowing. Although border crossings were still possible at that time, whilst the two aggressor countries wrangled over the border details, hundreds if not thousands of refugees who had fled from the Germans had managed to filter through and back to their homes. Nonetheless, risks were considerable since it was the Russians who did their best to prevent this exodus, showing little mercy to those they apprehended. Shades of the Berlin Wall? How my mother managed to remain a 'free' person was a puzzling question since, according to all the rules, as an enemy alien she should have been arrested and sent to an internment camp. She was not alone in this precarious position, as there existed a handful of British and French nationals who had also failed to escape the occupation and still remained largely unmolested, although subsequent events eventually took care of that. In the meantime, I rejoiced at the fact that she still appeared to be free.

Life in Albertyn became grimmer by the week. The wood mill became state property and a new-style works committee consisting of a group of local communists was set up to supervise the work force. Having fled before the advancing Russians, the previous owner's position as director was taken over by a Russian.

The activity of the works committee became, in fact, an extension of the secret police when all employees were vetted for their political reliability, and anyone known to have had any kind of political affiliation, even in the slightest measure, was either fired or arrested. Here Vacek was fortunate. Although he had served in the Polish Army as a conscript in the early 1920s, he had never been involved in 'politics'. As in any small community, it would have been difficult if not impossible to conceal one's political views or allegiances. It was a sinister scenario added to which there were a number of informers with long memories who were only too willing to ingratiate themselves with the new masters. This chilling state of affairs extended to society in general so that one lived in a perpetual state of uncertainty and fear. The Church and clergy then came under attack and gradual elimination, the lie being that the right to worship was guaranteed by the Soviet constitution. The method of elimination was both cunning and simple – or plain crude, such as prohibitively high taxes being levied upon them which were impossible to sustain, resulting in churches having to close down. Worse still hundreds of clergy were accused of anti-state activity and arrested. The churches throughout Eastern Poland thus remained empty, depriving communities of the very stuff which had bonded them for generations. Having achieved their aim, the churches were taken over by the Army and used for storage and stables. It all fitted into the pattern. The sudden disappearance of a colleague at work, the local shop owner or an entire family next door served to create fear on a daily basis. Even entire villages and communities disappeared overnight, an instance we witnessed for ourselves, when an entire housing estate was raided during the night and left bereft of a living soul, like a ghost town. Raids of this sort were always carried out at night by units of the NKVD. The inhabitants were allowed about fifteen minutes to collect whatever they could carry and then marched to the nearest railway station in Slonim, there to be packed like animals into a long line of cattle trucks. The following morning there was panic when news of the raid had spread and friends and relations flocked to the station to see what could be done to help. Armed troops ensured that no one got near the victims. For ten days the train remained on the sidings completely isolated, after which it began on a slow journey somewhere into Russia. It would have been bad enough in mid-summer but this was winter. As far as I knew, no more was ever heard regarding the ultimate fate of these people. A more detailed description of one young man's experience told how he was bundled into a cattle truck packed to capacity. His journey into Russia lasted two weeks, during which time many perished from starvation and exposure. The train would come to a halt occasionally in a remote area where the dead were afforded burial close to the track, but when children perished, the guards would not bother so the only way of disposing of these pathetic little bodies was to push them out of the narrow windows, allowing them to fall into the deep snow outside. The transport ended up in a remote forest area not far from a settlement and, having disgorged from the train, the people were given a few basic tools and told to build their own shelter. At this time they were approached by some of the inhabitants from the settlement who appeared ragged and emaciated in the extreme and begged them for food! The young man said that had he not seen this with his own eyes, he would not have believed that things could be so bad in Soviet Russia. However, he was strong, survived his ordeal and by sheer determination and guile, managed to escape; after wandering for many weeks, he eventually returned to Polish soil.

In this constant climate of fear, it was very much a case of wondering whose turn would come next.

Chapter Five

Christmas 1939 was one of the worst I can remember. Officially it had been abolished, as were the customary titles of address – Pan and Pani (Mr and Mrs). We were now made to address everyone 'comrade' and anyone overheard using the old title was severely admonished. Unofficially, these rules were ignored whenever possible. Those brave enough smuggled home a Christmas tree around which to 'celebrate' the holy day and privately addressed each other in the traditional manner. Friends and relations still continued to drop in for a chat, albeit furtively, and partake of a fast-disappearing stock of alcohol, but even worse was the ever-decreasing stock of food. Shops became empty and what Maria was able to purchase at the butchers in Slonim, if available, proved to be highly suspect – Jurek, having judiciously divided up his diminutive portion of sausage one evening, revealed a cat's claw lurking within it.

In schools, Russian became the official language and a typical manifestation of the prevailing trend came when the caretaker at the Slonim hospital was appointed its director. There was, nonetheless, a humorous side to this whole charade which the Poles quickly seized upon. The occupying troops, as well as their officers, were basically primitive creatures who were totally bemused by their new surroundings – it was true to say that they reflected in every sense the type of society they had sprung from. For years, isolated from the outside world and conditioned – brainwashed by their propaganda to despise and distrust the rest of humanity – they were more than surprised to find that life elsewhere was not as bad as had been painted. Furthermore, it was obvious that they had been well schooled in parroting praises to the Soviet Union and one found that their responses to various questions were absolutely identical and pathetic in their naivety. So, for example, when asked if oranges were grown in Moscow, the reply would be an enthusiastic affirmative. Whatever one cared to name and however ridiculous the question, there was always an abundance of it – everything was just fine. One wag innocently enquired if there was a large supply of Thames water available in Russia to be told that there was plenty of it, although I hasten to stress that I was not the questioner. This form of baiting became a popular pastime at one stage but it did serve to relieve the terrible reality of life under the Soviets. Running tap water and water closets were a never-ending source of wonderment, in their ignorance many mistaking the true purpose of a water closet for a wash basin, the only complaint about it being that when the chain was pulled, so the soap vanished.

Shortly before that first depressing Christmas, Leonie, an old friend of Maria's, paid us a visit. She lived and worked in Slonim but hailed from

Warsaw. She explained how she had managed to make two successful trips to Warsaw, smuggling back goods and provisions unobtainable in the Russian zone with the help of a local man who was familiar with the border area. Obviously she was a resourceful woman. Furthermore, as the border was soon to be sealed off, illegal crossings of this sort would become impossible. She then suggested that if Jurek and I wanted to take the chance she would be prepared to escort us on one final attempt, whereafter she would remain in Warsaw. The idea needed careful consideration. It was easier for one person to cope with the various obstacles which presented themselves than a party of three or more, and certainly safer for a woman than a man, or men. As far as Jurek's mother was concerned, her safety was in no doubt – it was my mother's freedom that hung in the balance. But as there was no time to lose, we decided to go ahead with the plan. These tensions only served to add to the subdued Christmas atmosphere in our household. The broad plan of action was then worked out: our departure was set for New Year's Eve, on the 8.30 train from Albertyn. In order to avoid arousing suspicion we were to book tickets to Slonim which was the next station, and in view of the severe weather and deep snow, was an entirely reasonable thing to do. If questioned with regard to the purpose of our journey, the answer would be 'a visit to relations'. This was the easy part. We would then have to alight at Slonim and make a dash for the ticket office where tickets to Hajnowka would have to be bought, and then get on board the same train again. The mind boggled at the thought of it, however Leonie assured us that it could be done! The main point of the exercise was that whereas we were known at Albertyn, word of our departure to a place as obvious as Hajnowka could soon spread and reach the wrong ears, but in a town like Slonim we would be part of the crowd. The trouble with Hajnowka, however, was that it was a well-known hub for all wanting to effect a crossing to and from the German side, not least to the NKVD. But there was no option. The other aspect to all this was that the NKVD had never been known to be at Albertyn station because of its insignificance and most of our waiting time would be spent there. But although Slonim crawled with these undesirable characters, in theory our time obtaining tickets there would be minimal, or so one hoped. Leonie would arrange to spend the day previous to our departure with a friend in Albertyn and our meeting at Albertyn station would take place half an hour before the train's arrival. We would remain apart as though we did not know each other. The arrangements for the actual border crossing were left in her capable hands.

On the evening of 31 December, we said our farewells to Vacek and Maria and made our way to the station. In order to avoid the centre of the village we decided on a circuitous route over snow-covered fields away from habitation and approached the station from the 'wrong' side of the track, at the same time gaining a clear and unobstructed view of it. Nothing stirred the silence of our progress, save for the steady crunch of the crisp snow underfoot, while the stars glinted brightly above in a blackened firmament begging admiration. If only things had been different we surely would have done just that. We were close enough now to distinguish a solitary figure pacing up and down the station platform, obviously trying to keep out the freezing temperature. It was Leonie. Refraining to seek shelter in the tiny waiting room we too proceeded to march up and down the platform briskly in an effort to keep warm and in passing, Leonie giving only the slightest sign of recognition. However, not being suitably clad to withstand this sort of weather and at the risk of getting frostbite, our resolve weakened and we entered the hut. It was full of peasants wrapped up to the eyeballs and huddled around a wood-burning stove with their tobolki (bundles) spread around the floor, however they showed scant interest in our presence. We stayed there for a while relishing the warmth but soon left, braving the elements once again. Try as we might by stamping our feet and with vigorous arm flapping, realized that we were on a losing wicket. As Leonie continued pacing up and down the length of the platform undaunted, we sneaked back into the hut. It was against the 'rules' and, we were soon to discover, a big mistake.

Minutes ticked by with exasperating slowness as the time of the train's arrival approached. Suddenly a pair of powerful headlights flashed across the window, for a second illuminating the hut's interior, followed by the sound of an approaching vehicle. It jolted its way across the railway line and gradually disappeared into the distance. We knew instinctively that it was an NKVD patrol. Within minutes the door was flung open and a civilian in a long black coat strode in. Crowding the doorway behind him stood several armed troops with fixed bayonets. With piercing eyes the civilian scanned the huddled crowd and, as though choosing the most likely victim, pointed a finger at Jurek, demanding to know where he was going. Taken aback and completely forgetting his lines he blurted out 'Hajnowka'. The damage was done in this instant. He then examined Jurek's old railway pass. 'So, you come from Warsaw? All right, then go to Hajnowka!' The inference was all too obvious. Then, turning to me he demanded to see my 'documents'. 'And you, where are you going?' I reasoned that the two of us would sink or swim together and also replied 'Hajnowka'. At that he grunted and stalked off. His choice for picking on us was obvious, since we looked different to the others crowded in that waiting room.

If we had had our wits about us we should have left the station there and then. Instead we heaved a sigh of relief at his departure, glad not to have been arrested on the spot, which we had fully expected.

The train was now minutes overdue and as we pondered the incident, the door was flung open again and a grotesque character, rifle in hand, entered. Two other armed men stood in the doorway. They were from the local militia, communist civilians acting as police. In a scruffy black coat padded out against the cold so as to make him appear twice his normal size, with thick shapeless *valenki* (felt boots) on his feet, his pock-marked features were half concealed under a dirty flat cap pulled tightly over his ears. He had no hesitation in picking out the two of us, demanded that we hand over our 'documents' and, having pocketed them, ordered us outside. It was clear what had transpired: briefed by the roving NKVD patrol of our presence at the station, it became the job of the local militia to effect our arrest. In the meantime, Leonie, having witnessed everything from outside, beat a hasty retreat. The distance to the police station was short and once inside we were confronted with a Russian. He wore a tall grey fur hat, cocked to one side and eyed us blandly before speaking. He wanted to know everything about us down to the smallest detail, all that was said being laboriously written down by a young militiaman. It was pointless concealing the fact that we wanted to get to Warsaw – they knew that already – but our homes and families were there and that was reason enough. As usual he wanted to know who our parents were and what our fathers (stepfather in Jurek's case) did for a living. As I had no intention of telling the truth, I said that my father worked in an office as a clerk which seemed to satisfy him. On the other hand Jurek's description of his stepfather's employment in a bank caused the Russian to grimace. He was in fact chief cashier in the National Savings Bank (PKO). Our education came under scrutiny as well – what subjects were we taught? We explained the sort of curriculum prevalent in our school but he did not seem satisfied with that answer and then, stressing the point, said that surely we were taught political subjects as well, appearing surprised when told that that was not the case at all. (We were certainly taught about different political systems, types of government etc., as part of our history lessons).

When the questioning ended he searched through our pathetic little bags, turning everything out, examining each item meticulously. Even the small tub of butter Maria had packed was carefully probed with a knife. Secret messages were not to be found within it! If ever there was an example of a police state in action, this was it.

When it was all over we asked to be allowed to catch the train which was now much overdue, but he shook his head beckoning us to sit down on a bench in a far corner of the room. At this point we had no idea what their intentions were. Presently, however, the Russian departed and we were left in the company of two armed militiamen. For all we knew, missing our train would be the least of our worries! Then, sure enough, we heard the sound of the train pulling in to the station and made one final attempt at reasoning with our guards to no avail and our hearts sank as the train drew away a few moments later. Left alone during the night with a young guard who dozed fitfully by the door, we were overcome with the temptation to overpower him and make our escape. Perhaps in other circumstances this would have made sense, but in considering the consequence of such action it made one think again, for their retaliation would then be directed at Vacek and Maria.

The young militiaman finally stirred from his slumber and we talked for a time. He wondered why we should want to return to Warsaw, urging us to stay and enjoy the good life in Russia instead, but when we stressed the fact that our homes and families were there he seemed to understand. He appeared a decent enough fellow even if his politics were sadly misguided.

At first light our pock-marked militiaman arrived with the announcement that we would be on our way to Slonim. Told to march in single file, he positioned himself directly at the rear with his rifle pointing at our backs, whilst another guard followed on at one side with a drawn revolver. We had no illusions that our destination would be the grim NKVD headquarters in Slonim. We trudged the 2½ miles in virtual silence with the occasional gruff reminder to continue walking in single file and not side by side. The going was difficult because of the deeply rutted path covered in snow and icy patches. At the headquarters we were told to wait in a corridor whilst the pock-marked guard shuffled off into an office, leaving us with his comrade. He returned an hour later and, thrusting our 'documents' at us, announced that although they knew very well that we were agent-provocateurs (a favourite accusation), we were free to go, and free to go to Warsaw if we saw fit, but to remember that the Germans would feed us on bread and onions and then shoot us like dogs! He spat out these words with venom, but venom or not, it was like music to our ears and we hurriedly left the wretched place feeling weak at the knees. We cursed ourselves for failing to recognize the danger signs and not taking the precaution of making ourselves scarce from the station whilst the going was good. But the damage was done. We trudged on our way back to Albertyn feeling disconsolate and cheated, and ran into Maria and a friend hastening towards Slonim. Greeting us with tears of relief, she had never expected to see us again when Leonie had alerted her and Vacek as to our fate. Indeed, we were very lucky to have got away with it. However, ever since, the ridiculous suggestion that the humble onion could present a threat to one's diet has never ceased to puzzle and amuse whenever I happen to recall that episode. Maybe it was the militiaman's idea of a joke. But in a way it wasn't far off the mark.

The failure of our venture left us rather more frustrated than bitter and as for herself, Leonie, shaken by the outcome, abandoned further thoughts of a border crossing for the foreseeable future. Nevertheless, the intrepid and determined person that she was, she was not prepared to give up lightly. Having geared ourselves up, Jurek and I now had to come to terms with the possibility of remaining there indefinitely. There were many worrying problems to consider. Vacek and Maria had been selfless in their care for us and our well-being, and a prolonging of this state of affairs could only make life more difficult for them.

Assuredly we would need to have something to do, work of some kind to help ease the burden, and yet Maria, with her protective instinct, urged us to stay at home as much as possible and out of sight of the Russians – a tall order indeed. In the event we spent many days sawing and chopping up logs in the back yard, which were used as fuel for the kitchen range and stacking them in the shed. In the -30° temperature we were enjoying, even this taxed our limits of endurance and by way of a change we took to venturing on long walks into the forests until, for some reason, the Russians put them out of bounds. The supply of water came from a well in the back yard and at these temperatures was usually frozen over, so the ice had to be broken up before the bucket could be filled. This was achieved either by allowing the bucket to drop onto the ice on the end of the winding rope, or failing that with the aid of a long pole. Sanitation was primitive and was provided by an outside toilet of the 'hole-in-the-ground' variety, but at -30°, the sheer torture of it can be imagined. Furthermore, the days when normal toilet paper was available had long since gone, this commodity being substituted with sheets of the communist daily *Pravda*. So even the normally scurrilous *Pravda* had its practical uses. But it had its other uses as well. For each evening, after the meagre evening meal of bread and minuscule portion of sausage or rissoles with potato washed down with a herbal Russian tea, we would sit round the table and, under Vacek's tutelage, try to read *Pravda* and learn the cyrillic alphabet. As much as we all detested its contents we realized that at least some knowledge of the Russian language might stand us in good stead. We passed the long winter evenings reading books from Vacek's extensive library and playing games of draughts and 'warships'. News from the world at large was at a premium. Unlike the Germans, the Russians had failed to confiscate all radio sets, which was out of character with all the other restrictions imposed on the people, nonetheless, in order to avoid trouble, many sets were discarded or hidden to await better times. Vacek steadfastly refused to use his radio despite our pleas. However, what news we gleaned came from our neighbours, an elderly couple who were not afraid to listen in to the BBC foreign news broadcasts.

When the Russians became embroiled in their calamitous campaign in Finland, it gave us heart and hope that some of their venom would be drawn away from Poland, but it was not to be. As tight as ever, surveillance of the population continued now with NKVD patrols visiting homes unannounced, and always in the hours of darkness. No niceties being observed, they simply barged in, as occurred in our case. At that time of the evening a sharp rap on the door was enough to make anyone's heart miss a beat. As usual, we were sitting around the table reading. When Maria answered the door, an officer strode in and sat down beside the table, whilst several armed soldiers stood by the door. He observed everything and everyone for a time in silence before uttering a word. Vacek, in an attempt to break the ice, said something which was answered with a grunt. His interest then centred on Jurek and I. He wanted to know who we were, what we did and where we came from. His demeanour was totally bland. After a further silent observation of the room, he left, remarking how well we lived. When the door had closed behind him Vacek exploded with indignation, 'We live in two rooms and a kitchen and to them that is good living,' then adding, 'You see, I was right about that radio set!'

The type of society the Russians had set about creating was one of equal blandness, even shabbiness. One was simply not expected to 'flaunt' trappings of the hated bourgeoisie such as respectable attire, since the hallmark of a true socialist worker was soiled overalls or coat, as well as a pair of hands to match. In that sense the Russian idea of colour matching could hardly have been flawed. Woe betide anyone who did not conform to that ideal. Since people generally in Poland were so much better dressed than any Russian, they were constantly being stopped and questioned, and most certainly, if you showed a clean pair of hands, you stood to be vilified and rebuked in the street, there and then. It was as insane as that. The upshot of this idiocy was that there was a run on shabby clothes as ordinary folk hastened to acquire this demeaning disguise in order to avoid attention. We both experienced this kind of treatment in Slonim one day for ourselves.

Landowners, property owners and even ordinary house owners came under the special attention of the NKVD, these people being considered as some of the worst 'exploiters' of the masses. Albertyn's own squire, Count Puslowski, had the foresight to flee before the advancing Russians, leaving his beautiful property set on the lakeside to the tender mercies of the Russian Army who stripped it bare, even down to the kitchen wall tiles, carting their loot away by the truckload back to Russia. Ordinary householders were tolerated but also had to pay a price. They were forced to occupy only a small part of their home and had to admit a 'deserving' working-class family to occupy the rest of it, rent free. Smallholdings were forcibly split up and handed out to other 'deserving' cases, the perversity of this move being that the 'grateful' recipients were ordered to grow produce on it which was then collected for the 'common good'. Again, this ruling meant that many recipients were unable to cope, for one or other genuine reason, but that was never taken into account. Failure to produce a required quota resulted in a heavy fine. What it all amounted to was that the entire population was in fact being punished in one way or another.

In Albertyn village hall, in the meanwhile, preparations were afoot for a mass meeting. Advance announcements aimed specifically at the mill workers urged full attendance with no excuses for absence allowed. In order not to compromise Vacek, Jurek and I attended as well and on the declared evening found ourselves in the tightly packed hall. Late arrivals were obliged to remain outside, crowding around the door in the freezing cold. We had little idea what it was all about, inevitably, however, it proved to be a series of political harangues delivered by three Politruks – Political Specialists (Politychiski Rukovodzitiel). At any rate five of them occupied the platform. The first speaker explained the great advantages people derived from the new socialist order and how they had been mercilessly exploited by the previous Polish fascist-bourgeois regime in the past. They would enjoy greater freedom and a plentiful supply of food. In fact, plenty of everything. A never-ending list of statistics was quoted which the Russians were always so fond of in those days. At first greeted with a stony silence, the mood of the audience changed to one of derision and open challenge, which spelt out the question: who are they trying to fool? For all the promises and guarantees had come too late. Having already trampled on all their rights, deprived them of food, imprisoned and deported thousands, they were talking of a good life under Soviet socialism! The only applause came from a bunch of communists ranged along both sides of the hall.

Rattled but undaunted the next speaker, in an expansive and confident manner, took the wider topic of European affairs, the thinly veiled implication being that Soviet Russia had embarked on a drive to liberate the countries of Europe from the evils of capitalism and the bourgeoisie who exploited the working class. Extolling the virtues of Soviet socialism he derided everything else which had in fact created a far better life for its citizens than they themselves ever had. He ranted on to an incredulous audience who, though very ordinary people and anything but highly educated, were anything but stupid. In conclusion to this diatribe of hate and lies, banging his fist on the table, he declared that Soviet Russia would go to war with Germany and when Germany was conquered, would smash France. Finally, they would destroy Britain 'with all its rotten Lords'. The accent, one noticed, was always on the act of destruction. His words were met with a barrage of heckling and derisive laughter which took him aback, causing him to flush. The reaction against this entire farce was so overwhelming that even the communists present were for once struck dumb into an embarrassed silence. Nonetheless, the last speaker's outburst was deeply disturbing, for if it represented a true picture of Russia's intentions and ambitions in Europe; the future looked extremely grim and spoke volumes for their pact of 'friendship' with Germany into the bargain.

Elections, which were to determine the final act of integration of Poland's eastern province to Russia, took place early in 1940, although appropriation by stealth is a truer description. These elections were preceded by a lot of publicity featuring candidates, all communists handpicked by the central party machine. Constant pressure was exerted on the population to ensure total attendance – avoiding it spelt trouble. We knew it was a total sham and at the same time we were being driven into a corner, the most disturbing aspect of it being that we were not only about to vote ourselves into the Soviet caucus and thus become the Soviet Republic of White Russia, but by so doing also become in effect Soviet citizens. The thought of it filled me with horror. The day came, and we cast our voting cards under the watchful eyes of the militia, some time later to be issued with identity cards stating that we were citizens of the Soviet Republic of White Russia. I was overcome by a feeling of utter misery and felt trapped like a rat.

Compounding our misery, deportations proceeded at an increasing rate with village after village being left devoid of its inhabitants, rounded up at the dead of night like so many cattle and spirited away, more often than not never to be seen again. We felt as though a steel ring was slowly but surely tightening around Albertyn and in the truest sense lived in constant fear of the midnight knock on the door. The border between the two zones of occupation was now hermetically sealed, the Russians having created on their side a security strip measuring several kilometres in depth which rendered it impossible to penetrate. All inhabitants who happened to find themselves within it were removed and deported. And yet early in May there appeared a ray of hope.

Chapter Six

Leonie called unexpectedly with the news that she had just returned from the border town of Brest (Brzesc), and had discovered that both Russians and Germans had reached an agreement for an exchange of refugees; furthermore a German commission was actually present there accepting applications from thousands of refugees anxious to return home to the West. Typically, the Russians never announced this move so it was by sheer luck that Leonie found out about it. Her elderly mother and two young nieces who had been stranded in Slonim since the outbreak of war all wanted to return to Warsaw, including herself, so she set about resolving the problems with typical determination. She planned to return to Brest immediately in an effort to procure travel permits for them and us as well. 'From now on you can be my cousins, it will strengthen our case if we go as a family,' she explained. She was adamant that she first went alone, declining our offer to go with her as the NKVD took less notice of female travellers. It all seemed too good to be true and we refused to allow ourselves to become over-optimistic. But if Leonie couldn't pull this one off, then no one could. We wrote a letter to our mothers hinting that we might be seeing them soon and, to our relief, later received letters of acknowledgement. This proved that my mother was at that moment still free. The question of for how long constantly burned itself in my mind.

The strangest twists sometimes happen in times of war, as the following event illustrates. A letter in a brown envelope bearing a Moscow postmark hurtled through the letterbox the day after Leonie's return to Brest. It was addressed to me. I think I almost guessed what I was about to find within it – a letter from my father perhaps? The blue embossed letterheading read 'The British Embassy, Moscow'. To the best of my recollection it was worded thus:

Dear Sir.
    We understand from your father Mr. G. A. Firth that you are at present residing with Mr. & Mrs. Dabrowski at this address at Albertyn nr. Slonim. Should it be your wish to proceed to the United Kingdom please complete the enclosed form on the strength of which you will be sent a British passport. Etc.

The impossible had happened and it all suddenly seemed so simple. My immediate impulse was to complete the form and post is as soon as possible, but I knew the time for a decision would depend on the success or failure of

Leonie's mission to Brest. A day later Leonie appeared wearing a triumphant grin.

'I've got them, I've got them – all of them!' she exclaimed, happily waving some pieces of paper in the air. She then explained what had happened.

Both German and Russian rehabilitation commissions sat in one building, a prerequisite for an interview with the Germans, being governed by the Russians. Moreover the Germans were no doubt deliberately lodged in a far corner of the building at the end of a long corridor. The main entrance was guarded by an armed soldier. Leonie joined the queue but soon realized that not only did the guard behave in an officious and unhelpful manner, but many applicants were being turned away in a state of despair by the Russian commission. She wondered what chance she had, the thought growing on her whether she could circumvent the Russians altogether. She bided her time when, suddenly, a heated argument broke out between the guard and a disconsolate man. With the guard's attention diverted she sprinted along the corridor and into the room with the Germans. They listened to her story and eventually issued her with the six travel permits she had asked for. This was all very well, but by her quick-witted action she had failed to obtain Russian permits without which her efforts could well be in vain. Nevertheless we were prepared to take that chance and hope for the best. Curiously, the question of our pseudo-Russian 'citizenship' never arose and never presented an obstacle.

I was now faced with a dilemma. Whereas Jurek's position was clear cut, I had to make a choice: that of returning to Warsaw and the unknown, or escaping to England and freedom. If my mother was still free, she would need all the help she could get for surely her state of 'freedom' was extremely tenuous. On the other hand, my journey could be in vain. As happy as my friends were for me to have the golden opportunity of going to England, they did not wish to exert any kind of pressure on me regarding a decision. It had to be mine alone. I was in a terrible sweat, my agony lasting for three days and nights during which I hardly slept a wink. After that, my mind was clear and I knew what had to be done. With all the dangers it entailed, I knew I had to return to Warsaw, for if my mother was still there, it was unthinkable that she should have to face an uncertain future alone. With a heavy heart I wrote a letter to the British Embassy in Moscow thanking them and explaining that due to circumstances I now found myself in a position to travel to Warsaw and would be taking this opportunity to do so. Although to my annoyance I had omitted a request for this vital message to be conveyed to my father, in point of fact this the Embassy did. Having now made my decision I tried to put it out of my mind. To brood over it with eternal regrets served no useful purpose whatsoever. What was done was done. Of course I realized that not only would I be taking a gigantic leap from the frying pan straight into a fire, but that freedom would in all probably elude me for the foreseeable future as well.

Chapter Seven

Our German travel passes stated that we should present ourselves at Brest railway station on 12 May and on the evening of the 11th we set out on our journey. As tickets to Brest were not available at Albertyn's toytown station, we would be obliged to leave the train at Slonim, make a dash to the ticket office there, purchase tickets to Brest and clamber aboard the same train again – clamber being the operative word. We had arranged to meet Leonie and her party there, and this time all went well. At Slonim we dived into the main hall to be met with the sight of an impenetrable mass of people and, mingling among them, the unmistakeable green-capped NKVD security police. Catching sight of Leonie we decided to split up, with Jurek forcing his way to the ticket office and I to assist Leonie with what turned out to be a mountain of heavy luggage. First things first – with her mother and two nieces safely ensconced in an already overcrowded compartment, the luggage followed, most of it heaved through the carriage window, falling on top of protesting passengers inside. It was a matter of using brute force, with no time for niceties. Jurek in the meantime had managed to obtain our tickets. In a way it was the sheer size of the crowd which undoubtedly saved us from the attentions of the NKVD. Others were not so lucky.

The journey to Brest necessitated a change at Baranowicze where the luggage was stacked on the platform to await the next train, due in one hour's time. We were told by a railway guard that waiting on the platform was forbidden, and to move everything into the waiting room. When we explained about the sheer weight of it he protested, but went away. Not only for that reason did we choose to remain on the platform. Although there was no way in which the heap of luggage could be disguised, at least we felt safer in the relative isolation of a darkened platform than in the confines of the waiting room, which was the favourite hunting ground of the NKVD. As it turned out, it was the conspicuous mound of luggage which was very nearly the cause of our undoing. The railway guard returned prepared for battle, in no uncertain terms ordering us off the platform. We, in turn, told him in no uncertain terms that we had no intention of doing so as there was no law against it. 'We shall see,' he muttered stalking off. We thought we had seen the last of him but our hearts sank when he reappeared ten minutes later with two militiamen. Telling Leonie and her party to stay where they were, everything was removed and loaded onto a waiting horse-drawn cart. Jurek and I went with it. 'We are going to the Posterunek [police station],' they said. Now what? we wondered. In our minds eye we could see our train disappearing into the distance without us, yet again.

In the *posterunek*, two bemused militiamen then began searching through the cases with leisurely deliberation, and it was obvious that they had never seen such 'finery' before. Indeed all the trappings were there for them to admire! After half an hour we began to get anxious as it seemed that at their rate of progress it would take all night. However they must have realized that there were no secrets to be found and, daunted by the remaining mound of luggage, decided to call it a day and let us go.

On our next stage of the journey to Brest-Litovsk, a ticket inspector appeared with a plain-clothed security man who questioned passengers about their journey. We showed him our German passes, explaining the purpose of our journey and, having stared at them blankly, they were returned to us. We reached Brest close to midnight where our friends summoned a *droshki* and drove off to a prearranged destination, leaving us to find our own place to spend the night. We had agreed to meet up with them at the railway station the following morning. However, all this was easier said than done. Before parting, Leonie had given us an address to go to, but when we got there we were told that there was no room and to try next door. So this we did, but the landlady shook her head and said that the only available space was on the kitchen floor, as she too was inundated with refugees. By now we were too tired to search any further and accepted. At least it was a roof over our heads. As we settled down on the kitchen floor, we soon realized that sleep was impossible because of the continuous blast of propaganda poured out over loudspeakers, interspersed with strident martial music. They certainly seemed hell-bent on making our lives as difficult as possible!

Brest-Litovsk was bursting at the seams with human flotsam returning home to the German zone. The square by the railway station was a sea of forlorn humanity, most of whom had camped there during the night, possibly several nights, and it was by pure chance that we collided with Leonie in that teeming crowd. Under the circumstances we agreed that it would be impossible for all of us to remain together as a group, opting to split up and taking our chances separately, so we bade her and her family farewell and wished each other luck.

There appeared to be no proper organization or direction but after much searching we found a side entrance to the station with a queue beside it, as well as a 'green cap' (NKVD) security man, who told us that we had come to the right place. He took our passes and told us to wait. A number of people were being brusquely turned away for no apparent reason, and there was no argument about it. They were simply told to clear off. The anguish and distress caused by what must have been an arbitrary. decision on the part of that single security guard was extreme, for this was in fact a last chance for all those wanting to return home. He was in effect condemning hundreds to a life of misery and uncertainty.

It transpired that our passes were being scrutinized by a trio of NKVD officers seated at a table inside the entrance and presently the guard called our names and directed us to the trio. No doubt because of inefficiency or confusion or both, the question of the missing Russian passes, which Leonie had failed to obtain in the first instance, again never arose. The trio rubber-stamped the German passes and told us to go to the station platform.

We were directed into a cattle wagon, which was one of a long line waiting to be filled and finally, when that happened, the doors were bolted and the train moved off.

Then suddenly, as though on cue, a tremendous cheer erupted from every single wagon and the invective hurled at the Russians in classic Polish style was worth hearing! Fortunately the Russians were not there to hear it.

The journey was of short duration. We had crossed the River Bug and were now inside German-held territory, stopping at Biala-Podlaska. Here men and women were segregated, and underwent fumigation and cleansing in specially equipped Red Cross wagons. That was all very well, but we were made to strip and parade under the beady gaze of 'sexless' German female medics, and were given to understand that all the women suffered the indignity of having to do so in front of male medics. But it was a small price to pay in order to get home.

After that introduction, we awaited the next stage with apprehension, for we had no illusions about the Nazis whatsoever and realized that having escaped the fire we were now jumping into the frying pan.

All our luggage had to be left in the train whilst now, reeking of 'lysol', we were marched to an army barracks compound. Here we were to join an endless queue in order to reclaim our possessions which had been stacked into the largest mound of luggage I have seen and am ever likely to see again, for it must have been as high as a house!

As we stood there in the queue, I became acutely aware that I was being watched by a character standing some distance away. He then approached me and quietly but firmly told me to follow him. I did not need telling that he was from German security, his looks alone betrayed it. Why did he have to pick on me, out of all the hundreds of men milling about? Did they already know about me? He led me past an armed sentry and into a shed in which stood a table and chair. He told me to sit down and perched himself on the table top. He then asked where in the Russian zone had I been staying. I told him Albertyn, near Slonim, whereupon he said that I looked the sort of chap that might notice interesting things, such as, for example whether there were any Russian troop concentrations in the area. Whereas on the one hand I was relieved that it was not my identity that was being probed, on the other hand I felt that if this line of questioning continued for much longer, I would get out of my depth. However, there was really nothing I could tell him. I told him that we hardly saw any troops at all. Would I know what units they belonged to? 'No'. Surely there must have been some tanks in the area – did I not see any? 'No'. By now he had begun to lose his cool which made me wonder desperately how I could change the subject and I decided to take the bull by the horns.

'You know, I am not in the slightest interested in military matters because I am an artist by nature. I am far more interested in the sky and trees. Anyway, Albertyn is so small and remote that we never saw a thing.' I said.

He took the bait and exploded, 'You don't know anything, do you, you … you, you're useless!' he spluttered. 'Go on, get out of here!' And with that, he propelled me through the door.

Jurek, meanwhile, had been engaged in conversation with someone in the queue and to his consternation had only just realized that I was missing.

'Where the devil did you get to?' he asked anxiously.

I began to explain, 'Well, there was this chap. I'm sure he's a Gestapo. He wanted to know …' My voice tailed off as through the corner of my eye I caught sight of my inquisitor standing right behind me, listening intently. I turned away and started to whistle a tuneless tune, but Jurek, unaware of the situation, demanded to know what the chap wanted.

'Oh, nothing,' I replied casually.

'What do you mean, nothing?' demanded Jurek.

'Just shut-up!' I retorted, grimacing furiously.

The man stood watching us for a while, then uttered a disdainful 'HUH!' and, turning on his heel, stalked off.

That brush with German Security left an unpleasant foretaste of things to come and I began to wonder if I stood half a chance of getting anywhere with a name like Firth.

We stood in the endless queue until dusk until it was our turn to enter the compound containing the mountain of luggage. We searched for ages to no avail. So there our precious possessions remained to the benefit of the Germans after we had all long departed from the wretched place.

After that fiasco we were to face an identity check, the thought of which filled me with fear. Thankfully, up until now, my surname had not aroused interest or questioning, but a closer examination could be a different matter. What if they already had a black list of 'wanted' persons? Although no spy, I was still an enemy alien and a fitting candidate for internment for the duration of the war.

Now faced yet again with another marathon queuing which was to stretch well into the early hours of the morning, we managed to force our way nearer the front. Inside the main administrative block, in the centre of a vast and otherwise empty assembly hall and seated behind a large table, were three sombrely dressed German civilians, behind whom stood a bevy of grim- faced SS officers. To reach them it was obviously necessary to traverse the expanse of floor area all the way under their withering scrutiny, a most intimidating experience – obviously intended so.

We watched those before us approach the desk, then the questioning, after which each individual was directed to another room and out of our sight. The process took about five minutes.

As my position didn't look too rosy we devised the idea that Jurek would go first and only should the questioning prove tricky would he pretend to use his handkerchief as a signal to be on my guard when my turn came. 'After all, as a mere Pole, what have I to lose?' he said.

I watched with bated breath and when they had finished with him he managed a glance in my direction, giving a faint, reassuring smile. Then it was my turn and with pounding heart I stood before the cold, glaring eyes of the SS men. My name, Firth, was read out from a long list in the hard, phonetic manner, as though it was a German name. The ensuing questions were straight-forward enough and routine. There was no problem at all. The scene which confronted me in the next room, however, was a different one entirely!

Here, many of my predecessors were being practically stripped naked, manhandled and abused by two vile young SS men who, along with a female companion, were frantically searching for smuggled goods and secret messages. One poor young woman was in floods of tears as the heals of her dainty pre-war shoes were roughly ripped off and searched. Others seemed to stand about in various stages of undress, bewildered and humiliated. It was sheer bedlam.

Luckily Jurek and I fared better than some, for although our caps were swiftly knocked off our heads as an introduction, and we were generally manhandled, we otherwise got away lightly.

It was almost three in the morning when we were directed to the main barracks where we managed to find two empty bunks, hoping to get some much-needed sleep. But the general din of masses of humanity tramping around the building quickly put a stop to that, added to which our neighbour, who appeared to be in a high state of nerves, wouldn't stop talking. Who could blame him? Some talked endlessly, others were thoughtful and silent. In the morning, the news filtered through that German forces had begun their attack on France. The Germans, eager to justify their action, then distributed newspapers free, for us to read all about it!

All the men from our party were made to assemble on the barrack square where we were addressed by a group of German civilians. It transpired they represented various industrial groups or companies in the Reich, and called for volunteers to step forward and register with them for work in Germany. However, that morning they were severely out of luck, for there were no takers. A Polish prisoner of war put to fatigue duties in the barracks told us that we were very lucky to have got away with it since all the men who had gone before us had had no option and were without exception bundled off to the Reich for slave labour.

We thanked our lucky stars, and were eventually allowed to leave and make our own way to our destination. Wasting no time we made for the railway station and boarded a train bound for Warsaw. The journey was trouble free and within a couple of hours we arrived at the Dworzec Glowny (Main Station) in the very heart of the city. As soon as we stepped outside the station we were presented with the sight of a city in ruins, so much so that it left us speechless. Buildings, streets and shops we once knew so well had disappeared into piles of rubble. Could this be our city, or were we imagining it all? We hastened our step.

As though that wasn't enough the sight of so many Germans swaggering along the pavements made us sick. Pedestrians were ordered to step out of their way and the Jewish population, already singled out for 'special treatment', was forced to wear armbands sporting the Star of David and walk along the gutters. Transgression of these rules met with instant retribution – at best a beating up, at worst, arrest.

As it was by far the nearest, we made for Jurek's flat which we soon reached. Luckily it had remained undamaged and once inside we were greeted with tearful affection by his mother. To my intense relief I learned that my mother was still free but had been obliged to move to another flat, albeit in the same suburb, and I was able to call her straight away on the telephone. An hour later she had joined us and our reunion was complete.

Now we had to take stock of the situation and discuss at length our next course of action. Our entire lives had been turned upside down, so much having changed since we left Warsaw for that 'short holiday' in the August of 1939!

In the first place it was imperative that Jurek and I equip ourselves with identity cards, without which our survival would be short lived. As a boom industry in the production of false identity cards had come into being since the German occupation, the procurement of these invaluable documents did not pose a serious problem. Whereas Jurek was able to register with the authorities in the normal way, I had to make a risky journey to a 'certain address' in town in order to collect my phoney one, complete with fingerprints and photograph. I now became Tomasz Kopystynski, born in Kiev, January 1920. (Kopystynski was my mother's maiden name). In order to avoid the currently enforced registration of young men up to the age of eighteen, an extra two years were added to my age. This omission could well have ended with a call-up for direct labour, or more accurately, slave labour, probably somewhere in Germany.

My cover story now sounded thus: I was born in Kiev of Polish parents, orphaned at an early age and subsequently taken care of by an aunt, now deceased. Attended such-and-such a school in Warsaw (now disbanded anyway). Just returned to Warsaw, having spent ten months as a refugee in the

Russian zone. Regarding former addresses of residence, I had memorized two properties in town which had been conveniently destroyed in air raids. In effect none of the story was verifiable, added to which the city authorities had prudently burned most of the records and archives prior to its occupation by the Germans. It was as good a cover as any and I could only hope that it would see me through whatever lay in store in the days ahead.

It wasn't until our arrival at Jurek's flat that we realized how famished we were. The events of the past few days had deadened our appetites, but now as we began to relax and return to some sort of normality so our appetites returned with a vengeance. We had had nothing to eat for three or four days, and when we sat down to that first meal we became aware of just how bad the food shortage was. Jurek's mother apologized for the meagre fare and explained about the severe rationing that had been imposed on the population.

In turn, I learned how my mother managed to survive the German onslaught on Warsaw. Although the suburb we lived in had not suffered any great damage, an artillery shell had passed clean through our flat, luckily exploding somewhere beyond, consequently most of our possessions remained intact. Sadly looters, taking advantage of the chaos, stole some family silver and jewellery. But my mother came through it all unhurt.

As I recall, money had always been a problem in our household but now the situation seemed impossible. My mother had managed to cash a cheque which father had sent just before all communication ceased, but that was barely enough to last a month. Unable to afford the repair to the flat she decided to move. Curiously, with the exodus of so many souls escaping the war, living accommodation was not too difficult to find and she rented a very pleasant flat in a modern block in the same suburb, overlooking the River Vistula.

Up to the time she decided on the move, she had been registered as an enemy alien, which meant that she was obliged to visit the Gestapo headquarters every week on the Aleja Roz. She was not the only one to have to do so for there was a small band of French as well as British nationals who were stranded there as well. In fact most of them were elderly people who had been domiciled in Poland for years. Curiously, and for reasons that I have never understood, the Germans left them alone until the very day that they launched their assault on France.

In the meantime, since my return to Warsaw, and still without the all-important identity card, I was strictly 'confined to barracks'. With the constant checks and raids carried out in the streets, it just wasn't worth the chance. But an identity card alone meant little – the only document that could prevent arrest and a journey into the unknown was proof of employment with a company which was contracted to carry out work for the Germans, but even that was no guarantee.

Since it was too risky to visit my mother, I stayed with Jurek and his mother, who had selflessly and unstintingly offered to shelter me. But the journey to collect the phoney ID card had to be made, and only I could do it. Once it was in my possession I ventured out into the streets and began visiting my mother, albeit mostly on Sundays when SS street patrols remained fairly dormant.

So when my mother moved to her new flat she made the decision never to go to the Gestapo headquarters again and simply 'vanish', bearing in mind that sooner rather than later she would have found herself in an internment camp. Her move had been carried out surreptitiously, without notifying the local police. With one exception, most of her friends and relatives had no inkling of her whereabouts, and better that it be so. Mother trusted the person who knew implicitly, for she had proved a staunch friend and neighbour over the years. Her name was Natalie. To avoid registration she took in a distant cousin and her husband who had lost their home in western Poland, and the flat was registered in their name instead.

And then the inevitable happened. A breathless Natalie appeared at the door with the news that the Gestapo had called at mother's old flat. Unable to get a response they knocked on the door of Natalie's flat to enquire whether she knew anything about Mrs Firth's whereabouts. Naturally Natalie 'hadn't a clue', and they went away. Now the question remained whether the Gestapo would pursue their search or not. Mother seemed confident that she had given them the slip, but the uncertainty remained. To make matters worse, she was obliged eventually to register with the local police upon the insistence of the house owners who, though unaware of her true identity, only wanted to abide by the rules in order to keep themselves out of trouble. As at this point in time she had not yet managed to acquire a false identity, she had no option other than to register in her real name. As luck would have it the local police were discreet and helpful, although in fact knew exactly who she was. But all this was obviously still an insufficient safeguard against possible ferreting of the Gestapo. A foolproof cover had to be devised soon if she was to keep out of their clutches.

My pleas that she should move away from Saska Kepa to another area where she was completely unknown fell on deaf ears. And in the meantime the Gestapo had not been idle, as we were soon to discover.

My mother had been going about her business in the normal way and had just returned to the block of flats where she lived, but held back abruptly when she noticed a drab grey saloon car with German registration plates parked at the main entrance. Her heart missed a beat but, sizing up the situation, she entered another part of the building and knocked on the door of a neighbour. Happy to be able to help, her friend led her to a window which overlooked the main entrance and from which they were able to observe all movements in and out of the building. Presently the figure of a leather-coated civilian emerged, followed by two high-ranking officers; clambering into the car, they drove off. Thanking her friend she wasted no time in returning to her flat. There was no doubt that it had been entered and, although little had been disturbed, some of my father's business papers were missing. However, the surprising aspect of this affair was that contrary to their usual practice the flat was not sealed by the Gestapo, which would have effectively prevented my mother from entering it. Stirred into action, my mother, with the aid of a few good friends had everything packed off on hand carts to another apartment within twenty-four hours. Again my pleas for a more distant place of residence came to nothing, and to my dismay the new flat was only a few hundred yards away!

There was now no doubt that my mother was sailing very close to the wind, to say the least, but argue as I might, she would not on any account consider moving to an area unfamiliar to her. From that time the Gestapo seemed to give up their search, as far as one could tell, but scares were to follow with alarm bells ringing loud and clear.

One wondered why the Germans began arresting British and French nationals when we had already been at war with them for 8 months. How was it they knew nothing about me and my brother George's existence since, according to my mother, they never made any reference to us at all? Not that I should complain about that! Far from it, for their ignorance about my existence certainly allowed me valuable breathing space in the early days of my arrival. And why did they not confiscate mother's property and seal off the flat as they had done in all other cases? My only thought on the latter was that it was intended as a trap. By leaving everything intact, my mother could have been led into a false sense of security. However, she never subsequently heard of any further intrusion at the flat.

Now installed in her new flat, the burning problem of her identity still remained. Eventually, after much deliberation and heart-searching, only one scheme seemed to answer it – she would have to 'marry' an obliging and understanding gentleman, thereby not only adopting his name but also his Polish nationality. Once again her friends rallied around and eventually produced a single gentleman who said he would be willing to help. In fact the whole affair took on a light-hearted turn. A church wedding was duly arranged with everyone sworn to secrecy including the priest. The joke of the day was that Mr Zaworski was in fact already engaged to be married to a Polish lady! She must have been an exceptionally kind-hearted soul. After the ceremony was over, for appearances sake, the good Mr Zaworski even agreed to spend a couple of nights in Mother's flat, and that was the end of it. Now, as Mrs Zaworski, she was able to register in her new name with impunity.

Chapter Eight

For several weeks since my return to Warsaw, and with no employment, I never stayed in one place for very long. As kind as they were I could not impose myself on Jurek and his mother and, once my mother's problem became resolved, I was able to remain in her flat, albeit temporarily. Life in Warsaw was extremely precarious and the business of both evading the system and the Germans was a stark and harrowing reality. This engendered a whole new attitude to one's existence, at times so unreal and unnatural that it filled one with revulsion. In one's daily life one moved about with the utmost caution from the moment one stepped outside the house. Instinctively, one glanced up and down the street for any suspicious signs or unusual Security Police movements which usually heralded a large-scale raid. This was a time for quick decisions, either to dart into the nearest doorway or continue on one's way casually, with the hope of attracting little attention. However, if there was a row of parked trucks as well, the only course of action was to make oneself scarce. Travelling on the trams was no better, for these were swiftly brought to a halt and surrounded – in short one was liable to be trapped like a rat.

I was able to spend a few days with one Stefan Kiesewetter and his wife in the relative peace and quiet of Saska Kepa, and not very far from my mother's flat. Before the war Stefan had worked in the state telecommunications establishment as an electrical engineer, but had since resigned, refusing to work for the Germans. Now he eked out a modest living fabricating small domestic appliances which he sold here and there. He also undertook electrical repairs to help out with finances. Much to the despair of his long-suffering wife, his workshop was the kitchen and the resultant mess was indescribable – not an inch of space was free, with wires and conduits festooning the walls and swamping the floor like so much spaghetti which had been hurled about by a demented chef.

Stefan assured me that there was method in this seeming madness and promptly began to demonstrate what he meant. Having connected up various odd lengths of wire he handed me a set of headphones. 'Now, just listen,' he said, and sure enough, I was listening to the BBC foreign service loud and clear. It was inadvisable to listen to these broadcasts for too long in case the signals were picked up by detector vans which cruised around secretively in search of illegal radio sets and transmitters.

Although the news coming over was depressing, just to be able to listen to English voices was a tonic and the feeling one got was one of unruffled stability and calm. On the other hand the apparent lack of action made us impatient and frustrated, and when the latest cricket scores were read out I didn't want to know! It just seemed too trite and irrelevant for words, but we did rather expect the impossible in those days. And yet things had to get so very much worse before the turn of the tide.

'If the Germans ever pay us a visit they will never be able to unravel this mess in a million years!' laughed Stefan. His wife just stared and remained silent. Luckily they were never found out.

It was about this time that the first Red Cross parcels began to arrive. To many, this was their salvation and only hope from starvation. What delicacies they had sent us – tins of sardines, cocoa and tinned meats! And much-needed clothes as well. The International Red Cross had persuaded the German authorities to allow these life-sustaining consignments into the occupied territory. They were, in fact, paid for and sent by friends and relatives of Poles all over the world through the auspices of the Red Cross in Lisbon.

In the meantime, back in England, my father fretted and worried over our fate, having no idea what had happened to us at all. Nevertheless he decided to send a small parcel as a trial, addressing it to an old friend of the family with a note simply saying: 'Please hand to Halina'. It was a shot in the dark but a successful one.

Unfortunately this was the only time it worked. Mother's frequent moves, which were effected with necessary secrecy, served to confuse matters, furthermore, when it became possible to send letters – the statutory twenty-five words in all – also via the Red Cross, Mother used a friends name for that purpose. The 'old friend' in this case being Kathleen Smith, a long-time resident in Warsaw and a lady of Southern Irish nationality who, thanks to her 'neutral' status, proved to be of great help to my mother.

In pre-war days, she had taught at the English language college on Mokotowska Street. Kathleen identified completely with the Allied cause and later was to play an important part in activities which would have earned her instant deportation, if not imprisonment, had she been found out.

Life in the capital deteriorated steadily as reports of hostage-taking and mass executions spread alarmingly by the week. Save for the dark forests that abounded in Poland, nowhere was it safe from the hounding of the Gestapo and the SS punitive squads. With this background my mother understandably became more and more concerned about my safety. Above all, however, the problem of funds reared its ugly head, for we could not live on thin air, neither would I expect my mother to subsidize me while she was herself desperately short of the necessities of life. It was a fact of life that she had no qualifications whereby she could secure some paid occupation, however mundane, in order to revive her dwindling resources. As it was, her jewellery became her currency.

Accumulated during our years in the Far East, she found a ready market for it now, whilst it lasted.

The job I was looking for was one which would provide me with a 'sound' certificate of employment. I was lucky and presently called at the firm of Z. Balcer in the district of Praga to apply for a job. Their main work was manufacturing breeze blocks for the building trade. Mr Balcer himself explained the nature of the work and what would be expected of me. Because the company had secured a contract to supply the German Army with 10,000 breeze blocks, or slabs, they were in need of three extra overseers to supervise the increased workload. As a new plant had to be set up quickly somewhere near the town of Kielce, I was to receive a crash course in all aspects of manufacture before proceeding to the new site, where I was to take charge of a production unit. As distasteful as it might have been to be in some way 'working for the Germans', there were very few options available.

Working conditions were basic and the pay low, but at least I was earning a wage. And with it I was able to help my mother, having moved into her flat and stayed there until my departure to Kielce and the provinces, three weeks later.

It was arranged that Balcer, the director, Wladyslaw the works foreman and I would meet up early on a Sunday morning at the railway station and travel to our destination together. The journey to Kielce lasted two hours. From Kielce railway station, which was situated on the outskirts of the town, we struck out on foot across country following a rough dirt road, lugging our heavy cases as best we could. It was usual to hire a farm cart and horses, whose drivers plied for this sort of trade outside most railway stations, but for some reason Balcer had decided against this modest luxury with the result that after about a mile I had had enough. My mother had ensured that I travelled well prepared, with the result that my heavy suitcase, weighing a ton, literally fell out of my hand as the handle parted company with it. This was no joke and there was no way of effecting a repair to the wretched object, however Wladyslaw, strong as a horse, picked it up and, slinging it onto his shoulder, proceeded on his way as though it was a mere trifle. In exchange I was able to carry his luggage. Soon, as the scorching sun rose higher into the sky and the going became rougher, he too became exhausted and we had to switch our load several time in order to keep going.

In the end we caught up with a slow-moving farm cart whose driver not only agreed to take all our luggage aboard, but let us 'hitch a ride', one at a time, in order to save his horse's strength. When my turn came I jumped onto the back of the cart and, settling down on some straw, soon dozed off. After what seemed an age I awoke from my blissful slumber with a start to find with horror that we were surrounded by Germans. Luckily they were unarmed and obviously heading to the canteen or bent on some other peaceful mission, and didn't bother us.

We now entered a forest and followed a track for about another mile, flanked by tall pine trees, eventually arriving at a long rough clearing in which stood a low concrete building or bunker which stretched ahead of us into the distance, looking completely out of place in such unspoilt and natural surroundings. As we passed by apertures where doors should have been, we could see through the narrow building and the thick forest immediately beyond it. Presently a young man appeared from one of the doors and grinned broadly as soon as he caught sight of us. We had arrived.

He took us to a stubby wing of the building which was to serve as our living quarters. Our new companion introduced himself as Alex, explaining that he had arrived several days before us, along with two others, in order to prepare some of the groundwork for the new factory. He was a personable chap, a little older than myself and I got on well with him in the weeks ahead.

I soon learned that the Germans were planning to build a vast military camp and depot in the area which entailed the employment of hundreds of workers – contractors, sub-contractors, architects, engineers, electricians and the whole gamut of supply services which were eventually to bring the gigantic project into being. It meant the clearance of vast areas of forest as well as shelters for the workforce, which in large part was recruited from the capital. There was also an army of unskilled labour recruited by the iniquitous method of co-opting large numbers of men and women from each hamlet and village within a large radius. That presented the inhabitants with an intolerable burden since without exception they came from peasant communities where their presence was badly needed to help with work on the farms.

There was also a dreadful irony in the whole situation because whereas no one would ever wish to work for the Germans and aid them in their war effort, projects of this sort did provide work as well as financial reward for scores of men, at the same time affording them the best kind of security against random arrest, because of the importance of the work. Perhaps not so surprisingly this set-up also provided an almost ideal refuge for individuals who were being pursued by the Gestapo or needed a place to lie low, for in the two and a half months I was there, no one had either seen or heard of the Gestapo. So it did say something for the notion that the best place to hide was right under their noses. This worked for a time at any rate, because later, when I left the place, it was raided by the Gestapo and two Polish engineers were arrested.

As for our own efforts at setting up a production plant, things moved apace. As the saying goes, our feet hardly touched the ground. In the first week or two we had to turn our hand at everything from paring down logs into finely planed planks, to supervising the unloading of bales of wood shavings at the railway sidings a mile away in the forest. These bales were then loaded onto military lorries and delivered to our site. We were completely reliant on the military for all our major supplies and transportation needs.

Evenings were therefore the only time for relaxation when we congregated in our bare concrete room, filthy and tired out. At first three of us shared these inhospitable quarters, sleeping on stout, tiered wooden bunks, the rule being to sleep as high off the floor as possible to avoid the attention of fleas. Wladyslaw, our works foreman, was ensconced in an adjoining room, later to be joined by his wife, and in the next one, also enjoying the comforts of a home life, was our manager, Kaszynski, with his wife, though I hate to think how they survived the utterly spartan and isolated existence.

The mystery as to why the entire concrete structure was built here, buried in the depths of the forest was soon explained, for it was intended for the production of explosives and never completed at the outbreak of war, which also explained the massive steel doors in which the place abounded, as well the numerous solidly protected cubicles and chambers, some of which we were in the process of being used for our own needs.

Its total length must have stretched to several hundred yards, yet in width it could have been no more than 40 feet. It had two 'wings', one of which, as I have explained, served as our living quarters. However, at the far end a larger 'wing' was now used as a canteen serving the workers from other areas of the construction programme. We were able to make use of it on two occasions in the first days of our arrival and were pleasantly surprised with the standard of fare provided, everything considered, and thought we were onto a good thing. However, whether it had anything to do with it or not, immediately after Balcer's departure early in the week, the place was declared out of bounds to us. All they agreed to supply us was bread. This was a blow, for without the precious canteen meals we were faced with a process of slow starvation unless something could be done about it. All our representations to the wretched canteen manager, Ptaszynski, fell on deaf ears. In fact, nobody seemed to care and there seemed no possibility of organizing an alternative supply of food. This predicament, I must add, did not apply to either our foreman, Wladyslaw, or manager, Kaszynski, whose wives must have arrived prudently well stocked with provisions. In the end the weasel Ptaszynski did the dirty by absconding with the canteen funds after a series of near riots over bad food and 'we', alas, were doomed to live on bread alone – and dry bread it had to be, for some time to come.

When the wooden forms, over which we had slaved for the past ten days, were installed and all the other necessary changes to the building effected, we were ready to start our first trial production run of breeze slabs. The only thing now lacking was the labour force, but on the following day about a hundred men and women turned up to be selected for the work. Out of this number forty or so were taken on, the brawniest men to do the heavy and physically most demanding work on the production lines, and the rest to do the various ancillary jobs in and around the plant. So commenced a brief period of intensive training for these raw recruits under the watchful eye of Wladyslaw, the senior foreman.

For some reason, which totally eluded me, I was not only put in charge of one of the three production units, but also in charge of the storeroom and all the tools, as well as transport and supplies of raw materials – a daunting task for someone so young and inexperienced. In practice this meant that whereas Wladyslaw and Alex had only to look after their own 'back yard' and ensure that they maintained a steady production flow, I had to be, more often than not, in several places at the same time. I found myself placed in an impossible situation and had it not been for the good offices of Wladyslaw things would have got completely out of hand. It never occurred to me either to complain or try and remedy this obvious imbalance by discussing it with Kaszynski! I simply tried to get on with the job as best I could.

The two main ingredients in the manufacture of 'breeze slabs' were wood shavings and cement. The shavings arrived on site, courtesy of the German Army, tightly compressed in bales of about a cubic metre each and bound with wire. They then had to be stacked neatly in order to facilitate the checking of their number, each batch and truckload having to be accounted for. Then I discovered that the specified loads often did not tally, the reason for this being that they simply dropped off the lorries as they bounced and lurched their way along the forest track. When I drew the German driver's attention to what was happening he didn't want to know and would not go back and collect them. This resulted in a galling situation for me, for we had not even the most rudimentary form of transport to call our own, on which the wretched bales could be retrieved. Summoning help from our own people eventually became a futile pastime as well, so in the end it was up to me to retrieve them. I would head down the forest track at dusk and seek out the offending bales, one by one. Sometimes hundreds of yards separated them but I was not to be put off. I literally 'rolled' them back, painfully slowly, yard by yard, until tears streamed from my eyes in a rage of futility and self-pity.

However, there were compensations to be enjoyed as well. Once away from the site, one found oneself in a deep, silent forest in which abounded the most delicious edible mushrooms. But to pick them it was vital to do so at the crack of dawn, since one hour later they would have practically all but disappeared. Because we were simply too tired to make this effort, our combined effort at picking these delectable fungi was quite pitiful. As we had no means of cooking anything, and had nothing to cook anyway, except the mushrooms, they were stored in jars and dried in the sun for future consumption. But whilst they were undergoing the process of drying, the aroma was simply mouth-watering!

We rested on most Sundays, did the chores and washed out our heavily soiled clothes which had become thoroughly impregnated with cement dust. The only supply of water came through one standpipe at the end of the corridor, but again, the means of heating, let alone boiling, it was nonexistent.

When Poles talk in terms of outdoor entertainment, they usually mean netball, which has always been one of their favourite games. So with that in mind we set to clearing and levelling off a patch of ground on which two stakes were erected and linked by a length of rope which served as a net. Even this took hours of hard graft in order to remove several stubborn tree stumps before we could enjoy a game, and enjoy it we certainly did, thanks to one thoughtful individual who had actually brought a ball with him.

Andrew and I managed a trip to the nearest small town one Sunday but found it to be a depressing, dusty little place inhabited by orthodox Jews, as so many small towns were in Poland, whose poor inhabitants had managed to survive, but only just, before a matter of weeks later being cruelly swept away to the various ghettos being set up by the Germans up and down the country. Andrew, who was Alex's younger brother and had found himself a job as a carpenter with one of the construction companies, shared our infamous bunker for his lodgings. He was a handsome lad, somewhat lacking in discipline and suddenly announced that he intended to find himself a girl to sleep with – as the hot sunny day wore on his desire for this carnal treat seemed to increase by the hour.

I liked Andrew, but could not help treating his sexual appetite as a joke. 'Anyway,' I said, 'this is the last place on earth that I would wish to seek out such casual frolics.' But he was not to be put off. By sundown he became impossible and I said that we ought to think seriously about getting back to base, but he wouldn't hear of it and begged me not to leave him. Why don't we spend the night there and get going at first light? He was bound to find the damsel of his desires between nightfall and sunrise, he moaned.

I promised not to leave him and that I saw no reason why we could not travel back first thing in the morning, but it was entirely up to him how he wanted to spend the night. And so we trudged around the dimly lit streets and alleyways, Andrew hungrily eyeing any female who happened to pass us by, in the end ruefully deciding that they were not for him after all. Women apart, there was precious little else to do but walk in circles which by the nature of the late hour could only be of the ever-decreasing variety and it was high time to think of somewhere to sleep.

We knocked on the door of a darkened old house and presently it slowly opened revealing an ancient, wizened Jew holding a flickering candle in one hand. He was dressed in the manner of all orthodox Jews, in a long black coat and a small black peaked cap perched on his head. Almost silently he invited us inside and bade us to sit down on a bench by a large solid table. There was little he could offer in the way of refreshment, but we were welcome to some bread and milk, he said. When we had finished this meagre offering, he took us to another room and, opening the door without uttering a single word, indicated with outstretched arm the bed we had to share. He then lit another candle which he placed on a bedside table and in a barely audible voice bade us good night.

Inevitably we overslept after the exertions of the previous day and had a frantic scramble to be on our way back to work. We had enough money to pay the old man something for our stay and were gone. But how to get back was our problem. We had taken all morning getting there, in leisurely fashion, mostly on foot and by hitching the odd lift on a farm cart, but now speed was essential. We wandered about for a time wondering what to do until we spotted a railwayman passing by and told him of our predicament. He pointed in a certain direction and said that if we hurried there was a goods train, due to leave any minute, to where we wanted to go. This was an incredible bit of luck! We raced along in the direction he had indicated and across a meadow, where surely enough stood a goods train obviously ready to go – no sooner had we climbed onto an open and empty wagon when it pulled away. And so we travelled in great style revelling in our good fortune and the glorious morning sunshine. However our joy was to be short lived for there ahead of us on the single track stood in all its defiance another goods train, ready to head in our direction. Obviously something had gone seriously wrong and when we had pulled up to within yards of our adversary, the two drivers alighted from their cabs and proceeded to have a verbal set-to, accompanied by a great deal of arm waving. For a while we waited to see who would win, but in the end decided that a stalemate had been reached and there was nothing for it but to continue our journey on foot, which we did, reaching our destination in mid-morning and, of course, more verbal trouble as well.

After that little episode my own trials and tribulations did not last for very much longer, because we had by now come to the end of our contract. And in a final tally of breeze slabs which were supposed to have been supplied to the Wehrmacht, we were about 800 short! Or so the figures seemed to indicate. Luckily I was due for some leave and decided the best policy would be to leave straight away, return to Warsaw and never show myself in Kielce again to face an inquest on the missing slabs.

In the meantime, my mother had moved yet again. Her new flat was but a hundred yards from the previous one but now, living under her assumed name of Zaworski, she had reached a safer haven, at least as safe as anything could be in the circumstances. It therefore seemed reasonable for me to move in as well. The house in which we now resided belonged, by coincidence, to the parents of an old school friend of mine who naturally knew me well, but we had no fears on that score since they proved to be the epitome of discretion.

The climate in Warsaw had eased somewhat and whilst my certificate of employment with the company of Z. Balcer indicated that I was engaged in important work for the Germans, I felt reasonably safe, but it was important that I find alternative employment before its date of expiry. I met up again with my old friend Jurek, who was attending an engineering course by now, but for several weeks I found myself at a loose end.

I eventually got a job as a technical illustrator with a small engineering company on Nowy Swiat, in the middle of the city, but was able to do the work at home, only needing to call at their office once a week. This suited me well in as much as I enjoyed the work, but it did not offer a convincing enough certificate of employment.

The proverbial 'grapevine' was a wonderful institution and it was through this medium that I secured a job with a firm which was contracted to supply camouflage netting for the Wehrmacht. It was situated in a drab, industrial quarter which entailed a lengthy journey through town, with a change of two or more trams and therefore not a prospect I looked forward to, for all the reasons I have already explained. But at least it did provide me with a good enough certificate of employment.

Most of those employed were women who worked on the looms, or frames. Here I joined a group of manual labourers who did all the heavy, menial work around the place. But beggars can't be choosers and the first job of work I was put to was clearing rubble from one of the bomb-damaged buildings. As it was a four-storey building, the top two floors of which had been partly demolished, this meant carrying large wickerwork baskets filled with rubble down eight flights of stairs and emptying them in a heap in the yard. Two of us were employed on this exhausting and backbreaking work for several weeks before I was transferred to other duties. In the meanwhile, I had been casting longing glances at the two lorries which the company ran and struck up a friendship with one of the drivers. As cars had always been my great love in life, I said to Olek, the driver, that there was nothing better I would wish to do than act as driver's mate should a vacancy for the job ever occur. Olek had obviously been impressed with my enthusiasm because several weeks later he told me that he'd persuaded his manager that he badly needed a 'mate' to help him with the heavy workload, and the manager had agreed.

I soon found that the new job really did require the extra pair of hands. We had a tight schedule to stick to, with journeys which took us to all parts of Warsaw and beyond, but our vehicle, a 1930 Ford, long past its prime, simply couldn't cope, with the result that we spent countless hours in repair garages, over and under it, sometimes working halfway through the night in order to try and get it mobile again. Breakdowns in remoter areas were an ordeal we could have done without, while starting the thing up in sub-zero temperatures in the winter of 1941 taxed one's strength and patience to the limit. One could call it hell on wheels! But, after all, I had volunteered for the job.

The acquisition of petrol was a constant problem, since the official ration was far from adequate. As with everything else which was in short supply, however, a flourishing black market existed. But one had to have the right contacts, speak the right sort of language and in short, 'be in the know' to get this precious commodity. The secrecy that surrounded the whole business was understandable, because the Germans, like ourselves, badly needed it too. Human nature being what it is meant that some military personnel were not averse to doing some illicit business on the side in order to line their own pockets, a universally typical facet of life in time of war. The German authorities were naturally well aware of this trade, with the consequence that civilian vehicles were frequently stopped and checked, and if it was discovered that a car or lorry was running on the pale blue aircraft petrol of the highest quality, there was trouble aplenty. Olek, no fool that he was, also had his contacts, though not directly with the Germans, and we often used the pale-blue liquid which propelled our aged mount. But we were lucky and never got caught.

It was just prior to taking on the job as driver's mate that I met Hania. She was a petite brunette who worked on the looms along with the 150 or so women, but she had a personality which I found immediately attractive. She was one of several girls who had opted for this menial work, primarily with the aim of keeping out of sight of the Germans.

However, Hania did have a secret to hide, for her parents were Jewish. In order to further protect herself, like my mother, she too had undergone a marriage of convenience, adopting a new name and religion. Her father had died years before and her mother later married a Christian, which only gave her scant protection. As Hania had her father's name, Klotzmann, which was obviously Jewish, she had spared no time in righting that situation at the earliest possible moment, to avoid arrest and, in all probability, the dreaded concentration camps. As in my mother's case, the 'marriage' was purely an act of generosity on the part of the 'husband', with no strings attached.

Hania now rented a small flat on Mazowiecka Street, a busy thoroughfare in the centre of town and almost directly opposite the discretely elegant Mazowsze Cafe. Because of our long working hours, especially mine, our subsequent midweek meetings were both infrequent and brief, this situation also being exacerbated by the 9 o'clock curfew which had been imposed on the population of the city. But on the occasional glorious Sunday, in the summer of 1941, we would escape the claustrophobic confines of the city and spend a few carefree hours together in the peace and tranquillity of the countryside.

Chapter Nine

There is no doubting the fact that wars have a way of throwing up some strange and unlikely events and I recall one such instance which occurred early in 1941. The following event concerned my mother and the Japanese, with whom she had, before the war, enjoyed a rapport, thanks to her own mother's humanitarian activities related earlier.

The Japanese embassy had lingered on after the German occupation of Warsaw, but was eventually forced to close its doors to normal business, leaving behind a skeleton staff to wind up its affairs. For a time the premises remained as a stopping-off point for Japanese diplomats travelling between Tokyo and Berlin and although they had thrown in their lot with the Germans, they were not yet at war with the Allies at that point. And so it happened that a former official of the embassy, who was known to my mother as well as the small group of Poles who had also had a friendly association with the Japanese before the war, happened to stop off in Warsaw, on his long journey from Tokyo. He must be given credit for his fidelity towards the Poles, because he promptly made contact with members of that group, disregarding the vulnerability of his own position. Evidently their meeting was brief but warm and he confided in them, albeit guardedly, about the general situation. He was a much saddened man and said that things would be getting a lot worse.

One member of this group immediately contacted my mother, informing her about the extraordinary meeting. Upon hearing about it, she promptly decided that a meeting with our Japanese friend could prove useful and this was duly arranged. Her subsequent meeting with the envoy took place in Warsaw under a cloak of secrecy, the Japanese explaining with a wry smile that he was obliged to resort to some subterfuge before proceeding on the way to his destination. The outcome indeed proved fruitful as my mother asked him point blank if he was willing to convey a letter addressed to Father. As it was about a year since she was able to send the usual, cryptic letter through the Red Cross, she saw this as a golden opportunity to write a lengthy letter explaining about life in Warsaw and how we were managing to survive.

The Japanese knew full well that we were British, but never demurred. Then, after a brief, silent deliberation, said that his best bet would be to try and get the letter into the hands of the Americans in Berlin and promised to see what could be done. He explained that he would be returning to Warsaw for a final trip, after which he was due to return to Japan for good and the Warsaw embassy would be closed down. The letter was handed to him the very next day. He was as good as his word, for three weeks later word got through that he was back and wished to see my mother. This was, of course, an exciting moment for her, and what he had to say was equally so.

One has to imagine the atmosphere prevailing in Berlin in those tense war days, the distrust as well as the secrecy which must have pervaded foreign diplomatic circles in that city, and if the position of the Americans there was already tenuous, then surprisingly neither, it seems, did the Japanese escape suspicion, as 'close' as they were to the Germans.

Having decided that the American embassy was indeed to be the target of his mission, our faithful Japanese proceeded to reconnoitre the territory surrounding it, in order to find out how best to deal with his mission. However, after three abortive trips he concluded that it was not possible for him to take that risk. Firstly, he explained, he was too well known to the German security service, and secondly, the American embassy was too well guarded. Undaunted, he then persuaded the caretaker in the Japanese embassy to take the letter and try to deliver it. Under the cover of darkness and looking quite inconspicuous, the Japanese caretaker circled the building and then, seizing his chance, approached an unguarded door at the rear of the building and deposited it in the letter box.

Some time later my father received a letter from the Foreign Office in London to say that a communication had been received via the American embassy in London, addressed to him, and in order to claim it he should call at the US embassy. The letter depressed him intensely, added to which Mother's change of name was misunderstood, for he somehow concluded that she had re-married. Mother had not explained the situation regarding her faked marriage due to an oversight, although I believe this was primarily because she was being cautious lest the letter fell into the wrong hands and gave the game away.

This illuminating episode served to show, that even in times like those, one could never tell who one's friends were.

Whilst this was happening, other events were now gathering momentum which, for me, were to have far-reaching consequences.

I have already mentioned Kathleen Smith, the lady who, because of her Irish nationality, had enjoyed immunity from the German authorities. This however did not mean that she did not have to take great care, and because of this our meetings with her were rare. Her 'immunity', however, totally belied her sentiments because on the day she decided to pay us a visit, she had already become involved in activities which would have qualified her for instant imprisonment.

There were, she explained, a number of escaped British prisoners of war in hiding, in and around the Warsaw area, desperately in need of food and shelter. Some were already taken care of, but more volunteers were required to take them in on a rota system, so that they did not stay in one place for too long.

Would we help out? We agreed without hesitation. She then departed, saying that we would be hearing from her within a fortnight.

We were both staggered by this news and felt elated, yet not without a tinge of apprehension, for the dangers were only too obvious. But the overwhelming feeling was that at last we would be involved in something of positive use to the cause we were fighting for and that we would be of assistance to men who would come to rely so much on people like ourselves. And the Poles, who came to be involved in this dangerous game, never lacked that quality of selfless courage.

So it was that several days later a knock on the door heralded the arrival of Kathleen in the company of two of our escapees, John Grant and George Newton. Both had been captured at the fall of France and had been 'on the run' for about a month. John, a fresh-faced Londoner, could not have looked more British if he tried, but George, a 'true Geordie', much less so. If my memory serves me correctly, they both served in the King's Royal Rifle Corps. This was to be their second 'safe house' since their escape and we made them as comfortable as possible. Fortunately Mother's flat had a small room which I had been occupying, so I moved out to make room for them. Feeding two extra mouths was a serious problem but we managed. Even more serious was the problem of keeping them out of our neighbours' sight as much as possible, for the appearance of two strange young men within our suburban community was bound to raise questions – moreover men who spoke not a word of Polish! Fortunately we could rely on the owners of the house. We took them into our confidence and to give them their due, they hardly batted an eyelid, their only plea being that our two lodgers did not stay for too long a time, which was only reasonable, as the last thing that was wanted was for the police to be alerted.

It was extremely difficult to set a rigid routine for escapees, such as remaining indoors during the day as much as possible, and venturing out only at dusk, not visiting '*knajpy*' (inns) and not trying to communicate with strangers. All this was anathema to young men who had escaped their prisoner-of-war camps precisely to be free and, rather naively at times, might have cherished the notion that it was fine to talk to all and sundry. Unhappily wagging tongues were a real menace and the presence of informers a stark reality.

At weekends I would go for walks with them and indulge in a charade of conversing in Polish to them whenever we passed someone by. I had taught them two basic words, '*tak*' and '*nie*' (yes and no), which they could say at appropriate moments, but as their pronunciation was so bad we decided that silence was preferable. I also insisted that they try and look as inconspicuous as possible, which not only meant wearing drab clothing but also a drab expression! For that is exactly how the Germans expected to see us – downtrodden and glum! John's clean-shaven, Anglo-Saxon face was also cause for concern, but there was nothing to be done about that. However, all went well and after a fortnight I was requested to escort them to a certain address in Warsaw.

George Weeks arrived several days later and also stayed for a fortnight. As he required some medical treatment it became necessary to see a doctor but, as one would expect, his discretion was unquestionable and he refused to charge a fee. Bless him.

Our fourth escapee was Alan Potter, a quiet and rather vague individual who for some reason aroused in me a suspicion that he might not be what he claimed, and I promptly got in touch with Kathleen Smith expressing my doubts concerning him. However she assured me that his credentials had been checked out and that he was a genuine escapee. One could not be too careful. He too was to be escorted to another safe house in town, two weeks later.

Thus the whole operation depended on so many stout-hearted people who were prepared to risk their freedom and their lives to help those in need. A vital feature of the organization was to know as little about it as possible so that we never knew where such-and-such escapee had been or who he had met. All we knew was the address to which he had to be taken. And at this stage all we knew was that Kathleen Smith was 'up to her eyes' in it.

Among several others I met were two prominent escapees, Lieutenant Michael Sinclair and Major Littledale who, interestingly, were harboured at the time by the Whiteheads. The Whiteheads, originally of Lancashire stock, in the days before the First World War had gravitated to Tzarist Russia. What they did there I do not know, but they fled the Revolution in 1917 and established themselves in a newly independent Poland. There were four sons and after the death of his wife Mr Whitehead married a Polish lady and adopted Polish nationality. However, whatever he did in Russia and subsequently Poland, he must have done well, for he was able to take over ownership of the well-known confectionary business of E. Wedel, which became a household name and achieved some renown abroad, including Britain. My father knew the family well and I recall meeting them on occasion. Two of his sons, Alfred and George, escaped to Britain after the collapse of Poland in 1939 and joined the RAF, when my father met them once again.

It was a curious experience meeting these two British officers in these strange circumstances; unhappily they were later recaptured and confined to the notorious Colditz Castle. Mention of them is to be found in the book written by P.R. Reid, entitled *The Colditz Story* which was published in the 1950s.

In the meantime the Germans were making gigantic preparations for their assault on Russia. The inhabitants of Warsaw had been aware for weeks of the unusually large movement of military hardware heading in an easterly direction and reports from other parts also confirmed it. At first it was put down to a routine regrouping of forces, but as time went by it became obvious that something far more serious was afoot. The entire population waited and wondered. Could it be that the impossible was about to happen? When it finally became patently clear what was about to happen, we all prayed that these two evil giants would fight to the death and tear each other apart on the distant steppes of Russia. But it wasn't quite like that, as we now know.

What everyone had hoped for was that whilst the Germans were absorbed in their life-and-death struggle with the Soviets, they would be obliged to reduce their repression and cruel regime on the Polish population. Sadly it did not turn out that way. We had underestimated the Germans, for rather than ease their efforts, they seemed to redouble them with incredible venom, as though to demonstrate their complete supremacy. The truth was that there was to be no respite.

Olek and I continued on our rounds as usual during these goings on, whilst indulging in our own private battle with the recalcitrant Ford. That too had not changed. However, sometime early in 1941, I was summoned to a meeting by Kathleen Smith. The purpose of it was to gather together a number of escapees for a briefing which was to take place in a flat on Mokotowska Street. I was to call at a certain address in Warsaw, collect John Grant and George Newton and escort them to our destination. This went without a hitch and the three of us entered the crowded city streets. The drill was for me to lead, followed several paces behind by John and George. There were many Germans around, possibly troops on leave, but there was no reason to fear them, provided one gave them a reasonably wide berth. All went well on Marshalkowska Street, but then I became aware of a minor commotion which appeared to be taking place behind me and, turning around, to my horror I saw Grant and a German standing in the middle of the pavement eyeing each other with obvious distaste, the German letting forth a stream of invective. Both seemed to have reached a point where fists were about to fly but as the German raised his hand I grabbed Grant by the arm and dragged him away.

The German stood his ground glowering and muttering dire threats, whereupon his companions, who had gone on ahead, turned round and came back towards us. Now, I thought, this is the end, for there were seven of them and they were obviously coming to the rescue of their friend. But their mood did not appear to be hostile and in a jocular manner called on the bully to pack it in! Luckily he took heed of his comrades and we melted away into the crowd. When it was safe to talk, John explained that he had accidentally kicked the German's ankle in the ensuing crush and that he was ready to fight him. Grant seethed with indignation and regretted that the chance of 'getting even' with the German had gone. But better to take an insult than a trip back to a POW camp!

Observing the usual precautions, John and George entered the building on Mokotowska Street first and waited for me in the darkened lobby. Meanwhile I walked on, carefully observing whether there was anything suspicious nearby –

a parked car with the usual dour characters lurking inside it, or others 'casually' hanging about in doorways pretending to read a newspaper – and, having allowed about four minutes to elapse, as instructed, entered the house. Some had already arrived at the flat and we waited for a further half hour for the rest to trickle in, singly and in pairs.

All the escapees who I knew were present, as well as one other who I did not. Lieutenant Sinclair and Major Littledale were absent for the simple reason that they had not yet arrived on the scene. In fact, this was to be one of several similar meetings, for so high was the number of escapees in Warsaw (the figure was put at twenty-two in 1942) at that time that it would have been folly to try and gather everyone under one roof at the same time.

Also present were the leaders of the organization: Kathleen Smith, Olszewski, Romanski and a Mrs Markowska.

Olszewski, a thoughtful man of middle age and a civil engineer by profession, spoke excellent English. Romanski, a stocky man in early middle age, had been a serving officer in the Polish Army, whilst Mrs Markowska stood out as 'the leading light' of the group. She was English, had married a Pole many years before and in her younger days, prior to the First World War, had been governess to the ruling family in Austria. In spite of her age, she displayed a remarkable energy and enthusiasm for the dangerous work she had now undertaken. Also present was a tall young Pole, a courier who had been parachuted into German-occupied territory.

At first the discussion revolved around organizational matters, then proceeded to the question of the escapees' welfare, and finally to the order in which they would be passed along the escape route, which led to the south of Poland, into Czechoslovak territory and eventually Turkey.

Plans for the operation had already been set into motion and were obviously far more advanced than I realized. Indeed, the problems as well as the dangers involved in such a complex plan were daunting.

Broadly, it was to work on the principle of 'first in, first out', thus John and George would be on their way first. The second group was to consist of George Weeks and myself and so on. The whole operation was to commence in July (1941). As the meeting came to an end and we left the building singly or in pairs, just as we had arrived, the feeling of excitement became overwhelming, the prospect of the dangers that lay ahead utterly daunting.

I was later to escort Alan Potter to a similar meeting, but to a different address, where there were other escapees present, as well as the courier from England. The courier explained that a regular financial allowance could be arranged for me 'through London', as he put it, which was an extremely attractive thought, but my instinct told me to decline, much to his amazement.

The third and last meeting I attended took place in the autumn, in the lovely flat belonging to the Whiteheads, on the corner of Bracka and Hortensii, and involved Sinclair and Littledale. In the meantime, John and George's July departure had been delayed and they were obliged to stay a further week with us in Saska Kepa before being passed on to another safe house. I briefly caught sight of them two and a half years later!

Now I had to wait patiently for the signal telling me that it was my turn to go.

The winter of 1941/42 was a severe one. The Germans, having counted on a swift and victorious campaign in Russia, sent many of their men to the front ill equipped for what turned out to be a protracted and hard-fought war, if not to say a cruel one.

All went well for them in the first few weeks and their famous blitzkrieg tactics proved a great success, as it had done both in Poland and France earlier. Thousands upon thousands of Russian prisoners were taken, an entire army under General Vlasov surrendering to them. The Soviet Army reeled with each German hammer blow, but at the same time withdrew to the deep and distant fastness of 'Mother Russia', leaving in their wake dedicated groups of partisans to harass the Wehrmacht.

But that winter was the Wehrmacht's undoing. Lacking suitable clothing, their units became decimated with cases of severe frostbite and it was then that the evidence of their own misjudgement became only too obvious on the streets of Warsaw. Having requisitioned most trams in the city they ran a continuous shuttle service between the railway stations and the city's hospitals. This went on day after day and the sight of these trams crawling on their way in a crocodile, laden with their human wreckage, was something to be seen.

There was no denying that at first each tram load of wounded was silently cheered on its way by the population. We were glad of their suffering. But as time went by the feeling wore thin, for in purely terms of human suffering it would have been an obscenity to have continued.

Desperate for warm clothing for their troops, the Germans devised a simple method of procuring this precious commodity at no cost to themselves. An order went out demanding that civilians possessing furs, fur coats and ski boots were to hand them in, but they did not waste any time waiting for a response and began literally stripping people of their clothes in the streets. It became a common sight to see some hapless individual going on his or her way in stockinged feet, or minus an overcoat in freezing weather, having just been stripped of it. It happened to Jurek, who was told to remove his ski boots by two officers, fortunately within sight of home, but it could be said that he had the last laugh for the ones stolen from him were old and worn, and a brand new pair, carefully preserved since before the war, lay safely closeted in a cupboard. These he promptly took to a local cobbler who cut them down to resemble shoes! But this was yet another illustration in the way the Germans 'turned the screw' on a population already suffering terrible privation.

As though that wasn't bad enough, people were forbidden to keep their hands in their pockets. This cruel order was issued because of the growing number of killings which the resistance movement was inflicting on members of the German armed forces on the streets of Warsaw, and anyone seen with their hands in their pockets would be presumed to be concealing a gun! If one placed oneself in that position, it literally meant that one would be shot on sight, and the self-discipline required to conform to that iniquitous order, in the very depths of winter, taxed one to the limit.

And so the respite we had hoped for never materialized and the atrocities against the population continued unabated.

My long tram journey to work each morning at one point ran parallel with the high wall which surrounded the Jewish ghetto, the partly destroyed buildings within it standing out like gaunt, darkened skeletons. As the tram trundled past this ghostly apparition, fifteen or so bodies hung in full view, men put to death as a reprisal for the killing of German soldiers. This message to the people could not have been clearer and soon became the norm.

It did not weaken people's resolve, however, and I discovered that Hania too had become deeply involved in some clandestine activity, although I never asked any questions. By now she had left her work at the factory and was employed as a personal secretary to the director of an engineering firm, and we saw even less of each other than before.

It was during one of our rare meetings that she said she had something I ought to have and pressed on me a small object wrapped in paper, which on closer examination appeared to be a piece of confectionary – a sweet – with the famous word 'E. Wedel' printed on it.

'It's not what you think it is, you know,' she said in a matter-of-fact manner.
'

'Oh, what is it then?' I replied, puzzled by this unexpected little gift.

'Well, it's a cyanide pill. Put it in your pocket and keep it there. I've got one as well. My stepfather made them up for me, he's such a clever old stick.' (Her stepfather, a Dr Kielbasinski, was a professor of chemistry and physics.) I gingerly dropped it into my coat pocket.

It was at about this time that I got to know more about Mrs Markowska, as i had to take various messages to her that had been passed on to me by Kathleen Smith. This was largely done to protect Kathleen, since she was in a far more vulnerable position than I was.

Mrs Markowska and her elderly husband lived on Ordynacka Street, which was a short walk from the busy thoroughfare, Nowy Swiat. It was rather a curious arrangement, because they occupied part of a large ground-floor premises which constituted the offices and showroom for a firm of wholesale suppliers of industrial tools, i.e. picks and shovels. Presumably to make ends meet, she taught the English language to a number of people with an eye to the future, or who simply wanted to widen their horizons, having decided that even in the prevailing circumstances, the risk was worth taking. Learning English, in fact, generally became the all-absorbing ambition of a large number of people. Of course, what her pupils were unaware of was her secret activity with the escape line.

In January of the following year, a much agitated Kathleen called at our flat on Saska Kepa. The news was disturbing. Rumours were in circulation that all was not well with the organization. Information was scant, but it was suspected that two British escapees had been recaptured. As it was obvious the Germans would want to keep it quiet, the wisest thing to do was to lie low for a time and await developments.

Whilst I packed a bag and made tracks to my good friend Jurek, my mother decided to stay in Saska Kepa and promptly scoured the flat for any incriminating material, in anticipation of a possible visit by the Gestapo. Time passed by and as neither I nor Mother had word of further trouble, I returned to her flat about a month later.

Observing greater care than usual, a further meeting with Kathleen revealed that the rumour was true and that the identity of the captured men was now in no doubt. Although it was impossible to gather further details, everything pointed to the organization having been 'blown'. The situation was even more serious than we thought and there was nothing for it but to disperse and keep our heads down. However, before yet again taking advantage of Jurek and his mother's hospitality, I had decided to call on the intrepid Mrs Markowska in the hope of gleaning more information on the situation.

Having returned to the factory after completing our usual rounds in the old Ford at about 6.00 p.m., I caught a tram, travelling as far a Marszalkowska where I alighted and cut along a street which led me to Hania's flat on Mazowiecka Street. She was in, and when we had talked for a while I said that I had to be on my way to Ordynacka Street before returning home to beat the curfew. My time was short. Hania knew very little about my involvement with the escape organization, but had remembered how on some previous occasion I had mentioned Ordynacka Street. With true feminine intuition, she demanded that I turn out my pockets and check there was nothing incriminating lurking within them. And indeed there was. The first thing that came to light was a screwed-up clandestine newspaper, of the sort often passed around factory floors, followed by one or two other small items that Hania deemed worthy of confiscation. But two items somehow got overlooked. One was the stub of a small pencil which had belonged to one of Father's old diaries, on which, in decipherable gold letters, was imprinted 'CHAS. LETTS'. The other was the old First World War tunic which I wore under my overcoat. It would normally have been of little consequence, but it happened to be a British one – not that Father had ever had occasion to wear it – and it was one of those things that always just happened to be around. My mother had wisely replaced the lovely gilt buttons with ordinary ones, and I had worn it every winter since the war began. Nevertheless, to the trained eye, its cut and style revealed its obvious origin. Also removed was a small label with the manufacturers name and date, 1918.

Not wishing to worry mother, I had decided against telling her about my intended visit to Ordynacka Street but as it was as well to let someone know, who better than Hania should know?

A gentle snow fell as I stepped out into the street, and for a moment I stood and listened to the muffled, lilting tones of music wafting from the Mazowsze Cafe opposite. The orchestra played 'Jealousy', one of my favourites, so I crossed over to be a little closer to it and for a brief moment be able to bask in the yellow pools of light which reflected on the pavement from the elegantly draped windows. Lucky people, in there, I thought – but were they really lucky, or happy? Anyway, most of them were probably Germans. With that thought I moved on.

Hurrying now, I crossed Nowy Swiat and presently turned into Ordynacka Street. It was a black night with not a single street light to illuminate the way, but I found the house without any trouble. There were no tell-tale cars parked nearby and the coast was clear. I rang the doorbell and presently the door was opened by a small, rotund man, which surprised me, since Mrs Markowska always answered the door herself. But I supposed she was busy with her pupils and the little man, awaiting his turn, had been asked to admit other callers. Hesitating, I asked if Mrs Markowska was in and he stood aside to let me in, at the same time gesturing that I should enter a room where presumably he, too, had been waiting for her. But there, huddled in a corner, sat four people in a state of obvious distress – I knew by his blue peaked cap that the man in the group was the caretaker. His presence suddenly struck me like a thunderbolt – he and his family were being held there to prevent them from warning off callers to the flat.

For a moment I stood in the middle of the room in a state of shock as it dawned on me what had happened. The Gestapo's old trick! When I turned towards the little man, I found myself peering down the barrel of a Luger. And all the while not a word had been spoken. Waving the gun, he motioned me to sit down on a chair in a far corner of the room, away from the door, at the same time placing himself on a chair by the door, all the while nursing the gun on his lap. I cursed silently a thousand times. It had all happened so easily and undramatically. How could I have fallen for this neat little trap? At first, confused thoughts crowded my head, but this was no time to panic, I told myself. For the sheer enormity of events and the obvious calamity which had befallen the organization, with all its consequences, could easily have overcome reason.

In the other corner of the room, the caretaker sat with his head buried in his hands while his wife protectively clutched both the bewildered children in her arms. I felt desperately sorry for them.

As silence descended on the room, I decided on the 'innocent' approach by explaining to the little man that my visit to see Mrs Markowska was unimportant, that it did not matter whether she was in or not and that I ought to be on my way in order to get home before the nine o'clock curfew.

'No, we have to wait for the others,' he replied blandly. It had been worth a try but now at least I knew that reinforcements were on the way, which was not a happy thought.

I surveyed the room for a possible route to escape. A dash for the door seemed to be the least likely method to succeed. A header through the window might work, but the heavy drapes were drawn and it was impossible to tell if the window was heavily protected with bars, as they often were in ground floor premises. Reluctantly, I discarded that idea. The massive brass lamp which stood on a large desk looked attractive – if I could only hurl the thing across the room and knock the little man out with it before he fired his gun. But lamps are, in a sense, tethered to the wall by a flex, so how far would this one travel before falling onto the floor? Not far enough. There was no way of rehearsing such daring acts to see if they worked – they would have to the first time!

In the hour which had elapsed before the arrival of the 'heavies', no one else arrived to fall into the trap. But it gave me ample thinking time in which to formulate a plausible excuse for my presence here. Beyond that, I would have to wait and see, for there were too many imponderables at this stage.

My worst thoughts, however, concerned my mother. I prayed that the leads the Gestapo were now following would miraculously fall short of Saska Kepa and knew that in one hour's time, at the nine o'clock curfew, my absence would cause alarm bells to start ringing. I had little fear for Hania's safety, since she had no connection with the organization whatsoever. Her own commitment lay in another direction, but she was the only one to know of my movements that night. Then there was Kathleen Smith, Mrs Markowska, Olszewski and Romanski, as well as the whole group of escapees. The vision of the tragedy unfolding itself in my mind was too much to take in. And surely there would be many more victims caught in the spider's web.

Presently I heard a car draw up, followed by a knocking on the door. It was opened by the little man and four tough-looking individuals entered the room. All four stared at me for a minute before two of them went into another room (the one which was used as a showroom for industrial implements), where Mrs Markowska would always see me. The two who remained stood directly in front of me and demanded to know why I had come here.

I started to reply but was struck across the face and told to tell them the truth, because they knew exactly why I had come here anyway. I managed to complete my story, explaining that I had intended to find out about English language lessons. At this, both proceeded to punch me until my head began to strike the wall. It hurt. In a more menacing manner, they once again demanded to know why I had come here, repeating that they knew all about me anyway and it was pointless lying. My repeated answer brought another vicious flurry of punches.

They had worked themselves into a towering rage and the same process continued over and over again. It got progressively more painful for me, but for them, nowhere. Instinct told me that they really knew nothing about me at all. Not yet, anyhow. When they had finished, I was dragged into the other room where they told me that I would be given one more chance to tell the truth about my visit here. Should I fail to do so, I would be beaten to insensitivity with shovels, screamed one, pointing to a rack of new shovels. Perversely, I thought, if they have to bash me with shovels, they should at least use the flat rather than the edge!

I composed myself and as calmly as I could, told them how I had always been interested in foreign languages – as I already had a fair command of German, I wished to learn Italian as well as English. I had heard that Mrs Markowska taught English and indeed had called once before to discuss her terms, but she had been too busy to see me on that occasion. In no uncertain terms, they yelled, did I expect them to believe that kind of story and did I not realize that they knew everything about me?

For the tenth time, I told them that was the truth and if they cared to ask Mrs Markowska, she would verify every word I had said. They then demanded to know who had told me about her in the first place. I said it had been someone I had once worked with in the net factory.

'What's his name?'

'Pawlowski,' I replied (there had been a Pawlowski at the camouflage-net factory, but he had long since left). A check at my place of employment would have confirmed this, but I knew Pawlowski would never be found as he was a casual worker and no record was kept of his whereabouts.

'Right! We shall now see if what you're saying is right – bring him in!' he said to his companion.

Mr Markowska was then brought in looking terribly frail and frightened. 'Now tell us who he is,' the little man, Gustav, said, pointing at me.

'He is an Englishman. I heard him speaking in English to my wife during a previous visit,' came the shaky reply.

'You see. He is English!' Gustav cried, thumping his fist on the table. 'Now what have you to say?' He leered at me triumphantly.

'I don't know how he can say this because I only saw him once before, that's true, but as to my speaking English …!' I made a dismissive gesture. 'I came here to learn the language so he couldn't possibly have heard me speaking it. How can I be an Englishman? Why don't you ask Mrs Markowska? She will verify it!' I replied with as much indignation as I could muster. For a moment Gustav looked nonplussed, no doubt wondering how, if I was English, I could speak such flawless Polish.

'Search him!' Gustav ordered and, grabbed by two others, I was hauled into the middle of the room and told to empty my pockets. How I blessed Hania for her intuition! But what if they discovered the cyanide tablet? Trapping the 'sweet' between two fingers like a magician, I proceeded to empty my pockets of the odd harmless items, when suddenly out fell the tiny pencil which had lain at the bottom of my pocket. I could have cursed and hoped that stubby little pencil would be overlooked, as surely the name of 'CHAS. LETTS.' embossed on it would not escape their attention. To my relief it did. After all, a pencil is a pencil.

'Now take your clothes off!' demanded Gustav.'

No sooner had I removed my top coat when I was set upon by a young SS officer. 'Oh yes, oh yes!' he exclaimed excitedly, fingering my tunic. 'There's no doubting this one!' For a moment everyone joined in – pulling, pushing and cursing me.

'Where did you get this tunic!' shouted Gustav.

As casually as I could I explained that a farmer had given it to me since I hadn't anything to wear during the winter of 1939 when I was in the Russian zone (the British government had sold large quantities of British Army surplus issue to the Poles after the 1914–18 war, so my story was not a wild one). I also volunteered the information that there had been a label sewn to it, somewhere inside.

'What did it say?' demanded Gustav eagerly.

'I think the date 1918,' I said and noticed Gustav's disappointment. A thorough search followed – every seam, nook and cranny was scrutinized and examined by fingers feeling for a tell-tale rustle or thickening of the fabric, which might conceal something. My bare body was also searched. Gustav never ceased to remind me during all this that they knew all about me and what I had been doing – yet never once actually spelt it out. When my heavy boots were searched I was reminded of the way the young SS men had ripped shoes apart during the search at Brest in 1940 and couldn't resist uttering in a sarcastic voice, 'I trust you won't wreck my shoes,' which was a mistake.

Gustav took a swipe at me and muttered to the SS man, 'Er ist ein intelligente – aber er ist sehr stolz.' (He's intelligent but very proud). Which I took as a compliment!

Back in the first room again, there was now no sign of the caretaker and his family.

A portable typewriter was brought in and a statement was started:

'Name?'

'Tomasz Kopystynski.'

'Date of birth?'

'1920.'

'Place of birth?'

'Kiev.'

'Address?'

'Obroncow 22, Saska Kepa.'

'Who else lives at that address?'

'My aunt, Mrs Zaworski. She has looked after me since childhood after my parents were killed by Bolsheviks.'

'We will search the place,' was his cryptic comment. 'Now tell us, what you were doing here?'

I repeated the reason for my visit and after a pause said as innocently as I could, 'Can I go now?'

'You are coming with us,' laughed Gustav.

Grabbed firmly by both arms I was hustled outside and pushed into the back seat of a small DKW car which stood outside. With Gustav sitting on top of me, we moved off.

After a quarter of an hour we entered one of the checkpoints which separated the city from the Jewish ghetto and stopped in front of the huge forbidding gates of the dreaded Pawiak prison – now a prison within a prison. I was checked in at the reception desk and handed over everything which I carried in my pockets, except the cyanide tablet.

'What are you in for?' asked the bored clerk with pen poised to enter me in the appropriate column.

'I don't really know,' I replied.

'Well what did you do?' he pressed.

'Nothing as far as I know. I was arrested in this flat …'

'They all say that,' he interrupted casually without looking up and noted in his book the word: 'Political'.

It was long past lights out and the whole prison was in darkness. A Polish guard led me down stone steps, our footsteps echoing in the dungeon corridors. Unlocking a cell door he switched on the light for a few seconds, revealing a tiny, dingy cell crammed full of reclining bodies. At the far end, beneath a tiny window, sat an elderly man. In an instant I recognized Olszewski, one of the leading figures in our organization whom I had met at the briefings. Nobody showed any interest, so gingerly treading between the grunting bodies I edged forward and sat down beside him.

'So they've got you too,' he whispered. 'Where did they get you?'

'At Mrs Markowska's", I whispered.

'God! That's about the worst place you could have been. Listen, we must not be seen talking, you never know who's in the cell; they have informers everywhere, but if they ask us, we don't know each other. OK?' I was desperately tired and had to lie down. I managed to slide onto the stone floor and stretch out whilst Olszewski lay down on the bench.

My thoughts turned to my mother and I prayed that the threat of a visit by Gustav and his gang wouldn't take place that night, thus giving her sufficient time to escape. I judged the time to be after nine o'clock when, hopefully, the alarm would have been raised. I went over the evening's events, making a mental note of everything I had said and searched for any hopeful signs. Only one emerged: there had been no sign of Mrs Markowska in the flat, otherwise why did they not produce her instead of bringing out poor old Mr Markowsksi, who had obviously been threatened and frightened into making a statement against me? Surely even the Gestapo realized what an unreliable witness he was – but only time would tell. I wondered who else had been arrested and how they would stand up to the trials and tribulations of the days that lay ahead. Olszewski, and Romanski, who I was to meet two days later, were up to their necks in it and were in a terrible position.

The following morning 'appel' was at the crack of dawn, when the prison came to life again amidst shouts and clanking of keys. All new arrivals were marched off to a separate building for delousing and a shower – always at the double. There was hardly time to undress and get dressed again under the malevolent glare of SS guards wielding whips. Because of our excursion to the baths and delousing we missed 'breakfast' altogether and were forced to sit on the floor of our tiny cell like sardines, making any movement impossible. In the corner of the cell stood an open bucket – the smell was beyond belief! I wondered how long I would have to endure this hell-hole when the cell doors were opened up amidst shouting and the noise of hundreds of boots tramping along the stone corridors. Everyone was assembled in the yard for exercise, in columns of four, under the watchful eyes of the SS guards. Many prisoners were glad to see their friends, exchanged greetings and passed on messages sending a constant buzz of voices which began to irritate the guards. Their roars for silence had little effect and we were threatened with punishment if the noise continued. We soon found out. 'Alle nieder!' (Everybody down!) roared the guards, closing in on the columns with whips raised. We were made to crouch on our haunches and then frogmarched round and round the prison yard. We had to balance unaided and anyone caught supporting himself on the man in front or with his hands on the ground was whiplashed. This was a gymnastic feat only a fit man could perform. Not surprisingly, therefore, the whips cracked all the time. One cheated at every possible opportunity, though. I was at the end of my tether when they suddenly called it off, but we had to carry several elderly men back to the cells as a result.

In the early hours of the following morning a distraught young man in our cell attempted to hang himself from the bars on the window, causing a commotion as everyone made a grab for him before he could do himself any harm. He was inconsolable and kept moaning, 'They will kill me, they will kill me!' The reaction from the other cell-mates varied from sympathy to impatience and left us all rattled for the rest of the day. We were all in the same boat, living through our own private hells, so a loss of nerve on anyone's part was unwelcome. The senior inmates requested the unfortunate's transfer to another cell and the Polish guard duly obliged.

The following day I was transferred to a larger basement cell and met up with Romanski, the other leading member of the organization. However, neither of us gave any sign of recognition, knowing that we might be watched. I could see no other reason for my transfer other than the gross overcrowding of the previous cell. I knew Romanski rather less than Olszewski, but came to admire his quiet courage and flashes of dry humour. As an ex-serving officer he probably stood to lose more than the rest of us. Months later, during a brief conversation with Olszewski, he said, 'Poor Romanski was caught red-handed – he hasn't a chance.'

Almost a week after my arrest I was called out along with Romanski and Olszewski to the reception office. Several others were already gathered there: Dr Dabrowski, Ignatowicz and two women, neither of whom I knew, but guessed that they were connected with the organization (they were Mrs Borman and Zubrzycka). All our belongings were returned to us and each of us was issued with a small brown loaf and a chunk of bacon. During the course of this toing and froing Olszewski whispered to me, 'I think I know what this is all about – we must be going to Krakow. The whole case is being handled by the Krakow Gestapo.' Gradually it emerged that the reason for our transfer was because the two prisoners of war (mentioned previously) had been recaptured in the south of Poland and imprisoned in Krakow. Consequently, the follow-up operations in Warsaw were also handled by the Krakow Gestapo. Considerable rivalry existed between the Gestapo groups operating in various parts of the country, and no doubt the Krakow branch saw this catch as a feather in their caps, whilst at the same time denying their Warsaw comrades some of the glory.

Significantly, both Olszewski and Romanski were initially taken to the Aleja Szucha Gestapo headquarters in Warsaw for interrogation and then promptly removed from it by the Krakow Gestapo. I myself was never taken there, but much later Gustav made an interesting comment during my own interrogation: 'You can count yourself lucky that you were arrested by us from Krakow, because the Warsaw Gestapo would have given you a much harder time.'

Chapter Ten

We filed into a grey truck waiting outside. I was made to sit forward immediately behind the cab, and the last to get in was Gustav, after another civilian Gestapo and two uniformed SS officers carrying Bergmann sub-machine guns. We jolted our way over the cobbled streets of Warsaw and joined the main highway leading to the south-west. It was bitterly cold with a leaden sky above and thick snow blanketing the countryside.

Olszewski, sitting next to me, whispered, 'If we turn right within the next two kilometres we're all finished because it will be to Palmiry, so let's pray we carry straight on.' (He was referring to the execution grounds where countless numbers of hostages and political prisoners were summarily executed and buried in mass graves.)

A lump came to my throat and I prayed, however the truck continued on its journey and we relaxed somewhat. Later, we pulled up at a roadside inn which emptied on our arrival, as if by magic, as we all trooped in. The innkeeper, looking petrified with fear, ushered us to a long table where we sat down with the senior SS man at its head. Two plates of sausage sandwiches were ordered, but our guardians ate most of them leaving just a morsel for the rest of us to share. We were also made to pay for them. For us starving prisoners, the smell of bread and garlic sausage was almost too much to bear. Then the senior SS man in charge made a speech for our benefit, telling us how Germany had to be constantly on her guard against disruptive and subversive elements that were ready to strike against Germany's war effort – presumably we fell into that category. 'However,' he added, 'Germans are a humane people and after a fair hearing' our own position 'will be duly resolved.'

During this little pep-talk I noticed Dr Dabrowski getting more and more agitated and red in the face. Indeed, he seemed to be the least likely of all of us to do so, but suddenly, unable to contain himself any more, he leaped to his feet.

'Please tell me, then,' he blurted out, 'why is it, if you say you are so humane, do you have to arrest thousands of innocent people and send them to concentration camps?' All eyes turned on him and a truly pregnant silence descended.

'Sit down, Doctor!' hissed Romanski.

'Shut up!,' added Olszewski, blanching visibly whilst the rest of us were quickly overcome by a fit of coughing and shuffling of feet.

Curiously, with the exception of Gustav, our guardians seemed to ignore this outburst save the senior SS man who rose red faced from his chair and repeated emphatically, 'We Germans are "hart aber menschlich"' (firm but humane).

On the road again, ensconced in my corner directly behind the cab, I began to contemplate the chances of escape. With the truck in motion one way would be to take a header over the tailboard between the two armed guards – an exercise fit enough for a most experienced acrobat, but not for me! Along the sides of the lorry the canopy was fastened down on hooks spaced about every ten inches apart, but it was far too taut for my body to squeeze through even if I managed to loosen one or two hooks. Moreover the driver was bound to see what was happening in his rear-view mirror. I made one decision, however, and with a mixture of defiance and optimism stealthily extricated the poisoned sweet from my pocket and let it drop onto the road. Would I regret it? I wondered.

The night was spent in a prison at Kielce, roughly midway between Warsaw and Krakow. We were split up and placed in different cells, the two women having to spend the night in a male cell. Later in the evening a number of young Russian prisoners of war were brought in, frozen and hungry. One poor soldier, excruciatingly thin, weak and as white as a sheet, was carried in by his comrades. When he spoke his voice rasped horribly and the poor fellow could obviously not last many more days. The most articulate amongst them was a sergeant of about thirty years with whom we struck up a conversation. By far the fittest of the bunch, he understood German and had acted as camp interpreter, but said he had no idea where they were being transferred. Russian prisoners were treated abominably and perished in their thousands from disease and malnutrition.

We checked in at the Pomorska Street Gestapo headquarters in Krakow the following afternoon, moving on again to disembark at a military prison. After the usual preliminaries in the reception office, we were dispersed into separate cells. The din throughout the building was deafening as guards bawled out orders to scores of young German army offenders who clattered their way up and down the metal stairways and along the galleries. Locked in a freezing cold cell, the thought of being here somehow seemed preferable to being in the care of the Gestapo.

Hunger was now constantly gnawing at my innards. I had devoured the last of the bacon at Kielce, leaving only a small but precious chunk of black bread from my Pawiak issue. This ration had been eked out sparingly for there was no way of knowing when the next meal would come. All the noises indicated that it was mealtime and suddenly the tiny hatch in the cell door flew open and a chunk of stale bread dropped onto the floor. At first I was unable to bring myself to pick it up thinking, That's how they feed animals in the zoo and I shall certainly not stoop to that level! My contemplation was cut short as the door was flung open and four or five SS men flung themselves upon me. In a matter of seconds they had whisked through all my pockets, tore my tunic open, called me a string of choice names and then vanished as suddenly as they had appeared – like a whirlwind! It seemed as though it was a pastime devised to relieve their boredom with a strong 'finder's keeper's' connotation. I slept fitfully in the icy cell upon the straw-filled palliasse without a blanket – needless to say I ate the last stale lump of bread.

My cell door was opened by a simple-minded sergeant who summoned me with the words 'Come on, Englishman!' I was taken to the reception office where he insisted that I was English and had been overheard talking in English in my sleep. I felt the fool was trying to score a brownie point and could only comment icily that I was not prone to sleep talking, certainly not in English. Olszewski, Romanski, Ignatowicz, Dr Dabrowski and the two quiet, dignified ladies were all there too. At no time had the Gestapo hinted about the presence of British prisoners of war, yet the Sergeant's outburst served as a warning that I should be very much on guard if my bluff was to succeed.

Once again Olszewski was to whisper a few words to me: 'I'd hoped that we would come under the jurisdiction of the Wehrmacht. But it looks as though we will be handed over to the Gestapo for good.' Shaking his head wistfully, he went on, 'I'm sure that they have the two British prisoners here as well and I fully expected a confrontation with them but for some reason they seem to have decided against it.'

Later, the two women were taken to Helclow Prison, the rest of us arriving at Montelupich, a former military prison on the outskirts of the city. This was to be my home for the next fifteen months.

Unlike Pawiak, which was built by the Russians in the nineteenth century, the Montelupich and Helclow complex – grey, forbidding and emanating an atmosphere of eternal suffering of all the past generations of persecuted Poles – was built much later under the Austrian occupation of southern Poland. The complex was built for the military and consisted of army barracks and administration blocks which stood within tree-lined avenues, but the overall effect was altogether much less forbidding. The prison block itself was surrounded by a high wall, but the windows were mercifully of a normal size and fitted with minimal screens in order to prevent a direct view of the public road outside. The road ran at an oblique angle to the prison grounds, but with a good deal of craning we could see it. At least there was an unobstructed view of the barracks opposite and the sky above.

After a two-hour wait outside the reception office with our faces to the wall, we were taken to the showers whilst our clothes were taken away for fumigation. This delousing process lasted twenty-four hours and our clothes reeked of gas for hours afterwards. In the meantime, given wooden clogs to wear and a blanket with which to cover our naked bodies, we were dispersed to different cells. Mine was Cell 152 on the first floor and I was led to it by a giant SS man, Willi

Allkämper. If anyone could strike fear into the heart of a bewildered prisoner it was Allkämper. He was huge, with ape-like features and a bellowing voice which reverberated around the prison. He was an impressive figure, but I later found that his bark was often worse than his bite.

'TOMORROW MORNING YOU WILL BE SHOT!' he bellowed as I entered the cell.

'Take no notice of it – he says that to everyone,' comforted an inmate of Cell 152 as the heavy door slammed behind me. The cell was about 12 by 14 feet in size with six prisoners in it, which was a luxury at the time, although the figure increased to twenty-six at its worst during the mass arrests in the summer of 1942. In the corner stood a 'telephone booth' latrine, and that too was a luxury since most cells simply had a bucket and lid with no privacy at all. Against one wall stood a washstand which contained a zinc-lined trough and a water tank above with brass taps. This was refilled twice daily. Palliasses were neatly stacked against a wall and covered with blankets. These were spread out in a row on the floor at night-time. Our furniture consisted of a heavy pine table, two benches and a small wall cupboard.

Discipline was extremely strict with military-style reporting in German being the order of the day whenever a guard entered the cell. Each cell had a 'senior', usually appointed by the inmates themselves, who was responsible for maintaining discipline and general order in the cell. Any sign of sloppiness was promptly and painfully dealt with by the guards, so it was in everyone's interest to look sharp and comply. The trouble was that some guards went around looking for someone to beat up as a pasttime!

Kempa, our cell senior, hailed from Warsaw. An educated and articulate man who spoke fluent German, he helped me through the initial shock and bewilderment which most newcomers suffered. I had cause to be grateful to him later on in the harsh days that lay ahead and we became good friends. There too were Otahalik, a railwayman from Krakow – still wearing his uniform – and his friend Peszkowski, a shopkeeper from Rzeszow. Dr Guzek was our distinguished companion. Well into his sixties and looking every inch a 'professor', he was Principal of the Krakow Bacteriological Institute. All had already spent several months in Montelupich and it showed in their physique. All prisoners except 'arbeiters' (prison workers) had their heads shaved.

It was a tacit agreement that no questions were asked about the circumstances or reasons surrounding one's arrest. However, over the weeks and months, with most topics of conversation exhausted, invariably, some talk, however guarded, touched on this painful question. Kempa spoke more freely than anyone about his arrest and I gathered that he had been involved in black market dealings with two SS men who, as accomplices, were also jailed in Montelupich. He was a brilliant and versatile conversationalist with a strong and complex personality.

The sixth prisoner was Dr Dabrowski who had travelled down from Warsaw with us. He'd had the misfortune to be arrested in Ignatowicz's flat, who he was visiting professionally in his capacity as a GP. He was fortunate to be freed several weeks later in spite of his outburst at the inn en route to Krakow.

My immediate reaction to incarceration in Cell 152 was one of dreadful claustrophobia which I had not experienced even at Pawiak in Warsaw, and that had been a terribly depressing prison. There was nothing for it but to get down to coping with the day-to-day routine, doing the chores such as were demanded and finding out what there was to know about Montelupich itself. Without doubt the worst aspect of prison life in 'Monte', quite apart from the eternal lack of food, was the inactivity. The daily chores aside, everything else was forbidden. Otahalik and Peszkowski, who were the eyes and ears of our cell, seemed to know everything and everyone in the prison. They had mapped out a chessboard on the underside of the table top, which was loose, and had fashioned chessmen out of the clay-like bread ration, so that surreptitious games of chess became our sole pastime. Even this was risky because of sneak inspections carried out by the guards which could result in a beating or withholding of food for a day. Kempa, as cell elder, was flatly against anyone using the chessboard, saying it wasn't worth the risk. However, he was overruled on two occasions by the persistence of Otahalik and Peszkowski who claimed that with everyone's help they could conceal the evidence before being discovered. A lookout was posted by the door whilst a game was in progress. Of course the lookout, or more accurately 'listener', had an ear glued to the door and gave a warning if suspicious noises were heard in the corridor outside. Normally, the heavy footsteps of the guards and the clanking of keys were audible for miles and, not knowing at which cell they would stop, the chess men were swiftly scooped up and the table top deftly turned over with everyone trying to appear as though nothing had ever happened. Luckily, we were never caught out. Two of the guards were known to prowl the corridors in carpet slippers and spy on the inmates through the judas (spy-hole). A game of chess, or anything which could bring about violent retribution, was definitely off the agenda during their spell of duty. Then the only sign that we were being spied upon was an audible click from the metal flap covering the judas on the outside of the door.

My clothes were returned to me the day after my arrival, reeking of gas and stiff from the steam-heat treatment they were subjected to. I was fortunate because nothing had been damaged, but pitied those whose clothes had shrunk, or whose boots had cracked up beyond wearing.

I wondered at the simple communications system which existed between different cells, and here again Otahalik was its prime exponent. It had been discovered that the loo kiosk afforded the best acoustics for communication with the next cell – perhaps it acted as a sort of echo chamber! A tapping on the wall brought an immediate response from our neighbours, but it was necessary to shout at the wall to be heard so messages were just audible if one pressed an ear hard against the wall. All this usually happened at dusk after the last appel, when the distribution of ersatz coffee and bread had taken place and the prison was at its quietest. Not surprisingly, the sound of tapping and calls could be heard all along the corridor as prisoners, starved of information, yelled out their messages. This means of communication proved invaluable since I discovered that Ignatowicz, my fellow sufferer from Warsaw, was in an adjoining cell and Olszewski was ensconced several cells away along the corridor. Thus cryptic messages of greetings, acknowledgments and so on were passed from cell to cell. Unquestionably, the star of the top floor was Stan, whose messages and 'news bulletins' worked wonders for our morale night after night.

'Who is this oracle Stan?' I asked.

Stan was arrested a year earlier and had managed to escape briefly with several others from a ground-floor cell. They had scaled the high perimeter wall and headed for the vast railway sidings nearby, where they were eventually trapped and Stan was shot in the leg. As a punishment they clapped him in leg-and-wrist irons for months and sentenced him to execution. Freed from his awful fetters, around the time of my arrival at Montelupich, he was allowed visits to the sick bay in order to heal the bullet wound and the weals caused by the chafing of his manacles. He was an indomitable character, hero-worshipped by practically all the prisoners and even respected by his jailers. I met up with him many weeks later, after he had been appointed chief prison medic and actually became his patient.

Alas, as we had anticipated, the days of our 'bush telegraph' were numbered. The guards had tried for ages to put a stop to the echoes of tapping and shouting which reverberated around the building, with unabated determination in the face of threats and the occasional beating. Yet it wasn't until the prison commandant had ordered a general crack-down as well as a total embargo on our Red Cross parcels that it all had to stop. Fortuitously our cell was on the top floor and near the far end of the corridor, for on that particular day, when the beatings commenced, a contingent of guards worked their way systematically from cell to cell armed with truncheons indiscriminately battering their trapped victims. When the key finally did grind in the lock, two guards entered looking decidedly unpleasant, but were either too tired by their previous exertions or felt a degree of compassion towards a cell full of predominantly middle-aged men (I was by far the youngest), resulting in nothing worse than a tongue lashing and a poke in the ribs with a truncheon.

Prison life was made either bearable or unbearable depending upon the prison commandant, although the Gestapo were in overall control, as masters of life and death. In theory, certain basic rights were afforded prisoners, but the practice proved otherwise. Montelupich was first and foremost a prison for political prisoners, functioning as a sorting depot. Those found guilty of political crimes against the Third Reich were dispatched to camps such as Auschwitz and Majdanek. Auschwitz was only two hours away by car. Many languished in Montelupich for months 'pending the completion of enquiries'. Minority groups such as Jews and gypsies were classified as expendable to the regime and were brought here in transit for Auschwitz and certain extermination. Similarly fated were known communists, criminals, vagrants and the mentally deranged. Jewish prisoners were always kept in the worst cells in the basement.

At the time of my arrival and until early 1943 the commandant, Martin, had a reputation for being both hard and callous. In his fifties, a huge and powerfully built man, he epitomized the swaggering arrogance of a Prussian officer. With his ruddy complexion, close-cropped, bullet head, piggy eyes and steel-rimmed glasses, he was a peacock who fancied himself as he strutted along in his beautifully tailored tunic and polished riding boots. The bitter irony was that his tunic might well have been specially tailored for him by the Jewish prisoners who worked in the *arbeitszelle* (work cell). It was said that he had been an Olympic athlete in younger days and was often seen jogging around the prison block in singlet and shorts, much to our disgust. To the starving and emaciated prisoners it seemed like an obscene and deliberate display of superiority.

In theory, once a month, prisoners were entitled to a *Bedarfschein* (request form) for food parcels or clothes sent by relatives or friends. But between 'applying' and actually getting a precious *Bedarfschein* lay an enormous gulf, for the guards were either too lazy or were in fact instructed not to hand them out, in order to make our lives as miserable as possible. However, largely due to Kempa's fluent German and the presence of a reasonably minded guard, I was able to obtain a *Bedarfschein*. I completed the request for some basic necessities, but deliberated who it should be addressed to. I decided that Hania was the only person, since my mother could well have moved from her flat or (heaven forbid) might herself be in the hands of the Gestapo. I hoped that should I receive anything in return there would be sufficient tell-tale clues telling me of the prevailing situation in Warsaw. I could only wait and see, but there was always the possibility that parcels would be stolen by the guards or left to rot in the prison cellars. On one occasion the prison authorities were actually prompted into assiduously distributing these application forms when an epidemic of lice occurred and everyone carried the pests.

There existed a laundry operated by women prisoners, and for a time bundles of soiled clothes were collected cell by cell and duly returned by the girls, accompanied by a guard. Even this little diversion would make our day, but all we could do was to say 'Thank you' and have the opportunity to smile and receive a smile in return. Clever girls though! Vital messages were often tucked away in amongst the laundry. Even this came to an end, however, and the lice continued to flourish in spite of our crude methods to eradicate these tough little creatures.

Almost two months to the day of my arrest my parcel arrived! Like all packages it had already been opened and examined, but luckily nothing was missing. I waded through it slowly, trying to keep calm. A welcome change of underwear, socks, a shirt and a blanket. These were my very own from home! This was sheer bliss, but I still needed more evidence. Then I noticed the labels on two jars of home-made jam. One was written in Hania's handwriting, the other – my mother's! That was all I needed to know and I felt as though a great weight had been lifted from my shoulders. My mother was still free. Not until the following year did I learn that she had never moved away from the flat at all, except for a few weeks' 'exile' at the time of my arrest. She was very lucky!

Otahalik, the railwayman, had established his own pet theories and predictions regarding interrogations. They went something like this:

a) Anyone called for interrogation within a month of arrest stands a good chance of being freed.
b) If your first interrogation takes place within two months of your arrest you have a reasonable chance of being freed.
c) After two months, your chances are slim.
d) It's preferable to be interrogated within the prison building rather than be hauled up to the Pomorska Street HQ, as they obviously do not think you are important enough to warrant the car ride (Peszkowski challenged this point) and the chances of a short stay in prison are more than likely (but he didn't say what was liable to happen next).
e) Always, no matter how much they torture you, ask for a cigarette. Because it's us (meaning himself and Peszkowski) who are less likely to survive without one, than you, after a beating. In fact we can't wait for you to go. The trouble is (he added) there aren't enough chaps in our cell who can be hauled up for an interrogation to bring us back cigarettes!

'Thanks,' I said. 'I'll see what I can do when my turn comes.' I meant it too – I admired Otahalik for his whimsical sense of humour. Poor chap – both he and Peszkowski were sent to Auschwitz a few months later. When Dr Dabrowski was called out for interrogation to Pomorska and then freed a week later, I steeled myself for an immediate interrogation, believing that our case was due for 'review'.

We often heard the dreadful, agonizing shrieks of victims undergoing torture within the confines of our prison. On these occasions a deathly hush descended over the cell-block as our blood was chilled to the very marrow.

Downstairs in the reception room I was confronted by Gustav, carrying a tommy gun. We drove in silence to Pomorska Street in the back of a large black Buick. The Gestapo HQ was a large modern block previously used as a students' hostel. In a fourth-floor room I was made to stand in front of a large desk behind which sat a high-ranking SS officer. Ringed behind him stood several others of similar rank and an unsavoury looking civilian wearing a neat, dark-blue suit. Gustav and his younger, blonde assistant, also from Warsaw, completed the picture. I never did discover his name, although he was of a more agreeable and civilized type than the rest of them. The fitting backdrop to this scenario was a huge Nazi flag flanked by portraits of Hitler and Himmler, and for a crazy moment I thought I was on a film set! On the desk there were several piles of paper and photographs. I was struck by the thought that somewhere in that stack they actually had photographic evidence of my associations with escaped British POWs.

The man at the desk began silently thumbing through the pile of photographs. Every now and again he would stop and look up at me as though trying to compare me with a photograph. No luck, so to the accompaniment of cryptic mutterings, he continued. Suddenly, he picked one out and flung it down on the desk, turning it around for me to see.

'Well, what have you to say about that?' he asked slowly and deliberately, eyeing me steadily. There was no doubt that the photograph was that of a British POW and at a pinch it could have been one of myself. I stared at the photograph for a while and then told him that I had never seen the man.

There was a further muttering and sundry growls of disapproval from the other SS men and Gustav scowled and hissed at me, 'You know damn well who that is!' Their mutterings continued for a while longer and, judging by the tone of their muted conversation, they appeared to be satisfied that I was not the man in the photograph. So ended the preliminary of the photo-fit session. The next instalment was about to begin.

Partly as a defiant gesture, but also out of necessity, I still wore the ancient British army tunic. Perhaps unwisely, I had pinned by hope on what could be interpreted as coincidence and/or ignorance of its origin. It was minutely examined by the 'committee' who continued to mutter incomprehensibly amongst themselves. Inevitably they asked me where I had got it from and so I repeated my cock and bull story about the farmer all over again. I breathed a sigh of relief as they eventually backed off.

The man at the desk leaned forward. 'Now tell us what you were doing at Mrs Markowska's flat?'

I started to explain about my desire to learn English and Italian, when Gustav interrupted and moved towards me, threateningly. 'Look, we know all about you and why you went there, so why don't you just tell us. Otherwise we'll beat it out of you!'

'I'm telling you the truth.'

Gustav made to strike me but was checked when the man at the desk held up his hand authoritatively and entered into a detailed cross-examination of my 'curriculum vitae'. This didn't arouse any suspicions and neither did a detailed description of my employment. At this point the others began firing question at me rapidly and my head buzzed.

'Why did you visit Mrs Markowska's flat?'

'You didn't say that the last time, so why are you lying to us now?'

'You'd better tell us the truth this time or we'll get it out of you soon enough!'

The firing rate hotted up with my inquisitors pouncing venomously at the slightest deviation in my story. 'Of course you knew what she was up to, didn't you, you liar. Tell us the truth.'

'I am.'

'Tell us the truth – the truth, you liar!' Gustav struck me a glancing blow to the head and all at once the wolf pack stopped its howling, leaving me reeling in total silence for a split second. There seemed nothing left to hold on to. It was then that the sleazy civilian moved forward and spoke in soothing tones. 'Now look, there's no need for any rough stuff. You can tell me who you are. Now take me, I'm a foreigner here, so there's nothing to fear from telling us that you might be one as well.'

'But I am a Pole, not a foreigner,' I replied indignantly.

He stepped back and the whole performance was re-enacted until I was weak with the effort of parrying their continuing barrage of questions.

At some stage they broke off for a brief consultation which ended when Gustav thrust a piece of paper and a pen at me. 'Now sit down and write your name,' he barked.

I was seized by a rising tide of panic. My handwriting! If anything could give me away now, it could be my handwriting. Taught from childhood in the English Mission School, and later by Mrs Phillips to write beautifully rounded letters in true British copy-book fashion. I had never, in all my previous years at school in Poland, adopted the rather spiky Polish style. Gustav yelled at my hesitation. 'Go on, write! Do as you're told.'

They watched me in total silence as I began to write my name. TOMASZ KOPYSTYNSKI. It was a mess.

'He's nervous,' muttered Gustav. 'Go on, write it again,' he ordered.

I somehow got over my initial shock and managed a passable signature in fairly typical Polish handwriting. The paper was snatched away, scrutinized and passed around from   hand to hand. Whatever they were looking for didn't seem to be there. Did they expect to see beautifully rounded English script?

Finally, Gustav threw down his trump card: 'Right, now we shall bring in Mrs Markowska and she will tell us all about you. You do want to see her, don't you?' he gloated.

'Yes I do. She will verify everything I've said.' The feigned eagerness with which I replied could hardly contain my fear.

Gustav stalked across the room to the door and half opened it, hesitated for a moment and then slammed it furiously. I had guessed it was a ruse and suddenly felt a tremendous surge of relief.

The interrogation came to an abrupt end. I was wheeled about and marched out of the room. My escort was a young lieutenant not much older than myself. He had been present throughout my interrogation, but had not taken an active role. His manner seemed civil enough and as we drove away in the Buick he drew out a cigarette and lit it.

Ah, the cigarettes!

'Do you mind if I have one?' I asked.

'Why? Are you nervous?'

'A little,' I replied.

He handed me a cigarette and I held it for a while before slipping it into my pocket.

The car pulled up outside an official-looking building and I was taken inside to a clinical photographic studio. Seated beneath strong lamps I was duly photographed with a strip of card on my lap displaying a number. After my fingerprints were taken I was returned to Montelupich well after lights out.

All in all, I felt relieved with the way the interrogation had gone. It had given me two vital clues: both my mother as well as Mrs Markowska had not been captured. In my mother's case it verified what I already knew from that clever little label on the jam jar, but of course I had absolutely no idea what had happened to Mrs Markowska and prayed that she would never be caught. Indeed she had disappeared into thin air, only to surface after the war ended and after liberation by the Russians, along with a number of British prisoners of war – a remarkable achievement for an elderly lady! No reference had been made regarding the others in the party, i.e. Dr Dabrowski, Olszewski, Romanski, Ignatowicz or the two women. My true identity had not been discovered, but time was not on my side and it was anybody's guess if my destiny ultimately lay in Auschwitz or anywhere else. The entire proceedings had been in German, much of which I understood, with Gustav acting as interpreter giving me valuable thinking time. Wherever possible I stalled for more time by saying that I had not understood the question. This had earned me more of Gustav's dirty looks, but it had worked well. I wondered what would happen next.

The cigarette which I had cadged off the young SS man went down very well with Peszkowski and Otahalik. 'I see you came back in one piece then,' grinned Peszkowski. Many weeks later, when I engineered a meeting with Olszewski in one of the delousing cells, he made a curious comment. 'You know, the Gestapo are handling our whole case with kid gloves and I don't know why. Apart from initial manhandling, they haven't laid a finger on any of us. It's as though they've been told to go easy on us.'

In the long run there wasn't much consolation in this, either for himself or Romanski, as both were to be sent to Auschwitz to perish there.

1942

Spring turned to summer and as usual it was very hot. We languished in our cell, each of us lost in his own private world of hopes and daydreams, without being able to unburden our sorrows or confide in anyone. We exercised by walking six paces one way and six paces back along the available floor space of our cell. Kempa told me a lot about himself on these occasions and about his aspirations for the future, which were viewed with scorn by Otahalik and Peszkowski. By then we were loosely split into two groups. Kempa, who did not always see eye to eye with those two, was quietly supported by the ever-pensive Dr Guzek and myself, but apart from the occasional exchange of words and 'atmosphere' which existed between Otahalik and Kempa, we really got on surprisingly well under the circumstances.

The early summer weeks saw an enormous influx of prisoners from all over southern Poland. Most were innocent victims of random raids which were designed to provide slave labour for the Reich, but the evil weeding-out process destined many for the concentration camps or execution. For several weeks our cell was bursting at the seams with twenty-six souls. There was literally no room to move around and it required all our patience and fortitude to stay rational. The system couldn't cope with this number of inmates – as the guards were unable to cope, they became irritable. There was insufficient sanitation with the result that everyone was gripped with a bout of dysentery, creating an extension to the hell which we had to endure, but the less said about it the better.

Two incredible characters were in this new group. Both were criminals and seemingly natural brothers in arms, but one had married and gone straight, whereas the other had no intention of doing either. The latter was quite the most grotesque individual I had ever set eyes on. He revelled incessantly about the 'jobs' he had done and was seriously planning to rob Wawel Castle, Krakow's royal castle, after his release. He did this openly and unashamedly and I listened spellbound to his endless chatter while his friend desperately tried to make him see the error of his ways. I was relieved when he departed, but his friend, alas, followed him to Auschwitz as well. In time our number dwindled to eight.

One night we were awakened by the sound of shooting in the prison yard below and, peering through our gap, we could just see what had happened. Barely discernable in the darkness we could see fleeing figures pursued by guards. All hell was let loose as they shouted and fired revolvers into the melee until eventually all was silent again. In the morning we counted thirteen bodies lying stretched out in the prison yard. A terrible pall descended over the prison which lasted all day, even affecting some of the guards. It looked as though an attempted escape by some of the new arrivals on the ground floor had gone terribly wrong. The poor devils had probably never known that the prison block was constantly patrolled and that they had not the slightest chance of succeeding in their bid for freedom.

During the seven months which I spent in cell 152 we had only been allowed outside into the prison yard twice. Each floor took it in turns to exercise. After being formed into a long column we had to complete ten circuits around the prison block at the double. In our weakened physical state two circuits were more than enough – to expect us to do ten was insane. It was Martin's idea and, surrounded by his cronies, he saw us off as though it was the start of an Olympic marathon. Guards, strategically placed, ensured that no one was caught cheating. After two laps we were glad to note that Martin and his entourage had disappeared. After three laps around the block we were all in, however, some of the guards turned a blind eye as we literally shuffled by. It proved that even they were half-human. It all deteriorated into a shambles and by lap six everyone lost interest and gave up. Another time, because of an infestation of lice, we had to carry our palliasses into the yard and dispose of the old straw, before marching through the gate into the women's prison yard, where we filled them again with a fresh supply.

The whole operation left us covered in dust and completely worn out, but at least it got us out of our eternal confinement. Similarly, the fortnightly visits to the showers provided a welcome change, as well as an opportunity to mingle with other prisoners. Chased at the double down to the basement, once in the shower room it paid to be quick in order to secure the best place under the showers, followed by a jostling crowd of naked bodies. However, in the ensuing crush it became possible to enjoy little more than a few seconds under the tepid liquid, and no drying-off time was allowed at all. Retrieving one's clothes from the haphazard mass piled on a wooden bench was another matter, with the quickest to get dressed avoiding the guards' whips. We ran back up those stairs like scalded cats and into our cells, there to shiver the time away in our damp clothes. But just now and again, and for whatever reason, there were exceptions to this rule.

As it happened, during a relatively unhurried trip to the showers some time later on, I was amazed to hear two elderly men attempting a conversation in English. With the solitary guard lingering in the corridor outside at that moment, there was no fear of being overheard. One of the men I knew through the bush telegraph as Meier, an engineering consultant from Cell 149.

'Do you speak English?'

'Oh yes, a little.'

Standing next to them under the shower in that instant my caution abandoned me and I blurted out, 'So do I, you know.'

They both stared at me, then Meier, eyeing me curiously, continued in Polish, 'This is amazing. You said "So do I". Only an Englishman would say that, because no Pole who has learned the language in the normal way would ever have done so. He might have said, "Yes I also speak English", or "I understand English", but never "So do I". It shows you have an innate knowledge of the language. Tell me, where did you learn your English?'

My outburst surprised me as much as it had surprised them. I found myself lost for words and, not wishing to become involved in further conversation which could prove embarrassing, I made some excuse and backed off, losing myself amongst the other inmates.

One of the great events of Montelupich life was the arrival of the Polish Red Cross truck, containing a consignment of food parcels. Officially four visits were permitted during the year: at Christmas, Easter, and the May and August Bank Holidays. Officially, every Polish prisoner was entitled to a package on each of these occasions. However, in a number of instances, they were diverted elsewhere by the prison authorities or left to rot in the cellars prior to distribution.
In the latter case it was then a matter of separating the maggots from what was still reasonably edible.

But who, having spent time in Montelupich, could ever forget the two indefatigable ladies from the Red Cross who arrived with each heart-warming consignment, often risking their freedom in an effort to communicate clandestinely with *arbeiters* during the unloading of the truck, under the noses of the guards.

Experiences which touched one profoundly abounded in Montelupich, whether it be the sight and sound of a manacled prisoner being beaten by guards, or someone facing certain death as in the case of Madej and many more like him.

Madej was a railway guard from Krakow. A slightly build man of about thirty, he had arrived sometime during 1942 wearing his railwayman's uniform, complete with four-cornered hat. By his own admission he was caught red handed setting fire to medical supplies destined for the German Army in Russia. 'There is no hope for me at all,' he said in a matter-of-fact way. 'You know what they do to people who do that sort of thing.' After two weeks he was taken for interrogation. 'They are going to execute me,' he announced blandly. The rest of us tried to help him as much as we could, but it wasn't easy. For the following two weeks he seemed to divorce himself from everything and everybody and sat on the narrow window sill as if in a trance, fervently and silently praying. Then one day several guards appeared at the door to fetch him. Madej roused himself from his prayers and stood up.

'Goodbye friends,' he said, struggling with his chains.
'Goodbye, Madej.'

As I briefly described earlier, the prison windows were only fitted with small blinds so that, except for the bars, we had a clear view across the yard to the perimeter wall and to the buildings on the far side of the wall. We could also glimpse the road outside by pressing our heads against one side of the window frame. The 'free world' with 'free' people walking by. What heaven! This small luxury was stopped when the Germans realized that it was possible for friends to place themselves at a certain spot in the road outside and mime messages to inmates. In fact, some women had been caught in the act and were hauled into the guardroom for questioning. What actually happened to them I don't know, but the upshot of it was that all the windows were almost completely shuttered except for a small patch of sky above. The work was carried out by the resident handyman and his mate, the handyman being none other than the former Major Josef Klink. In pre-war days he had been a military historian with several authoritative books to his credit.

By the fifth month of my incarceration I had lost an enormous amount of weight, and was feeling weak and unwell. My daily diet since the outbreak of war had been a very deficient one anyway. Weekly visits to the lazaret (sick bay) were permitted and it made a welcome change to the scenery. One hoped it would do some good in spite of the meagre variety of medication available. But if the guards were particularly nasty it was best to skip this ritual altogether. The resident physician, Dr Zajac, and Stan, his aide, did a lot for the morale of ailing prisoners. Dr Zajac suggested that he would try to persuade the guards to admit me to the lazaret for a week. 'You could do with a little rest and some extra food,' he said sympathetically and within a week I was his patient in the *krankenzelle*.

Although the conditions were far from approaching a proper hospital, it was nontheless an unbelievable luxury, including real beds with real sheets. No straw filled palliasses on the floor! Food was more plentiful, if not much better in quality, but occasionally a kind arbeiter or Stan would sneak in something extra. I left this haven feeling like a new man.

Not long after my sojourn in the lazaret, a new man was admitted to our cell. In the course of conversation he explained that he had already spent several days in the *kretzezelle* (decontamination cell) and that his companion there was Olszewski. When I pressed him further, he described Olszewski in detail. I was convinced that it must have been none other than my friend from Warsaw and wondered what he could be doing in the *kretzezelle* of all places. It was many months since we had last met and by now he would no doubt be able to tell me a great deal more about our situation – if only I could get to him. I was determined to see him and the wretched *kretzezelle* seemed to be the ideal place to meet! I confided in Kempa, explaining that there was someone I had to see in the isolation cell. Kempa looked puzzled.

'How on earth do you expect to do it. After all, there's got to be a damn good reason for them to admit you to it.'

'It might just work. You know how scared they are of another epidemic of lice and "itches". Well, I shall scratch my arms and chest for three days non-stop until they are red and inflamed, as though with the "itch". I only hope that they won't want to see the rest of my body or I'll get a thrashing.'

After three days, my efforts at simulating the 'itch' began to take effect and Kempa agreed to report me to the guard, but we waited until a reasonable one came on duty. I was marched down to the lazaret, with the guard keeping his distance as though I was stricken with leprosy. A stroke of good luck distracted the guard's attention during my examination and I whispered to the doctor, 'I'm alright really, but I must see Olszewski in the *kretzezelle* – it's vital!'

Without batting an eyelid, Dr Zajac proclaimed in a loud voice, 'Yes, this man must definitely go to the *kretzezelle*. He has the "itch".'

I couldn't believe my luck. Good old Zajac!

The *kretzezelle* adjoined the sick bay and was in every way a normal prison cell. Here, to my relief, I found Olszewski, although a young lad was there as well so we observed the usual precaution of avoiding recognition. I had to be patient. After a day or so, I was satisfied that the lad seemed harmless and quite disinterested. Early the following morning I found Olszewski vigorously performing physical exercises.

'That's very commendable. I ought to be following your example,' I observed casually.

'Yes, physical fitness is of prime importance now,' he replied. 'It will help me withstand anything that I might have to endure in the future. Anyway, I have a scheme going which might just work.' His remark struck me as a broad hint, but I had to leave it at that. However, it was obvious that the good Doctor Zajac was in on whatever he was planning.

Later, during one hot and drowsy afternoon when our young companion lay in his corner dozing, Olszewski and I exchanged experiences in brief and cryptic sentences. Olszewski shook his head with resignation indicating the seriousness of his position. He remarked how leniently everyone in our Warsaw group had been treated. 'They did ask me if I knew you, but I naturally denied it and they said no more.'

He continued with his exercises like a demon and we never spoke again. I returned to Cell 152 the following day, having been miraculously 'cured' of the 'itches'. On the one hand I felt sad about Olszewski, but on the other, encouraged by the fact that my implication with the organization still remained undiscovered.

Chapter Eleven

It was every prisoner's dream to become an *arbeiter* (prison worker). Each floor had a group consisting of about six arbeiters, who were housed in a cell next to the guard room. Their function was to perform all the chores, distribution of food and so on. Life for an *arbeiter* was far better. They were able to grow their hair and enjoyed a marginally better status than other prisoners. Their appointment apparently worked on an arbitrary basis, mostly being chosen by the guards themselves. Long-time servers stood a better chance and a knowledge of German was also helpful. However, approval for the job had to be given by Pomorska Street HQ. Kempa, with his brilliant knack of impressing all with whom he came into contact, including the jailers, seemed a natural choice. 'Tomek,' he said, 'if I ever become an arbeiter I shall do all I can to get you out as well – I promise you.' I knew he meant it. But for the moment these aspirations came to naught. Kempa was suddenly summoned for two interviews with his lawyer in quick succession, after which he became pensive and uncertain. Shortly afterwards he was summoned and told to take all of his belongings with him – no one knew where. He had been a staunch companion and I naturally felt a great sense of loss at his departure, but life had to go on. I was chosen by my cellmates to take his place as cell senior – a role I hardly relished.

During the summer of 1942 the prison disgorged more and more prisoners in a frightening procession of trucks destined for Auschwitz, Majdanek and Treblinka concentration camps. The strain showed on everyone as we waited for our turn. Dr Guzek and Otahalik sadly joined the exodus. Could the gentle doctor ever survive that hell? How could anyone ever know until the gates of these awful places were broken down at some distant time in the future and everyone was accounted for?

By now it was August Bank Holiday and all of us listened intently for the arrival of the Red Cross truck with its precious cargo of food. Peszkowski, eagerly peering through the narrow gap, gave a running commentary as though it were a popular sporting event: 'Yes, there it comes. I can see it now, it's pulling up – ah, there they are, the ladies are getting out and here come the *arbeiters* to unload – gosh, there's Kempa amongst them.'

Sure enough, there he was. Clever devil, I thought whilst wondering where he'd been for the last month? Certainly not in the *arbeitszelle*!

Kempa was as true as his word, for within a few weeks he stood at our cell door accompanied by a guard. 'Get your things and follow me,' ordered the guard, and this time I knew it wasn't for an interrogation.

I marvelled at his powers of persuasion. It was as if Kempa possessed magical powers, even over the devil himself. His first words to me were: 'I might have got you out sooner, but as a new boy myself I didn't want to push my luck.'

When we were ensconced in the ground floor *arbeitszelle*, which was recognized as the plum location, he explained what had happened to him since his departure from Cell 152. He had spent a month in Treblinka before being returned to Montelupich, but he was still uncertain what fate ultimately awaited him. His subsequent 'appointment' as senior of the ground floor *arbeitszelle* didn't surprise me as I had already experienced his extraordinary personality and knew that even some of the guards seemed to respect him.

There was no doubting that the ground-floor arbeiters had the absolute reward in terms of prison life, whereas the first- and second-floor arbeiters were very much restricted. Our ground floor cell was by far the largest, housing all those who performed general duties, as well as plumbers, carpenters, tailors, the *bademeister* and *gasmeister*. It is worth mentioning some of the more noteworthy arbeiters who languished in Montelupich during my internment there: Cyrankiewicz, a lawyer who later emerged as Prime Minister of Poland in the early post-war years, I remember well. Similarly, Count Dzieduszycki, whose wonderful tenor voice echoed throughout the prison, singing various arias. It was discovered that not all the words of the arias he sang so well were those intended by the composers, but were in fact snatches of BBC news flashes. No opportunity was passed up. There was Gajewski, the electrician, a quiet and unassuming man whose job it was to service radio sets belonging to the Germans. His workshop, tucked away in the basement, was also a store for hundreds of radios confiscated from the civilian population when the Germans began their occupation of the country. The Germans had the pick of the best sets, but obviously these required occasional repairs and, largely working on his own, with little supervision, Gajewski had a heaven-sent opportunity to listen in to the BBC Polish news bulletins, which he would repeat to trusted friends later on in the evenings. I am glad to say that I too became his friend, and thus we knew exactly what was happening in the world outside. It was from this very source that the singing Count's news flashes had emanated. Gajewski was never suspected and survived for a long time before he too was taken on the road to Auschwitz. He was never to be replaced during the rest of my stay in Monte and the loss of our news bulletins was a serious blow to morale. The best job in the prison was held by Vladek Czajka, 'hairdresser extraordinaire' to the SS. His establishment was located at the far end of the corridor on the ground floor, next to our *arbeitszelle*. He was a charming fellow and formally hairdresser to the Krakow Opera House, where he had once used his professional talents grooming well-known stage artistes. Now he shaved the heads of our jailers, including the pompous Martin.

The women who operated the laundry were also billeted here, as were the kitchen staff, amongst whom was a 'mad' German Army offender and a giant bully who was Ukrainian. Another cell contained a group of young German Army offenders who worked in the metal shop. All in all, its was a motley crew if ever there was. The duties of the *bademeister* and the *gasmeister* were defined thus: the *bademeister* operated the boiler for the washroom showers, whereas the gasmeister was responsible for the operation of the delousing chamber. Both of them were trustworthy men as, indeed, were most of the others in our *arbeitszelle*. Yet care had to be maintained, since the carpenter sharing our cell was a *Volksdeutsch* and suspected informer.

From above, the outline of Montelupich prison resembled a shallow 'V', having a central tower topped with a glazed cupola at its apex. The main entrance and the staircases were contained within the apex of the 'V'. The stairwell had thick wire mesh covering its entire area, presumably to prevent suicide attempts. The ground floor wings contained the prison administration, 'reception', office, interrogation cells, store rooms and some prison cells. The basement contained the kitchen with its store rooms, boiler room, timber store, workshops, the showers and several other cells. Most of the latter were large and grim where the worst excesses, as well as executions, were carried out. Here were kept the so-called 'undesirable elements' such as gypsies and Jews.

Still weak from malnutrition I found myself thrown in at the deep end, having to knuckle under the intensive workload which the job demanded. Kempa helped me yet again through a difficult period until I became stronger and was able to stand on my own two feet! Both Kempa and I, along with Kazek Japoll, formed a trio responsible for general duties on the ground floor. Two others had been seconded to the basement, but when they left we had to take over. Kazek had already spent eighteen months in Montelupich; in his early twenties, small of stature, but sturdy and as strong as a horse, in the days before the war he had been a member of the Polish Olympic swimming team. Korbas was another prominent *arbeiter* who had played football for the Polish national team, and he was made to work as a cobbler repairing boots for the SS.

As arbeiters, our first job of the day was to assemble by the cookhouse door in the basement where churns of so-called coffee were collected. We served our own area by distributing the stuff to cells in the basement as well as on the ground floor. This was the only time we mingled with arbeiters from the upper floors and I was glad it did not fall to me to have to hump those extremely heavy objects up all those flights of stairs three times a day. The task which came next was less pleasant and entailed collecting the zinc kubels which were placed outside every cell door. These had to be emptied, cleaned and disinfected before being returned. With that onerous task done, the entire area, stairways, offices, freshly vacated cells and every conceivable corner had to be swept clean and disinfected. Copious quantities of water were used in the process. The marble corridors had to be left spotlessly clean and all ledges kept dust free.

During the winter of 1942/43 only minimal heating was permitted, but with the lack of any decent sustenance we shivered away the days and nights, drawing some consolation from the dreadful coffee and soup, which was hot if nothing else. Extra portions were rare, due to the strictly adhered to head-count, the mad German cook and his helpers refusing to dispense the slightest favour to anyone. In spite of it all, Kazek and I managed to store a secret hoard of bread from our own ration, as well as donations from others in the *arbeitszelle*. The system worked well and over a period of time we were able to distribute it to those who were suffering most, especially the Jewish prisoners who were being deliberately starved of food. In this we were passively helped by one or two guards who were either inattentive or closed a blind eye to what was going on.

Where Jewish prisoners were concerned great care had to be exercised, for to be caught out helping them in any way would have meant the end. So we had to think up a different system of supplying them with food. We realized that when going to the rubbish dump at the far corner of the prison yard we had to pass by the basement windows which belonged to their cell. Although out of sight of the prison guardroom, they were visible by anyone crossing from it to the prison entrance, and vice-versa. But the sight of an *arbeiter* or two proceeding in the direction of the rubbish dump during the morning chores was perfectly normal, and it was this routine which was to provide us with the cover we needed. However, before we could put our plan into practice, two serious obstacles had to be overcome. Directly overlooking our 'area of operations' were barracks occupied by units of the SD (*Sicherheitsdienst*, or Security Service/Police). These, we had observed, appeared to be left empty for several days at a time, but on the whole their movements were unpredictable. Great vigilance would have to be observed in that direction. Even if apparently empty, it would require only one malevolent pair of eyes to put an end to our game, but that would be a chance we would have to take. Then there were the patrolling guards who plodded their way around the prison building at a steady, predictable pace, and whose movements were easy to gauge. Kazek and I decided that in order to succeed, we would have to do this run together, at least for a start. One of us would actually do the 'unloading' of the bread as we drew level with the cell windows, whereas the other would act as lookout, provide cover and create a diversion if necessary. In addition, a lot depended on which guards were on duty inside, and what they were doing. It helped us if they were involved with something which took their attention elsewhere rather than outside the building.

As our main area of work was inside the building there was the problem of keeping an eye on the two guards patrolling outside – once we had planned to do a 'run', we both contrived to be working close to the entrance at the same time so that we could watch them pass by, then allow a minute or so to elapse during which they would have turned the corner of the building. We had to act casually, but our hearts were in our mouths and our legs felt like jelly. With us we had our buckets, mops, brushes, dustpans, rags and dusters, but one bucket concealed chunks of bread covered by rags, instead of dirt. Exactly at the right moment we both walked out of the door carrying our buckets as well as a dustpan and broom, which was nonsense because there was nothing to sweep outside – at least it created the right impression.

Drawing level with the basement window, having ensured that the coast was clear, a tap on the glass brought an immediate response as though the inmates within had read our thoughts. The window was opened and outstretched hands eagerly and swiftly grasped each precious piece of bread. That done we proceeded on our way until we reached the rubbish dump, for a few moments indulging in some spurious cleaning activity before turning around and retracing our steps.

The first run was a total success, as indeed were several following ones. We had to vary our plan, at times and in a purely opportunist manner walking outside with the usual accoutrements and assessing the situation as we saw it, sometimes having to stall here or there or do two complete 'circuits' before getting it right. Later we felt it unwise always to do these trips together and undertook them singly, becoming very proficient at it, until sadly all the occupants of that cell were transported to Auschwitz.

Life in the *arbeitszelle* was strange and unreal – we lived so close to everything that happened, witnessing much of the horror which was commonplace within the confines of the prison walls. Strangely, of the many incidents which stand out in my memory was the one when a young SS officer was sentenced to the firing squad. He was incarcerated in a cell on the first floor and on the evening preceding his execution was allowed a 'last wish'. It transpired he wished to spend the night in the company of two women, and in the event Maria and another girl from the laundry were duly dispatched to satisfy his wish. At six the following morning a staff car awaited him in the prison yard; behind it stood an army truck with the firing squad and a simple wooden coffin. The prisoner was then led downstairs, flanked by fellow officers, in total silence and the convoy pulled away, disappearing through the main gate and into the chilly early morning mist beyond. Who he was or what he had done to deserve such an end we would never know, neither did we derive the slightest pleasure from it ourselves.

Another episode which affected us more closely concerned one of our own group of arbeiters, a quiet and diligent man, who like most of us lived with his own thoughts, hoping that a miracle would free him from this hell one day. He was later included in a group of thirty or so which was led down to a basement cell. Three mornings later, when we were preparing to distribute the coffee and stood in front of the door to the cell, our guard tapped it with his bullwhip. 'Not this one. They won't be needing it.' We hesitated, but continued our rounds. After we had finished the guard led us back to the death cell and unlocked the door. It was empty, but the floor was littered with palliasses, blankets and personal possessions, and worst of all the clothes which they had been wearing. Wearing just their underwear they had been herded into trucks and taken somewhere for execution. 'Clear it all up,' ordered the guard. This was one of those tasks that churned the stomach.

During the summer of 1943, we were joined by Stan, a likeable young art student who seemed particularly unconcerned by his imprisonment. In between chores he sat at the table happily sketching portraits of the various members of our cell. He certainly brightened the days with his sketches and his generally breezy demeanour. As I was fond of art myself, I soon found myself joining him and between us we had everyone discussing the merits and demerits of our work. The guards became perfectly aware of this activity, but instead of stopping it, encouraged us and visited us regularly to see what we had done. We had not bargained for this unwelcome twist, but there was nothing we could do except to cease sketching, which by now we were loathe to do because of the salutary effect it had on the whole *arbeitszelle*. How Stan managed to acquire a box of pastels is beyond my recall, but decent art paper was a problem. Most of my sketches were done on toilet paper, which was in very short supply, but nobody seemed to worry. Then one day I got hold of a sheet of Bristol board and really went to town! Using Stan's pastels I completed a seascape depicting warships sailing by a rugged coastline in fine weather. The theme of my drawing puzzled my companions because anything to do with the sea was not fully appreciated. No matter – I loved it. Especially the barely discernible White Ensigns fluttering from the stern of each warship. I didn't own it for long, however, because one of the guards asked to have it.

Presently, Stan was taken to Pomorska Street HQ where he suffered badly at the hands of his interrogators, before being brought back and locked up in a basement cell. The next day he was visited by three sadistic Ukrainian guards, Kruszewski, Gonder and one other, who were known for their brutality, and was beaten up mercilessly. This was repeated the following day and he was left unconscious. When Kazek and I realized what had happened, we told the one decent Ukrainian of the bunch that we wanted to see Stan, to which he agreed and we made him as comfortable as possible, but it was obvious that he needed medical attention urgently. At this point the guard became nervous and refused to help any more. However, we did what little we could whilst the Ukrainian was on duty, but orders had already been given that Stan be left alone and, by the tenth day, he was dead.

On one further occasion, a young man was brought in with three bullet wounds in his stomach. Although he was in great pain and in a state of deep shock, the system had to be complied with – he had to be stripped, washed and dressed again, carried to a cell and left to die.

To our certain knowledge, the three evil Ukrainians were responsible for the deaths of at least five prisoners.

There was also a case of four vagrants who were incarcerated in the basement wood store, of all unlikely places. The temperature there was freezing and strict orders were given that they should be left completely alone, with neither food nor water to sustain them. After several days their pitiful cries began to annoy the guards, who were dispatched to beat them up. It was too much for Kazek and I, and again we managed to co-opt our decent Ukrainian to give them some food, whenever he was on duty, but it did nothing to help in the long run. What made it worse for the two of us was that timber for lighting the stoves had to be collected from the store and these visits became a nightmare, for we were immediately set upon by the four starving, emaciated men who clawed and clung to us in desperation. The guard would then beat them off with a stick, although not, I may say, the young Ukrainian. They died later, one by one, save one, the youngest of them, who gained a dubious reprieve by being sent to a concentration camp.

As usual, it fell to Kazek and I to carry the pitiful remains of the three dead men out into the yard and behind the pile of coal to await collection by the municipal wagon.

The Almighty must have known how little dignity there was left in life and in death, and it was on these occasions, when we had to dispose of the dead, that Kazek would say, 'The least we can do is to lay them down gently and with dignity.'

When would this nightmare end, we asked ourselves! Would we be around when it did? Indeed, we all hoped and prayed that we should be there when the end came. For the feeling of revulsion and hatred towards the Nazis, and the need to avenge all the suffering, burned deeply and constantly in our minds.

Although the three of us, Kempa, Kazek and myself often worked together, Kempa, as head *arbeiter*, was occasionally called upon to help in the administration office. I was sure that if at times he couldn't convince the guards about something he would certainly confuse them. He knew how far to push his luck and never overstepped the mark. He often managed to make himself indispensable by taking charge of new arrivals. This was vitally important, in fact, because people arrived in a state of shock and bewilderment. Instead of being bullied and harassed, he talked to them sympathetically, explaining what they should do, and acted as a buffer between them and the bullying guards. One such instance typically illustrates his ingenuity. All new arrivals, including women, were checked in at Montelupich. The women were then separated and taken to the women's block across the road, known as Helclow (pronounced

Heltz–loov). About twenty women were brought in for questioning one morning, although no one knew exactly the circumstances of their arrest. Kempa took immediate charge, comforting them and telling them what to do. They were being questioned one by one in a separate room and in the meantime he spoke to them quietly and rapidly whilst they stood frightened and forlorn.

'Please listen. I can help some of you, but not all of you, that just isn't possible.' He observed them carefully and having made up his mind continued in a whisper, 'You, Madam, tell them you are pregnant – alright? They'll let you go because they won't want to cope with it. And you Madam, tell them you are racked with tuberculosis. You, Madam, tell them you have cancer. And you, Madam, also tell them you are expecting a child – good luck to you all', and so on.

The trick worked as one by one these women emerged after their interrogation looking pale, but happy as they walked away free from the dreaded prison. Alas, some of the others were not so lucky. Kempa often interceded for prisoners with great skill, sometimes saving them from a beating and I began to wonder how long his luck would last, for I had the distinct feeling that some of the guards would gladly be rid of him.

Lighting fires had never been one of my skills. I had always had to use up wads of newspaper and a complete box of matches before anything happened. Consequently, I was gripped with apprehension on realizing that I was responsible for lighting half a dozen stoves twice weekly, in order to keep a dozen cells warm during the cold winter months. Continental heating was provided by stoves which were akin to a chimney breast protruding into the room and covered with ceramic tiles from top to bottom. In the bottom half were two traps, one for the fuel and a smaller one beneath – the flue provided the up–draught as well as the depository for ashes as in an old kitchen range. In Montelupich these stoves were build into the walls so that half the heated surface protruded into one cell and the other half into the cell next door. The stoking and lighting was carried out from the corridor and the success of this operation depended upon the judicious adjustment of up–draught, as either too much or too little air current could easily extinguish it altogether. Kindling for the fires was one problem; the other was the correct adjustment of the draught to maintain them. I had forgotten that it was vital to get a healthy flame going before closing all the traps – to do otherwise was to court trouble. The stove in question served a large cell with German prisoners – SS men and civilians, who had the luxury of one complete stove in their cell. In my rush to get all six stoves going by eight thirty, by which time all the chores had to be finished, I slammed the flue door shut too soon with the result that fifteen minutes later a dull thud reverberated along the corridor, followed by a moment's silence and then a frantic banging and shouting. Summoned by the noise a guard soon appeared to investigate. The German inmates emerged coughing and spluttering, with blackened faces smothered in soot. Their cell was in a terrible mess. Obviously the slow-burning coal produced a build-up of carbon-monoxide gas which ignited suddenly, splitting the stove at the seams in a minor explosion. Rapid repairs were put in hand and some of the German prisoners hurled vitriolic abuse at me. I had long resented the attitude of some of these prisoners who treated us like dirt, so instead of turning the other cheek, I decided that another dose of the same treatment was definitely required. That indeed would be 'playing with fire' – but well worth the risk, I thought.

About two weeks later, I made a point of stuffing the stove with an especially volatile load of coal dust and, slamming the flue trap shut, walked away from the scene of the crime to await the fruits of my labour. Sure enough, within a quarter of an hour a mighty thud echoed up and down the corridor followed by frantic yells and banging. The result was devastating. Already weakened by the first explosion, this one had ripped the entire stove apart creating havoc in the cell. I reckoned that my days as an arbeiter had come to an end and later on I was hauled into the office for an enquiry. Miraculously I got away with a severe reprimand and strangely – not a word of further abuse from the victims.

My next misdemeanour occurred some time after this episode with far more unpleasant consequences. Usually, any sort of association with the women prisoners who worked in the *washerei*, other than purely as occasional helpers, was strictly forbidden. Yet, curiously, two *arbeiters* actually managed to carry on a more or less clandestine liaison with two of the women. Vladek Czajka, the hairdresser was one, and Tadek Stanczyk, an arbeiter from the first floor was the other. Only one or two guards with a spark of humanity in them turned a blind eye to these romances, and it must be said that in so doing involved themselves in considerable risk. Vladek Czajka's girl was Vladka while Tadek's was Maria, who had already spent two years in Montelupich. During the day the women worked in the basement laundry and after work were confined to their cell which was adjacent to ours on the ground floor. It was during one languid afternoon when most of the arbeiters were resting on their bunks that we heard a knocking on the wall. Nobody took any notice until the knocking continued and Ganter, the *bademeister*, stirred himself on his bunk.

'What's the matter now? It seems as though it's someone in the cell next door.'

'What, at this time of day?,' said someone.

'Ignore it,' said Ganter, rolling over on his bunk.

But the knocking continued. By now there was universal protest at the disturbance, and Ganter's request for a volunteer to investigate the problem was met by a vehement chorus of 'Nos'.

Presently the knocking grew in frequency and with a feeling of disgust, I said I would go to investigate. For all we knew someone could be seriously ill and my gesture was greeted by a good deal of light-hearted banter.

'Good old Tomek – yes, why don't you go,' a voice chided.

'Go on, Tomek – do your good deed of the day.'

'Be careful. Don't let them catch you,' rejoined Ganter on a serious note.

All was quiet in the corridor outside and my knock on the cell door was answered by a feeble bid for me to enter. It was Maria, lying on a top bunk, looking extremely fragile. She said she was feeling unwell and wanted to talk to someone. My immediate instinct was to make an excuse and leave, but she pleaded with me not to.

'This could be dangerous – I can't stay here with you,' I stammered.

As I tried to pacify her and expressed my sympathy at her state of health, at that moment I heard a click of the judas on the door behind me. Maria and I froze and looked at each other as we realized that we were being watched.

'Don't worry, it's only Holzauge. He's on duty this afternoon,' Maria said confidently. (Holzauge was the nickname given to a young SS man who was one of the sympathetic types). To make sure, I slowly opened the door only to find myself staring into the cold, pale-blue eyes of Scharfführer Froh, one of the worst guards in Montelupich.

'*Ach, so!*' he bellowed. Striking a melodramatic pose, one arm akimbo and the other outstretched, he pointed towards the offices. 'Los! Los!' he yelled.

Roused by the commotion, 'Frogface', another particularly nasty guard, emerged from the office and started to beat me with his bull whip. There was nothing I could do or say but try and fend off the vicious lashes. Marched from the office back to the *arbeitszelle* under a continuous rain of blows, I was made to collect my belongings, marched up two flights of stairs to the first floor and locked in a cell. My back and shoulders were burning painfully, but at least I was in one piece. I was alone in my misery and slumped to the floor with a feeling of utter dejection and realized I had really cooked my goose this time. I had truly paid for my mission of mercy.

Later, after hours of brooding, I wondered if there was a way out of the mess, but couldn't think of one. Then I suddenly remembered that the girls from the laundry would be doing their usual rounds distributing clean laundry the following day, and wondered if they had thought up a trick or two, but quickly discarded the idea since I was not expecting a change of laundry anyway. Nevertheless, the following day I found myself listening intently for sounds of the laundry basket being shuffled along from cell to cell and the clanking of the guard's keys as he locked and unlocked cell doors. They were drawing nearer, suddenly my cell door opened and, framed in it, stood Maria and Krysia. Maria handed me a small bundle of clean clothes which I knew were not mine – although not a word was spoken she looked me straight in the eye, which was all I needed to know. As soon as the door was locked I frantically searched through the bundle and out dropped a scribbled note, which read: 'Please forgive me for what happened, I have told them that it was all my fault and a complete

At home in
Warsaw, June 1939.
George and I with
our parents.

Warsaw with Father, 1936. Taken by a street
photographer.

Brother George with the
Intelligence Corps, Brussels,
September 1944.

Rowing on
the Vistula,
1938.

Albertyn Village, September 1939. Policemen shooting at low-flying Dornier bombers.

ALBERTYN. SEPT. 1939. DORNIER BOMBERS BEING SHOT AT BY ALBERTYNS TOTAL POLICE FORCE & ENCOURAGED BY JUREK & MYSELF. THE BOMBER FORCE WAS SPOTTED FLYING EAST HALF AN HOUR PREVIOUSLY & THEIR RETURN WAS ANTICIPATED, BUT NOT WITH SUCH SPEED. THE FIELDS AHEAD OF US NEAR THE RAILWAY LINE WERE PEPPERED WITH MACHINE GUN FIRE.

A highway teeming with refugees … and Russian tanks, September 1939.

Sept 1939.
We emerged from the forest and halted on the edge of an escarpment overlooking open, flat country. Jurek and I stood amazed at the panorama laid out in front of us. A road stretching as far as the eye could see was crawling with refugees. Stationed on and alongside the road were some tanks. I stared hard as they must have been at least half a mile away. 'They are Russian', I said but Jurek didn't believe me – but it was true.

Accosted by a couple of thugs. We pitied the poor policeman who happened to be there.

17 SEPT. 1939

YOU CONCEALING ANY GUNS?
DEMANDED ONE. THEN

THE TWO GUNMEN APPROACHED US FLOURISHING PISTOLS. HAVING QUICKLY ASCERTAINED THAT WE CARRIED NO WEAPONS THEY SET ABOUT TORMENTING THE POLICEMAN WHO FELL TO HIS KNEES PLEADING WITH THEM TO SPARE HIS LIFE. WE DIDN'T WAIT FOR THE OUTCOME . . .

In the darkness
we ran straight
into a hostile
crowd of
Communists.

Sept 39
In the darkness we ran slap into a group of comrades gathered in the middle of the road. No harm was done but they were anything but friendly grabbing hold of us and shouting 'back them up! 'Hand them over' the Red Army!

New Year's Day, 1940.
Jurek and I being led
by armed militiamen.

LED ALL THE WAY TO SLONIM THROUGH THE ICE & SNOW
BY 2 ARMED MILITIA MEN)
NEW YEARS DAY 1940.

YOU'RE LYING — TELL US WHY
YOU REALLY CAME TO THIS HOUSE!

A beating at the hands of the Gestapo,
March 1942.

OUR TWO GUARDS. MARCH 1942
A 250 MILE JOURNEY IN THE BACK OF A
MILITARY TRUCK .FROM WARSAW TO
KRAKOW ·IN FREEZING COLD & SNOW ·
THERE WERE SIX PRISONERS

Our two guardians, en
route to Krakow in the
back of a lorry.

Being led to Cell 152 after the de-lousing.

WE STOPPED AT CELL NO. 152. 2nd. FLOOR. WILLI ALLKÄMPER TURNED THE MASSIVE KEY IN THE LOCK & FLUNG OPEN THE DOOR & I WAS SHOVED IN UNCEREMONIOUSLY. 'TOMORROW MORNING YOU WILL BE SHOT!' HE BELLOWED.

My first interrogation at Gestapo HQ in Krakow.

A Russian plane dropping anti-personnel bombs, July 1944.

JULY 1944

The Russian aeroplane cruised casually overhead and dropped what we took to be propaganda leaflets because they appeared to shimmer in the sunlight like confetti — until we heard the whistling sound. Then everyone darted for cover.

Attempting to get through to the Russian lines.

BITS OF METAL THRASHED ABOUT ALL OVER THE PLACE - LIKE HAILSTONES

RUSSIAN GUN

UNBEKNOWN TO US- ABOUT 200 YARDS AWAY WAS THIS LONE '88 mm GUN WHICH WAS A TARGET FOR THE RUSSIANS.

The dubious pleasure of straying in front of a rocket launcher.

July 44

Unbeknown to us we had walked to within yards of a Katiusza rocket launcher which suddenly opened up with all barrells. The shock of it nearly bowled us over.

Aboard a Russian DC-3. We watched the spare engine gradually penetrate the floor of the cabin.

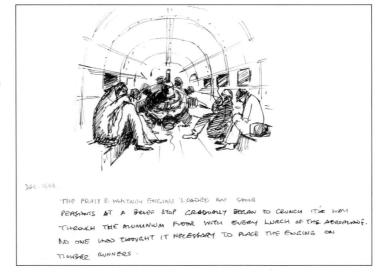

DEC 1944.

THE PRATT & WHITNEY ENGINE 'LOADED' BY SOME PEASANTS AT A BRIEF STOP GRADUALLY BEGAN TO CRUNCH ITS WAY THROUGH THE ALUMINUM FLOOR WITH EVERY LURCH OF THE AEROPLANE. NO ONE HAD THOUGHT IT NECESSARY TO PLACE THE ENGINE ON TIMBER RUNNERS.

Notice of embarkation.

End of the line at desolate Murmansk. I wave farewell to Tamara!

NURMANSK. DEC. 1944. ALMOST PERPETUAL DARKNESS

WE SET OFF ACROSS THE CRACKLING SNOW AND QUICKLY LEFT THE TRAIN BEHIND US. EVERY SO OFTEN I TURNED AND AND WAVED TO ... UNTIL I COULD SEE HER NO MORE. AFTER THE WAR HER VISION HAUNTED ME FOR A VERY LONG TIME AFTERWARDS & I WONDERED WHATEVER HAPPENED TO HER AFTER THE WAR.

PLANES SAVE CONVOY FROM THIS DECK

FLIGHT deck of H.M.S. Nairana, escort carrier, heaves up like a hillside during the recent voyage to Russia in which she helped to protect an important convoy with supplies for the Red Army. In such conditions Navy planes fought and beat planes and U-boats.

Convoy to Russia.

Duck!

The Swordfish slewed along the deck missing me by a hair's breadth!

The lower wing of the Swordfish missed my head by a couple of feet as it came to an abrupt rest, one front wheel luckily anchored by the cat walk and preventing it from toppling into the freezing sea.

Dramatic 'Phone Call to Blackpool

"IT'S TOM—TOM FROM WARSAW"

A CHRISTMAS Eve 'phone call to a Blackpool father must have been among the best presents to be received in Blackpool during the festive season.

The father was Flight-Lieut. G. A. Firth, of the R.A.F., senior Polish interpreter in the North-West—and the caller? . . . His son, Tom, from Poland, of whom he had heard only once since 1939, when the news leaked through that Tom had been put into a German prison camp.

Mr. T. Firth

Tom, who is 23 now, has lived a lifetime in five years. He could confirm all the reports of the monstrosities and tortures within Poland, but, having suffered some of them, he prefers to forget—or at least, try to do so.

He was a schoolboy when Germany and Russia occupied Poland. For many months, having complete command of the Polish language, he passed himself off as a Pole and lived a precarious existence under German domination.

ARRESTED BY GESTAPO

In February, 1942, he was arrested by the Gestapo and for 18 months was imprisoned in Cracow.

The fact that he was British was never discovered by the Germans or his fate would probably have been even more ·gruesome than it was.

After suffering the pangs of semi-starvation, beatings and other fiendish tortures, the Germans released him, having failed to pin anything on him. He remained in Poland until July, 1944, when he worked his way through the fighting lines into Russia.

Here he was detained for nearly four months before being handed over to the British authorities.

TORTURE SCENES

Having suffered the mental agonies of seeing mass executions and the torture of men and women—sights he and other prisoners were compelled to watch—Tom is not easily moved to emotional expression.

That explains why, when he spoke to his father by 'phone from London on Christmas Eve, his simple but expressive first words were—"I'm here."

"It's Tom—Tom from Warsaw," he enlarged.

F./Lt. Firth, at the Blackpool end of the line, didn't quite know whether to cry with delight or whoop with glee.

Now they are re-united and Tom is taking a well-earned rest. After that he is thinking about a branch of the Forces, but his father says they will talk that over all in good time.

ALLOTMENTS AWARDS

THE awards of certificates of merit by the Ministry of Agriculture and Fisheries, for the best-cultivated allotments in Blackpool during 1944, is announced.

The awards represent the 26 best plots out of about 900 inspected, and judged by experts of the Blackpool Corporation parks department.

The plot which earned the highest number of points and a special certificate, was on the Oxford Square site, cultivated by Mr. R. Seddon, of Fernhurst-avenue.

Other certificates were awarded to: F. Swain, Summerville; T. W. Allison, Handsworth-road; B. Tofts, Queensway; W. Ashton, Central-drive; M. Smith, Lindsay-avenue; T. Horsfield, Beechfield-avenue; C Salter, Scarsdale-avenue; A. D. Biles, Holmfield-road; A. V. Greaves, Rosebery-avenue; A Vardy, Babbacombe-avenue; G. O. Land, Central-drive; A. Walton, Westwood avenue; J. T. Leach St. Leonard's-road; J. R. Kirby, Stony Hill avenue; H. Hedges, Woodland-

Newspaper cutting, January 1945. Tom – from Warsaw.

Gillian and I in Cornwall, 1993.

misunderstanding. Kempa is doing what he can for you.' Kempa again. I knew he wouldn't waste much time! Restless with anticipation, I had one more day to wait before being rescued, when Kempa and a guard called for me.

'You know, you are damn lucky,' said Kempa later. 'I had a hell of a job persuading them to let you go. Maria told them that she was ill and as she needed "urgent" help could only think of knocking on the wall to attract attention – you were the one to answer. They gave her hell too, though.' He advised me to call in to the office when both Froh and 'Frogface' were next on duty and apologize. 'It would be the diplomatic thing to do in the circumstances,' he added.

The notion of apologizing to the two hounds stuck in my throat but I did as he suggested, in German, to boot. I thanked Maria at the first opportunity for her part in getting me out and could only smile at the thought of her fib about her urgent need for help.

The incident was logged in the official prison records and although it was subsequently brought up on one or two occasions which will be described later, did not appear to have made any difference in the final outcome of events.

Heaven knows, there was so precious little to laugh about in Montelupich, yet rare occasions presented themselves in stark and welcome relief.

The little *Volksdeutsch* informer and carpenter by trade, who ought perhaps to have been pitied rather than detested, was not surprisingly the cell pariah and at the same time the butt of practical jokes. His efforts at communicating with the rest of us were quite pathetic at times and often brought derisive responses, although he seemed too thick to realize it. Some wit screwed his clogs to the floorboards one evening when he was taking a nap, and then shouted, 'Mr Samek, you are wanted in the guardroom, immediately.' Looking like a tousled cockerel, Samek sat bolt upright in his bunk as though released from a catapult, banging his head on the bunk above. He then scrambled out of bed, complete in long-johns and, forgetting his trousers, leapt into his immobilized clogs. As they never moved he tipped over onto the floor, yelping, and, furious at being made a fool of, ranted and threatened to tell the guards, which he did. When he returned from the guardroom he was met by a cheerful chorus of voices demanding to know what 'they' had said about it. 'You'll see. You'll see,' he muttered, but nothing ever happened.

On another occasion the unfortunate Samek returned from work at Helclow one evening complaining of violent stomach pains.

'Mr Vladek [Czajka, the hairdresser] can you give me anything to relieve my pain.' he wailed. 'It hurts something awful. Last time you gave me some medicine it worked a treat.'

Now Vladek didn't possess any medicines. 'I haven't anything, Mr Samek,' came Vladek's bland reply.

Samek wouldn't take no for an answer and pleaded for Vladek's magic potion. 'But you must have something you can give me for this pain.'

'Really, Mr Samek, I haven't got any medicine.'

'But you must have something …'

Eventually, in desperation, Vladek suddenly 'remembered' he had something that would help. 'Alright, Mr Samek, I'll prepare something for you, but it'll take a little time. I'll bring it to you.'

'Bless you, Mr Vladek, bless you,' mumbled Samek humbly.

Presently Vladek appeared with a cup in his hand. 'Here you are, Mr Samek, you drink that, it'll do you good.'

Samek lapped it up eagerly, within a few minutes announced that he was feeling very much better and we never heard another word from him for the rest of the night. We later discovered that this infallible cure consisted of cold 'coffee', soap, eau-de-cologne and a dash of hair rinse.

Christmas 1942 was a strange experience. As usual, the highlight was the arrival of the Red Cross truck with its precious food parcels and churns containing traditional Christmas fare, rich and nutritious, which was ladled out to each prisoner. Although not intended for the German prisoners, one complete can was allocated to them by the guards. There was sufficient in a can to feed more than ten times their number of Polish prisoners.

On 24 December, Christmas Eve, we all sat around our table quietly enjoying the fare, talking and trying not to think about the ugly world surrounding us, and our tenuous existence. Kempa thought it might be a good idea if we invited the duty guards in for a 'drink' as a token of goodwill. 'We'll show them that we behave in a civilized way even if they can't,' he reasoned, but the idea failed to meet with general approval.

I said that I had no intention of wishing them a Merry Christmas, but Kempa still thought the idea would give us a moral advantage on the day, if nothing else. No vote on the issue was taken but grudging approval was eventually given by a majority. Not only did the guards on duty visit us as a result, but others, in passing, came in to wish us a Merry Christmas as well, including some of the German *arbeiter* prisoners. Zimmer, the mad German cook, sat down at our table with a mug of beer (which they were allowed) and joined in our fare. It soon became a sort of mad hatter's tea party with Zimmer, half drunk, and Kempa, stone cold sober, playing up to the German, both quite unwittingly putting on a kind of crazy double act. In between repeated toasts for peace and eternal friendship they both stuffed each other's mouths with rich pasta until it came out of their ears. Afterwards Kempa made a simple and seasonable speech, followed by Zimmer who, now somewhat sobered up, managed a surprisingly touching little speech of his own, in German. I never thought him capable of such genuinely human feeling. He stayed with us for a long time and seemed to enjoy our company. Some *arbeiters* received parcels from home, but I had not had any sign of life from Warsaw since the previous summer, which didn't worry me unduly for by now I was convinced that all was well and I didn't want my mother to make any further sacrifices, especially now that I was able to get by with more food and better conditions that the job of *arbeiter* allowed.

One day I became afflicted with raging toothache which persisted unabated for days to the point of distraction. Luckily, Vladek Czajka was able to give me some Kogutek painkillers which alleviated my misery. I knew that the sick bay had the necessary instruments but no one who could help. Dentistry was not on the prison agenda. Then someone said that there was a prisoner somewhere who had a marvellous knack of extracting teeth without anaesthetic. By this time I didn't care about the details and only wanted the offending tooth to be removed. Yes, the decent Ukrainian guard said, he had heard of this wizard and would find him for me. He was as good as his word and arranged for me to see him the following day. We waited in the sick bay at the appointed time and two men were led in by another guard.

'Here they are,' he announced.

'And who's the patient?'

'I'm the patient, but why the two of you?' I asked.

'We're brothers and always work together. My brother is the specialist and I'm his assistant – I hold you down.'

I sat on a chair whilst the assistant clasped my head firmly.

'Ready – here we go then, and it'll be out before you will have time to think about it.'

The specialist gripped the tooth with the tweezers and with one tremendous shove upwards, a twist and a heave, extracted the molar. After a rinse with permanganate, the ordeal was over. The method was crude yet effective, and the pain that followed was worth bearing.

'Tomek, I think I know you well enough to trust you. Kazek has been helping me for some time now but if the two of you can help me, that would be even better.' The speaker continued in a quiet, serious tone. 'What I need to know, from time to time, is information about certain prisoners. For example: do you know if a certain prisoner is in your area? If so, has he or she been interrogated and if so, what was the outcome? I shall also want lists of all newly admitted prisoners and what has happened to certain prisoners, that is, whether they were shipped to Auschwitz or elsewhere. I might ask you to try and find out any of these things about a given prisoner or prisoners at any time, and of course there could be other questions that will need to be answered if possible.'

The speaker was Vladek Czajka, the likeable, suave hairdresser, whose quiet, charming manner could fool anybody.

'Vladek, you know you can count on me, but can you tell me one thing? Don't if you'd rather not, but what on earth do you do with all this information?'

'I don't know whether you ought to know, but you'll be aware that I'm allowed into town [Krakow] for purchases. After all, I have to keep replenishing my stock. Of course, I'm escorted by one or two guards and we always visit the same pharmacy. Well, the pharmacist who serves me is my contact. As you can well imagine it doesn't always work if the guards are alert, but more often than not it is a chore for them, and they get slack and interested in other things in the shop; then I'm OK. Need I say more?'

I had no reservations about agreeing to help. Unbeknown to me, Kazek had been gathering information for Vladek for some time. Now with the two of us at it, the task could be carried out more effectively.

Two pairs of eyes observing the comings and goings of prisoners were better than one. One of our daily tasks was to count the number of prisoners in each cell and chalk up the figure on the cell door. The total figure was then passed on to the guardroom. This task, however, didn't always fall to the arbeiters, since some guards carried it out themselves. The way it was done was to knock on each cell door in turn and ask how many occupants there were. 'Solitary' cells did not, of course, call for any feat of mathematics. This routine gave us an excellent opportunity for gathering information, i.e. prisoners names, etc., as already described. However, great care had to be exercised, for to be spotted talking to a prisoner 'through the door' could be disastrous. Furthermore, the sound of voices carried clearly along the corridors. When it became necessary to do some urgent information gathering at an odd time of the day, for example, the bucket and broom routine proved invaluable. At that time I had acquired a pair of tracksuit trousers which were elasticated at the ankles and served my purpose exactly. After each information-gathering trip, having made rapid notes on a scrap of paper, I would slip it down my trousers where it was safely trapped at the bottom. When the information had been passed to Vladek, it would be torn into minute pieces and flushed down the lavatory.

Thus over a period of time Vladek Czajka was able to pass on to his pharmacist contact the names of many prisoners, with other details such as we were able to gather from them. We had long since known that apart from Vladek, others were searching for information as well. Ardent prison yard watchers such as Otahalik and Peszkowski, previously in Cell 152, were always observing and looking for any changes in the pattern of routine – new faces amongst the *arbeiters*, or anything else, however small. Even the limited vision available in Cell 152 proved sufficient to observe people's movements in the yard below, especially the arrival of the Red Cross ladies in their ancient truck. With a bird's eye view of the yard, it soon became obvious that whilst one of the good ladies engaged a guard in conversation, the other would gradually move over onto his blind side behind the truck and exchange words with one of the toiling *arbeiters*. Alas, they were caught at it on one occasion and hauled into the guardroom but presumably managed to convince the guards that it was an innocent exchange of words related to the business of unloading, and nothing more.

Then at Christmas 1942, for the first time, I was one of a group of arbeiters summoned to unload the little truck. I could hardly believe my luck. Working in silence, I became acutely conscious of the way the ladies discretely observed us all the time, perhaps wondering who I was, since I was a new face, whilst they knew Kazek well by sight. We couldn't even thank them for all the wonderful work they did trying to keep us alive!

On the next occasion, Easter 1943, at the height of our information-gathering activities, the prison bell yet again hailed the arrival of the Red Cross truck. Called out by a guard, several of us proceeded to unload the precious food parcels, however, as the unloading progressed I became aware that one of the ladies had moved over to my side while at the same time her companion had engaged the guard in conversation. The move was unmistakable. Deliberately fumbling with the packages I leaned over and murmured '*Slucham*' (I'm listening).

'Do you know of one Sasorski?' she whispered.

'Yes,' I replied and, jumping off the tailgate, carried several packages and stacked them inside the prison porch. When I returned to the truck she was still there. I leapt onto the truck and again pretended to fumble with the load, bending over in order to make myself less visible in the process.

'Is he well?'

'Yes, he's holding out well,' I replied knowing that the message would be passed on to anxious relatives. It was as cryptic as could possibly be, but even that shred of news meant so much. There was a hint of a smile on her face as she moved away and joined her companion.

I was happy that our efforts were proving to be useful, as illustrated by this incident, on the other hand the frustration lay in our inability to keep track of various prisoners' fortunes subsequent to their dispersal to other parts of the prison. This was of course due to the almost watertight separation of these areas one from another. In the circumstances we relied on our own observations as well as those of others and the odd remarks made by arbeiters from other areas, as well as speculation and rumour.

Usually ground-floor and basement cells were occupied for a relatively short duration; with the exception of Germans, other prisoners were eventually dispersed to the first and second floor. Among the exceptions, however, was a young woman. Amazingly, she always seemed cheerful and unconcerned until Kazek managed to extricate the truth of her identity.

'Oh, I'm a spy,' she told him. 'It is quite true – I'm a Russian spy and you know what they will do to me.'

As far as we knew she was never maltreated physically and at times managed to carry on a lively conversation with two young SS men incarcerated in an adjoining cell. In order to make themselves heard, this exchange took place at a high pitch of decibels which must have been heard by half the prison and, predictably, the guards put a stop to it. To pass the time she etched her cell walls with Communist slogans and patriotic sketches depicting Soviet soldiery and tanks advancing in a headlong charge. Curiously she seemed to be held in some esteem by her jailers and after many months of captivity we could only presume that she was taken away to be executed in the early hours one morning. At any rate, her cell was left empty, with only the defiant graffiti remaining as a stark testimonial to her indomitable spirit.

The spring of 1943 brought a sudden surge of new prisoners to Montelupich, most of them being Jewish women. The story surrounding this was that they were destined for deportation to Canada under an agreement arrived at between the Germans and an international relief organization. To us it all looked very suspect and only after the end of the war was it revealed that the Nazis did in fact resort to this kind of trickery. By promising the Jews a safe passage to the sanctuary of a neutral country, under the aegis of some international agreement, they in fact sent thousands to their deaths in concentration camps. Meanwhile, while they remained in Montelupich they were badly treated but, owing to the large numbers of them, there was little we could do to alleviate their misery. We could only manage it when our young Ukrainian was on guard duty, closing a blind eye to the extra portions of soup and bread we handed out to them.

Two British prisoners of war also spent time in Montelupich. The first one, Griffiths, a Welshman, told me that he had originally been captured on the island of Crete, and I spotted him later on two occasions after his transfer to an upper floor, looking haggard and thin. He spent many months there and I never knew what fate subsequently befell him. The other was Tom Blanche of the RAF. Ganter, the *gasmeister*, made a point of telling me of his presence in the delousing room – a fact which in itself caused me to ponder why he should have done so. Nevertheless, I decided to seize the opportunity and made my way to the basement under the pretext of sweeping the corridor. Luckily there was no guard to be seen and I readily picked Blanche out amongst the group of prisoners waiting for the return of their fumigated clothes. I beckoned him over and identified myself, but impressed on him that he should keep quiet about our meeting. We chatted briefly about the progress of the war and I remember him telling me about the death of the Duke of Kent in a flying accident. Blanche departed soon afterwards to spend the rest of captivity in a Stalag. The war was indeed responsible for many a strange encounter.

On another occasion I was summoned to the administration office, full of trepidation, wondering what awaited me. There, Zander, the chief of prison administration, announced that he needed help and led the way to a door which had always remained locked, causing us to wonder what dark secret lay behind it, for neither Kazek nor I had ever seen it used. Within it lay a gigantic pile of assorted bags, packages and tatty suitcases practically reaching to the ceiling. The sight took me aback when I realized that this was all that remained of so many poor souls who had been sent for execution over the months and years.

'You will help me search through these things. We will look for hidden messages. If you find any give them to me,' he ordered bluntly.

The mere thought of wading through people's private and intimate property made me feel sick. Could it not just be left alone? Had they not already done enough by killing all these people? Did they have to rake over the remains like scavengers and gloat?

Without further ado he set about his task with great gusto while I hesitated. 'Come on, come on – search!' he bawled.

Picking out a case I opened it carefully and peered at the contents, not wishing to disturb anything.

'No, no, no! You must do it like this,' he snapped and, dragging the case from me, tipped the contents onto the floor. Luckily he became so engrossed in his own efforts that he appeared to pay less attention to mine. However, it soon became very obvious that he had already uncovered several pathetic little scribbled messages which he held up triumphantly. Furthermore, he began to fish out various frilly feminine garments with a whoop of pleasure and set them aside on a separate heap. Damn you! I thought, no doubt these will in due course adorn the fat body of your Frau – or mistress!

There was one thing I could do to prevent this wholesale plunder, and I duly set about the job at a greater speed than his. Whilst not only preoccupied with finding messages, he was obviously bent on stealing as well and that gave me an opportunity, for in his eagerness he took less notice of me. I redoubled my efforts, making a great and convincing pretence, yet hardly touching the contents at all. I whizzed through package after package, and case after case, leaving a multitude of messages intact. So far so good, but I knew it wouldn't last. Zander was becoming impatient with my apparent lack of success so in the end there was no option and I handed him two bits of paper, which kept him quiet.

The following day the Red Cross truck arrived and we were made to load it with all those pathetic belongings, for their return to the next of kin. The whole operation left me with a feeling of sadness and disgust and yet there remained a spark of consolation – the pleasure of having fooled Zander.

News about the world outside our prison walls was scant, although in 1943 we had a very good idea that the tide of war had swung in favour of the Allies. The victory at Alamein in North Africa and the capture of Stalingrad by the

Russians were like music to our ears, and we prayed nothing would reverse this course of events. How the end of the war would find us here in Montelupich was a thought too difficult to predict and we never talked about it. At worst, what chance did we stand if the Germans decided to wipe us off the face of the earth before retreating into the Fatherland? We lived in hope, as we had never done before. My own optimism never gave in to the idea that I might never see England again, even if it took years to achieve.

It was close on a year since my first interrogation and though extremely remote, the possibility of escape was not to be dismissed. Kazek and I talked about ways of getting out of Montelupich and in the end concluded that only one had any chance of success. He recalled an unusual instance whereby an arbeiter had volunteered for work in the Reich and was, in fact, 'sponsored' by one of the guards. The scheme worked and the fortunate prisoner was sent to work on a farm. The idea, if it could ever be repeated, seemed a thousand times better than languishing behind prison walls, added to which, absconding from a farm would be a far easier proposition. The more I thought about it the more I liked the idea, although my optimism subsequently began to plunge to the very depths of despondency when I realized how improbable it was. Gustav and his cronies hadn't finished with me yet and after that, anything could happen. I had to put it at the back of my mind and be patient.

In the meantime, bizarre changes were about to take place in Montelupich. Commandant Martin departed to the accompaniment of silent cheers, his place being taken several weeks later by Oberscharführer Wedemeyer. If appearances were anything to go by, Wedemeyer seemed a different kettle of fish, and we were right. He was a handsome man of about forty who possessed that rare quality – civility. Unbelievably, there was an almost immediate easing of tension throughout the prison, which even began to reflect in the behaviour of the guards. Next, as though by magic, every single prisoner was issued a precious *bedarfschein* (request for a parcel from home), something that had been conspicuously lacking in the past months. There was also an improvement in the quality of the food and, to cap everything, we were given a ration of margarine.

I filled in my *bedarfschein* and decided to address it to Hania, although I had no idea if she was still in her flat. I considered it still too risky to send it to my mother's address – I could not be sure of her whereabouts anyway. But it was worth a try and, should Hania receive it, it would at least serve as a sign that I was still in Montelupich.

Sadly, Wedemeyer's 'magic' didn't last. For reasons we would not have known but could only surmise, Wedemeyer's benevolent reign came to an abrupt end within a month. Vladek Czajka was turfed out of his 'exclusive' salon, which was reconverted to a normal cell into which, ushered with due ceremony accorded to his rank, was none other than Wedemeyer himself. And so he became a prisoner in his own prison. He remained there for several weeks, eventually disappearing from sight altogether, and with him went our hopes of a better life.

It was around about this time that Kazek appeared pale and distraught one morning and told us that a young woman admitted to a basement cell the previous evening had been found hanged and, together with a guard, he had had to release the body. Although used to witnessing so many tragedies, he sank down and wept copious tears of sorrow.

On another occasion I was in the process of sweeping the main corridor when the young Ukrainian guard rushed by and disappeared into the office, only to reappear with a rifle and proceed to bound up the stairs leading to the first floor. But before he got there a shot rang out followed by a terrible commotion. He later told us that a prisoner he was escorting had grabbed his revolver from its holster and shot himself.

We well understood the awful traumas new prisoners suffered, especially when they were faced with the prospect of interrogation and possible torture. The shock of arrest followed by incarceration was quite enough to drive anyone to such a desperate measure.

In the summer of 1943, we noticed that some of the German prison guards were returning from leave in the Reich with very long faces and with less swagger than usual. Even the giant Allkamper, who had threatened to have me 'shot at dawn' at my introduction to Montelupich, had mellowed beyond recognition, to the point of almost seeming sympathetic towards the prisoners. We wondered whether we were about to witness an about turn in their general treatment of us in view of their worsening fortunes, one guard admitting that things were bad back home because of Allied bombing. But it never paid to be too optimistic. The arrival of a new commandant quickly dispelled any hopes we might have cherished on that score. A nonentity and complete bureaucrat, he reimposed the familiar old regime. So we were back to square one again.

It was Allkamper who called upon Kazek and I to assist him in an unusual task. Clearance for it had obviously been given by Headquarters and, not knowing what was demanded of us, we simply followed him as he led us through the forbidding prison gates and into the street beyond. Several minutes walk brought us to a busy part of the city and we mingled with the crowd thronging the pavements as though we were part of the scenery. It was heady stuff and in a sense caught us unawares – we were totally unprepared for it. Escape? With two of us it needed coordinated action and a degree of planning. For one of us to suddenly do a bunk could be disastrous. It was not as simple as it seemed for in spite of everything, Allkamper kept a close watch on us and 'discussion' between the two of us was *verboten*.

Eventually we reached the notorious Pomorska Street Gestapo Headquarters. Most city buildings had a yard set in the middle, with flower beds and space for parking. However, in the middle of this one, which was not altogether devoid of floral decoration, stood a horse and cart. Leading the way up to the fourth floor and entering a room full of furniture, we were told to carry sufficient downstairs to fill the cart. We toiled for an hour or two and when the cart was filled to capacity we returned to Montelupich. Allkamper explained that he was moving house and that there would be more to do the following day.

The next day Allkamper managed to 'hitch' a ride for us in the black Buick which inmates of Montelupich would remember with a shudder, as it served to ferry prisoners to Pomorska Street for interrogation. We would much rather have walked as we had the previous day. Although we were inexperienced in handling furniture of such size and weight – it was massive to say the least, and from the fourth floor – we managed it. Once the job was done and the cart loaded to the gunnels, we started off, the three of us following on foot at a slow pace. The cart was either hired, or more likely commandeered for this purpose, and the driver, to whom we were not allowed to talk, looked anything but happy.

It was slow going as we reached a suburban road of rough cobblestones, so that constant adjustment to the load had to be made in order to prevent damage. We finally came to a halt in front of a pleasant-looking villa which was Allkamper's new home.

Having unloaded the contents onto the pavement, the cart was allowed to drive off. When we carried our first heavy piece of furniture up to the first floor we were surprised to find Allkamper's wife and young daughter already in residence. At first Allkamper kept a watchful eye on us, following our every move, however, his vigilance soon waned and suddenly we found ourselves alone in the road!

'Christ, what a chance to run,' I remember saying to Kazek. But the moment wasn't right. Not yet.

For the first time we had the opportunity to talk freely and decided that we stood a better chance when it came to manhandling the heavier pieces of furniture, when there would be an obviously slower 'turn around'. To test Allkamper we dallied with a particularly weighty sideboard for as long as we dared, until he appeared in the doorway. We sized up the road and surrounding area. The road was as straight as a die and featureless, with most houses lining our side of the road behind which, some distance away, were railway sidings where we could hear the sound of shunting trains. The opposite side provided little or no cover at all and road traffic was nil – so no passing car or truck to leap onto. It certainly didn't look promising.

We dallied again with the next heavy object but Allkamper appeared once again, needless to say. He was taking no chances. We now realized that our only chance was to run like mad as soon as we had carried a piece of furniture upstairs and were on our way down again to collect the next one. That way, with luck, we could count on about four minutes head start.

But then came the crunch question – which one of us said it I can't now recall: 'You know, what will happen to the others if we do go? They'll show them no mercy. Could we honestly live with that?'

And of course, that was perfectly true. Neither the Geneva Convention nor any other convention of human rights applied to any of us. Our freedom would not be worth the reprisals which would be meted out to our friends in the *arbeitszelle* in the first instance, and inevitably to Kazek's family in Krakow in the second, not to mention my mother, should they track her down. That was the nub of the matter which stopped us in our tracks.

Our task finally over, Allkamper invited us indoors and ushered us into the dining room. There, seated at the table prepared with refreshments, were his buxom wife and daughter. Of all the weird experiences this one took the biscuit.

We sat around the table partaking of tea with the man who would shoot to kill us had we made one false move. As for his wife, she sat there expressionless with not a glimmer of softness on her large face; her daughter rather skinny, pigtailed and pale sat alongside her quietly munching a sandwich. It was like a mad hatter's tea party and the conversation was polite and stilted, but maybe somewhere in a different time and world we would all have been ordinary human beings. But not now.

Having worked ourselves up to such a high point of expectation, Kazek and I now felt deflated. But it served no purpose to feel sorry for ourselves after our failure to escape.

Anyone familiar with life in central Europe will in all probability have known of one of the scourges of ordinary daily life, although night life would be a more accurate description. I refer particularly to bed bugs. These little monsters have a habit of infesting convenient nooks and crannies of the ordinary bedstead, there to procreate and enjoy all their homely comforts. Primarily nocturnal creatures, they become a common sight, revelling in the hot summer season when they take to marching in single file or random formation, slowly homing in under the sheets with one object in mind – to deprive the recumbent human body of as much blood as possible, then fully sated to retreat slowly like so many bloated miniature balloons. Switch on the electric light suddenly in the middle of the night and watch them drop from the ceilings and walls from sheer surprise! There is a simple tale about a man who, having rid his bed of the pests, thought he had the perfect answer for keeping them at bay by placing each leg of his bed in a basinful of water, like a moated castle. Then, having retired for the night, happy in that thought, he awoke only to find the beasts parachuting from the ceiling. They were tough customers to contend with and the summer of 1943, which was hot and dry, suited them well as we discovered to our horror. Our metal bunks, which were stacked three tiers high, crawled with them and the only effective solution was to dismantle the bunks, carry them into the yard and blast them out with a blowtorch.

When a guard called one's name and then added the dreaded words '*Zum erhorung*', which meant a 'hearing', but in reality an interrogation, it was enough to make one tremble at the knees. In my case it was: 'Tomasz Kopystynski, *zum erhorung!*'

I wondered if this time it was to be a trip in the black Buick to Pomorska Street, but the guard led me past the administration office and into the adjoining interrogation cell. I was on my own patch, in a way, for I had swept it out on many an occasion! It was bare, save for a table and two chairs, and fixed to one wall, at a height of just over 6 feet, was a row of massive metal hooks with a gas mask dangling from one of them. Gustav was there, waiting with that cruel smirk on his face, whilst his sidekick, the same blond German, sat at the table behind a portable typewriter. This one, unlike Gustav, never seemed to get involved in beatings and manhandling prisoners, and simply got on with the job of typing. If anything he appeared to have a calming influence on Gustav.

It was a blazing hot afternoon and Gustav looked decidedly bored. The preamble followed the usual pattern: Name? Address? Date of birth? Where born? etc. The usual well-worn routine.

'Now maybe you will tell us what was your connection with Mrs Markowska?'

I repeated my story as I had on previous occasions, that my purpose for calling on her that evening was to enquire about English lessons, emphasizing that in fact all that I knew about her was that she was a teacher of the English language.

'Have you learnt any German since your imprisonment?' Gustav asked.

I said that I had, but would wish to take up proper lessons one day. At that he turned on me in a sudden burst of fury and shouted that my story about English lessons was my own invention and a complete lie.

'If you don't tell us the truth we will string you up on the rack and beat it out of you. So what's it going to be?'

Before I could say anything the blond man intervened: 'Now look, there really is no need for these sort of threats at all.' And he muttered something to Gustav.

I was convinced that by now they knew no more than they did a year before and it gave me heart. Again I said that the events I had described were true and that Mrs Markowska would confirm everything I had said. 'Damn Mrs. Markowska!'

Gustav snarled. Did I not know that she was involved in activities designed to help enemies of the Reich? I said that I was totally unaware of that, trying to appear horrified at the very idea. Did I not know that as her agent I was liable to be shot? He leered cruelly. I assured him that not only was I unaware of her activities but would not wish to have been involved in them. Things began to look distinctly nasty again.

There followed a prolonged silence during which both men observed me intently and it was the blond man behind the typewriter who finally spoke. 'When were you last in Dunkirk?' he said in passable English. I stared back blankly as though I didn't understand and asked for a translation, but my request was ignored and the two began whispering something in German.

When the interrogation finally ended, Gustav held open the door and told me to get out. As I left the cell, a voice called out in English, 'Hi, just a minute there.' I held my breath and kept walking. Then the voice began to call, '*Warte mahl, warte mahl,*' which meant the same in German. At that I halted and turned around in an uncertain sort of way. Perhaps I should have responded to their simple trick by saying 'Was there something?' in English. Both men had been waiting for my reaction, but with obvious annoyance waived me on. I had won that round and in spite of its relative brevity the ordeal had left me drained. I felt more certain than ever that they had found nothing in the past twelve months that could incriminate me. Mrs Markowska had still not been arrested and they had also not pursued the search for my mother, for she too was obviously still free.

Instinct told me that they wanted to finish with all the loose ends of the case and be rid of me in one way or another. How they intended to do so was the question and I had not long to wait for the answer.

Now I decided was the time to follow the slender thread of Kazek's story of the *arbeiter*-turned-farmhand. I had no time to lose. The next question was who should I turn to and how to set the plan in motion. Vladek Czajka seemed to be my best bet here. Once again, ensconced in his old salon after the strange episode with Wedemeyer, I waited for a suitably quiet moment to see him.

'Yes, that's right,' he began. 'It must have happened about two years ago. It was Bautz who pulled that one off and he has a farm somewhere in the Poznan area. He's really a decent chap, you know, and I wouldn't mind betting he would help if he could.'

Bautz had been in Montelupich ever since I'd been there and his reputation amongst prisoners as a decent and civilized man was well known. He was another phenomenon in Montelupich and a matter for surprise that he had managed to survive for so long. Although transferred elsewhere recently, he occasionally called in to Vladek's salon for a haircut. Vladek then revealed to me his technique for dealing with some of the guards, especially those who were closely involved with the preparation of lists of prisoners due for transportation to Auschwitz.

'You know, I sit them down in that chair, get them all nice and relaxed, let them forget about their problems and make them think of "blue almonds" [in Polish meaning "sweet nothings", "*niebieskie migdaly*"]. Then when I see they are in a receptive mood I begin to chat to them. Eventually I steer the conversation around to the things that really matter. I have to be patient, because it doesn't always work, but only too often they are glad to be able to talk. I've twice managed to get them to remove a prisoner's name from a transport list. God, was I lucky.' Suddenly we could hear the sound of approaching footsteps. 'Listen, leave it with me,' he spoke rapidly. 'I'll talk to Bautz about it and give you the nod when he's going to be here. You can then come in as though on a cleaning errand and I will be able to say to him "Ah, this is the very chap I was telling you about."'

I left his salon with dustpan and brush in hand as I had entered it, in the usual game of pretend.

Vladek's words were encouraging and from that moment I lived on tenterhooks, not wanting to think of failure. Days later a fellow *arbeiter* whispered into my ear that Vladek wanted to see me. When I entered the 'salon' Bautz was there and Vladek introduced me exactly as he had said he would. It was evident that Vladek had already primed Bautz about the plan, and his immediate response was that he would have to discuss it with the people handling my case before making a decision. I explained that I had been interrogated twice and he asked who was in charge of my case. I replied that I only knew one called Gustav. Bautz nodded, saying that he thought he knew who I meant. I thanked Bautz and left the 'salon'. It was as though I was applying for a job under perfectly normal circumstances and the prospective employer had told me that he would first have to obtain some references before making up his mind. But at least he did not turn the idea down flat.

The next few days were difficult to bear, with my mind almost running riot with ideas, not least how I could 'abscond' from Bautz's farm! I confided in no one except Kazek, whom I knew I could trust implicitly and who after all was responsible for putting the idea into my head in the first place.

Days followed any without further developments and I slowly began to lose hope. I wondered if Bautz would really stick his neck out this much knowing nothing about me and what I had been imprisoned for. I had to admire him though. Then one morning when I was going about my usual cleaning duties in the main hallway, Bautz appeared suddenly and raised his hand in recognition.

'Ah, Kopystynski. I shall be talking to Gustav about you – as a matter of fact he's in the office right now. Let's go and find him – you did say it was Gustav, didn't you?'

'Yes Herr Scharfführer, that's correct,' I replied.

As we reached the lobby Gustav had, in fact, left the office, and was already crossing the yard, heading for the main gate. 'Hi there!' Bautz called out, doubling after him. I watched the two of them from the lobby, eagerly trying to follow the tenor of their conversation. When they finally parted Bautz returned to tell me what had happened, and what he said was not at all reassuring.

Evidently my case was still under investigation and I should expect a further interrogation. There was no more to be said at present, other than he would try again another time. He seemed genuinely concerned and in no hurry to go, and we stood talking as man to man, in a perfectly normal manner. That was Bautz, a 'good chap' and a rarity indeed, who I hoped would survive the war to live another day.

The temptation remained to sift through every word of the conversation with him in order to find some hopeful sign or implied message, the only one in fact being in his words 'try again another time'. Was there a hint? On the other hand, the spectre of another interrogation began to haunt me more than anything, and somehow I felt there was a finality about it, the decider which would either condemn me to a concentration camp or Montelupich. The only remedy I had to counter the good as well as the bad thoughts which milled around the brain endlessly, and to no useful purpose, was to switch off and get on with my work.

Ever since the departure of Wedemeyer, food had become scarcer by the week, for not only was his faceless successor completely uncaring, but the adverse situation of the German war effort was also leaving its mark. Having put on weight since my inception into the *arbeitszelle* several months earlier, I now began to feel pangs of hunger returning on a permanent basis once again. I retreated to the cookhouse one day with the idea of scrounging some scraps of bread but to my disgust found the huge Ukrainian cook anything but helpful or sympathetic.

'Food, food? You must be joking,' he was lying through his teeth. 'No mate, there's nothing, but you can have a look in that cauldron there,' he added sarcastically, pointing at an enormous stainless-steel cauldron gently simmering away. 'Go on, take a look.'

Wondering what was so special about it I raised the lid, took one look and promptly slammed it down, for staring at me with a fixed mortal grin was a complete horse's head and neck, partially immersed in bubbling liquid. It had been dumped into this cooking pot whole, just as it had been severed from the carcass, with its yellowing teeth, eyeballs and mane.

'Good, isn't it?' the Ukrainian roared with laughter. 'Do you like it? I'm boiling it down for stock to go into the soup.'

The height of the summer of that year, 1943, were days I shall not easily forget. In a frenzy of activity, masses of new prisoners arrived, while truckloads were dispatched to Auschwitz at the same time. These activities became almost a daily occurrence, with familiar faces disappearing overnight. Without doubt I reckoned my number was up. There would be one more '*erhorung*', the case would be wound up and I would be carted away like all the others.

The prison services were stretched to the limit coping with all the bedlam, and both Ganter the *gasmeister* and Klink the *bademeister* worked around the clock, as regulations demanded that even those leaving had to go through the showers, cleansed in body. Then Klink's name was called from the dreaded list and he too went. In the ensuing melee that day a guard called for me and, leading me down to the basement, told me that I was now to be in charge of the boiler room.

It transpired that Klink had been told to nominate a successor before leaving, and had told the guards that I should be a likely candidate for the job, to which they agreed. Of course, I hadn't a clue how the whole system worked. It was a mass of pipes, stopcocks and a huge black boiler which was fed with coal. Poor Klink did his best in the little time remaining to him in Montelupich to explain the intricate workings of this monster – all I could do was to nod my head and pretend I understood perfectly well what he was saying. I did not dare turn the job down but I could see trouble ahead. What I did not foresee was the invaluable position I would be in with regards to 'intelligence' gathering, for every single male prisoner had to go through the baths at some stage. There could never be a better opportunity for acting as a contact between prisoner and the outside world, through Vladek Czajka and his trips to the chemist.

Next it was the turn for some of the girls who worked in the laundry to join the infamous 'transportation'. Among them was the tall brunette, Vladka, Vladek Czajka's girlfriend. The two had somehow managed to carry on a discreet liaison which was about to come to an abrupt end. Both were utterly distraught, but Vladek wasted no time in persuading the guard in charge to have her name removed from the list. It worked, for how long I could not say, and they both wept with relief and joy.

Our numbers were being ruthlessly decimated and the two Jewish tailors, who had already been living on borrowed time, were ordered out on the journey to Auschwitz. When that was announced Kempa and Ganter, our two senior men, approached the prison authorities without hesitation in an effort to try and get the order rescinded. Unbelievably, a postponement was agreed and the two men survived a little longer. However, two weeks later there was to be no reprieve in spite of Kempa and Ganter's renewed efforts. There was little doubt that the two of them risked their own necks, for to intercede on behalf of a Jew could have been suicidal, and the two sad men, whose fate was unquestionably now sealed, had always borne themselves with quiet and uncomplaining dignity.

As though a chapter was coming to an end Kazek and Kempa were both ordered to join the queue for a 'transportation'. They accepted it with fortitude and, typically, Kazek dressed in suit and hat, which he had kept stored somewhere, said that he might as well travel to Auschwitz in style. Kempa, however, as far as I know was destined to be incarcerated in another camp. I never heard what happened to Kazek but Kempa resurfaced after the war, only to be involved in other strange activities. But that's another story.

Maria's sudden release to freedom after three years in Montelupich came as the one redeeming happy event in those fearful weeks. And so with the departure of Kempa and Kazek I had lost two good and supportive friends.

The awful midsummer 'purges' finally ended and life returned to its usual norm – but not normality.

As predicted, my first effort at providing a hot shower for several score of inmates was a disaster and until I finally mastered the whole apparatus I got no thanks from anyone. There was no one whose advice I could seek. No one seemed to know, but when I discovered the secret I wholly made up for my initial failings. And that pleased everyone.

Even in Montelupich life had its pleasant surprises. Krystyna, a pleasant, dark-haired little girl from the laundry, secretively handed me a book which she had concealed under her apron.

'Thought you might like to read it, because I can't,' she said, glancing around to make sure no one was watching. 'You see, it's in English and I heard that you speak it.'

Touched by her kindness I thanked her and tucked it under my shirt. In reality I was more disturbed rather than pleased, for apart from that single faux-pas in the shower room many months earlier, my British connections were unknown to anyone. And now a virtual stranger, albeit a pretty one, had suddenly professed to the fact that I knew the English language! The book was a green Penguin paperback, the title of which I have long forgotten. To read it was folly, neither could I see a way of disposing of it, so in the end I shoved it under my palliasse and literally slept on it, praying that there would never be an unexpected inspection. And there it remained for a long time.

The next incident also came as a surprise, although not necessarily a pleasant one. At any rate it gave me food for thought. Thiele, a slightly built German inmate and a civilian who assisted in the office, surreptitiously beckoned me over. For some reason he seemed well disposed towards me – there was no side to him and he treated me like an equal. There was not a soul in the office. He opened a thick file, rapidly thumbing through the pages.

'You know that business with Maria. Well, it's all down here, but it's nothing to worry about.'

'Good,' I said. 'What else have they got on me?'

He pondered over the pages and whispered, indicating the place with his finger. 'Ah, yes. You're to have one more interrogation.' With that he closed the book and walked away, winking knowingly as he did so. Obviously there was more to it than he was prepared to tell me – I could put whatever interpretation on that knowing wink that I cared to.

In the meantime, Kazek's place was taken by a newcomer, Zbigniev. An inhabitant of Krakow, genial and outgoing by nature, and a good man to work with, we soon became great friends. His asset was his fluent knowledge of German, a point I had reason to value later on in different circumstances. He tolerated prison life with surprising equanimity and was well able to control a tricky situation when it arose. His confidence and optimism were infectious to the point where he warmly invited me to call on him and his wife when and if great and good fortune ever gave me the opportunity to do so. Three weeks later he was released and set free.

I was summoned for my final interrogation on the last day of July 1943. Unusually, it took place on the first floor in the building and, apart from Gustav and his blond friend, I found myself in the company of Ignatowicz, one of the original group from Warsaw, a sickly man who now, after months of imprisonment, looked in even poorer shape. His interrogation was almost at an end, when Gustav asked him if it was true that he suffered from tuberculosis, which Ignatowicz confirmed. The next question was most revealing, however. When asked what he planned to do should he be freed, he answered that he would return to Warsaw and resume his previous work. This sounded too good to be true and I prayed that this would happen for his sake.

It was now my turn and immediately Gustav's demeanour changed to one of sarcasm. It started with the usual preamble – name, date of birth and so on – then without further bullying and the expected threats, he posed the same question: what would I do if I were to be released? I took it as a joke in very poor taste and, remembering the advice of a certain inmate, said without hesitation that I would seek work in the Reich. Gustav's expression changed in an instant and he beamed with pleasure.

'You see, you see,' he said, addressing himself to Ignatowicz. 'He's going to work in Germany. *Schön, schön* [great, great].'

Whilst he was thus beside himself with patriotic pride, only Ignatowicz saw the joke and was hard put to stifle a smile. Having hitherto disbelieved everything I had said so far, I wondered why he should now believe such an obvious lie. But it didn't seem to matter any more now. It was as obvious as anything could be that our days in Montelupich were numbered. Whereas I felt certain that Ignatowicz would soon be Warsaw bound, I had every reason to question my own future, recalling Olszewski's words right at the outset in Warsaw's Pawiak Prison: 'God, you were in the worst possible place to be arrested,' – Mrs Markowska's flat. She had been the kingpin of the whole organization and she was still on the run.

In order that I may relate this next little episode, it is necessary to step back for a moment in time. It has, over the years, engraved itself indelibly on my memory, not only with sadness but also with humility. When it was the turn of the Jewish prisoners to be marched to the showers, their pleasure at seeing me in my role as *bademeister* was obvious and heart-warming. Now the opportunity for storing and smuggling bread was better than ever and I was not sorry to give up running the gauntlet with our supplies any more, bucket and broom in hand. The small wooden cabinet I had inherited soon became a perfect repository for an even larger hoard of bread so that, provided the guards were out of sight, I was able to hand the stuff out as a welfare worker would in normal circumstances. The look of sheer bliss on the faces of the poor inmates was wonderful to behold. I always made a point of distributing the bread as prisoners were leaving the showers on their way back to the cells, and not before, as it was safer to do so then.

However, on one particular occasion I became besieged by the Jewish prisoners as soon as they set foot in the shower room and, in spite of my pleas to be patient and wait until they were on their way out, they simply would not budge. This had the effect of causing a traffic jam, preventing the rest from entering, with the guard following up at their rear bellowing '*Los, los*' and cracking his whip ominously. Still they would not budge. Panic-stricken, I hurled several chunks of bread in the air and watched them disappear beneath shirt or coat as if by magic.

'There'll be more later,' I shouted, my voice being drowned by the general hubbub. It did the trick, but it was a close thing which left me in a sweat. Their exit, by contrast, was orderly and with the guard fortunately lingering at the far end of the corridor, it was an ideal situation, in fact, allowing a leisurely handout, to everyone's delight.

The last to leave the showers was Koper, the senior of the group of Jewish prisoners, and three of his companions. Koper was a selfless individual who had always, with great courage and dignity, borne the brunt of the terrible hardships which they all suffered, and whom we arbeiters much admired. This small group now stood before me, squarely, in what appeared to be an 'official capacity'. Koper then spoke.

'We all bless you and worship you. We will remember you for as long as we live. If there will be anything that we can ever do for you sometime in the future, if we come out of this alive, we will do so. We will do anything for you.'

The rest nodded in agreement. I thanked them and was left speechless, I remember, with tears welling in my eyes.

I just happened to be luckier than they were and was thus able to help them in their time of need. Had our roles been reversed, I don't doubt they would have done the same. Even fifty years on, it still brings a tear to my eye whenever this little episode comes to mind.

Chapter Twelve

One week after my last meeting with Gustav, a guard poked his head through the boiler room door and announced cheerfully, 'Thomek, *komm. Du gehst nach hause*' (Come on Thomek, you're going home).

'That, I do not believe,' I replied bluntly.

'Yes you are. Look, it says: Kopystynski zum entlassung.' He held a slip of paper in front of me to see.

With a little stretch of the imagination it almost became a silly game of 'Oh yes you are, Oh no I'm not', so suspicious had I become of their intentions. But I wasn't going to argue the toss. We repaired to the *arbeitszelle* where I collected my meagre belongings and only had time to say a brief farewell. It was a sad moment. There was so very little time to say anything. I collected a few more minor items from the depository which had been taken from me upon my admission to Montelupich, but the little money I had had was now retained as a contribution towards my 'keep' there so I was now completely penniless! I was then led outside where Gustav was waiting with the black Buick. We drove to the Pomorska Street Headquarters in silence.

On arrival we entered a room where Gustav's blond assistant sat thumbing through a sheaf of papers. He handed a couple of sheets to Gustav who glanced over them and lapsed into silence. It was an agonizing moment. Then slowly and with deliberation, almost as though it pained him, he started, 'Well now, we have decided to release you. You can consider yourself very fortunate to have been brought to Krakow – had you been arrested by the Warsaw Gestapo, not only would you have been beaten but probably shot long ago.'

Thrusting a printed form in front of me he added that unless I kept quiet about everything I had witnessed and experienced in Montelupich the consequences for me would be very grave, so if I was prepared to comply with that order I should sign the document. To this I replied that I would only sign it if I could read and understand the text (which was in German). He said impatiently that it was only a formality and told me not to be so impertinent. (For all I knew I might have signed my way to Auschwitz or to forced labour in the Reich). I signed. With that he told me that I was now free to go but should I become involved with either the Security Police or Gestapo on the journey to Warsaw, to refer them to him.

He telephoned the security guard at the entrance to let me pass unhindered and as I made for the door his last words were, '*Also, aufwiedersehen, du alte Englander*' (So, goodbye you old Englishman). Hamming it out to the last I merely gave him a puzzled look and disappeared through the door.

For a time I delighted in strolling along the pavement, savouring my freedom, inhaling the fresh summer air and mixing with the crowd. I had a compelling desire to run and run, as far away from Pomorska Street as possible and just be able to hide somewhere in some cosy corner and think. It also took a while before the I realized that I had not a Grosz to my name to spend on anything, all my money having been 'retained' by the prison administration. I had nowhere to go and worst of all I was in possession of a time-expired identity card from another city. At that moment, however, I could hardly be happier, so decided to make the most of it and find the famous Planty in the city centre. The Planty – the name betrayed its meaning, 'plantations', a place where flower beds flanked the broad avenue for nearly a kilometre in a gorgeous riot of colour to delight the eye. Added to that the cafes and bars dotted along the roadside all in all contributed to a splendid ambient atmosphere. It all looked so much sadder now than it must have done before the war, but to me it still looked like the next thing to heaven. It was then, lost in my thoughts, that I suddenly remembered Zbigniev's invitation. 'If we are ever released from Montelupich, come and see me,' he had said. He had been freed a month before me, so there was nothing now to stop me from doing so. I had memorized his address, 5 Zyblikiewicza, and without further ado set out to find it. Perhaps that would be my cosy corner where I could sit and have time to think. Stopping to ask the way I turned down a side street away from the bustling thoroughfare. It was when I turned another corner that I realized I was being followed. For a moment I pondered what to do and on a sudden impulse turned around to face my bloodhound.

It was the black Buick crawling by the kerbside with Gustav and his blond friend inside. As I stood there facing them, Gustav tossed his head with his usual sarcastic expression and shot off, disappearing around the corner. Damn you Gustav! I said to myself. One minute I was on top of the world and the next, who knew what they were up to.

Instead of proceeding directly to Zbigniev's flat I began to walk in circles in case I was being followed on foot, for in no way did I wish to drag him and his wife into my problems. Thinking furiously I concluded that I would be followed all the way until, as they hoped, I would eventually lead them to Mrs Markowska, and I decided that from now on I would have to take every care and precaution. Even if I was wrong in this assumption I would still have to do so. I simply could not be sure now.

I found the block of flats where Zbigniev lived, in a quiet street and walked past it. Turning the next corner I waited in the darkened entrance of another block of flats for several minutes. When nothing happened I retraced my steps and went upstairs. I rang the door bell and was greeted by a young man who introduced himself as Zbigniev's brother-in-law. I explained who I was and where I had come from, only to be told that Zbigniev and his wife were away 'on a business trip' and were not expected back until Saturday, in two days' time. He invited me in and told me to make myself at home.

Luckily, Zbigniev and his wife arrived the following day and greeted me like a long-lost relation. Zbigniev in his genial, expansive way couldn't do enough for me to make me comfortable. While his wife went out to get some food we sat and talked, ate the food she had prepared and talked well into the evening. I said that I wished to get away as soon as possible on my return to Warsaw, but hadn't the money for a ticket. That, he said, was no problem at all and thrust 400 Zlotys into my hand. However, he said it would be inadvisable to travel that night, Friday – it would be safer on Saturday because both the Gestapo as well as the Security Police were either too drunk or lax to carry out checks. There was only one train to Warsaw anyway and that was at 9.30 in the evening, which was after the nine o'clock curfew. This meant getting to the station before nine and hanging around for half an hour, giving even a drunken member of the Gestapo ample time to arrest me for possessing an out-of-date identity card in a place I had no permit to be.

However, Zbigniev's confidence was infectious. I was not to worry at all, he reassured me. We were going to leave at nine and get to the station just in time to catch my train. Just don't worry, he said. The following morning we went for a leisurely stroll to the ancient part of the city, so steeped in history and relatively undamaged, afterwards repairing to a small cafe for a snack and 'tea'.

At nine in the evening Zbigniev and I set out at a brisk pace on our way to the railway station. The streets were by now rapidly becoming deserted with the last of the stragglers scurrying home. In this unnatural and ghostly atmosphere the sound of our footsteps echoed alarmingly on the cobbled streets.

The station finally hove into sight but to reach it we had yet to cross a large open square. Presently we heard approaching footsteps and it was obvious that we were on a collision course. Out of the gathering darkness appeared an SS foot patrol and in an instant my heart stood still. What should we do now? We all stopped dead in our tracks and Zbigniev stepped forward, showed the Sergeant in charge his identity card and then, in faultless German and with absolute confidence explained the reason for our presence. The young Sergeant listened, nodded and we parted company, wishing each other 'good night'.

Reaching our destination with minutes to spare before the arrival of the train, I was relieved to note that there were no Gestapo in sight. Zbigniev insisted on paying for my ticket and when we stood waiting on the platform a railwayman stopped to ask us if we had heard of 'the accident'. What accident? we enquired. Last night's train to Warsaw had been shot up and derailed by partisans and there were numerous casualties. I thanked my lucky stars that I had taken Zbigniev's advice to take the Saturday evening train.

When the train drew into the station I thanked him for all he had done, with a promise to return the 400 Zlotys as soon as I could do so. His response was typical: 'Forget it – have a good trip.'

I was alone in the compartment and only one of a dozen or so passengers on the entire train – the evening train to Warsaw clearly wasn't very popular tonight following the events of the previous evening. In the dim light I could see that walls of the carriage were riddled with bullet holes and much of the glass had been shattered, which accounted for an uncomfortable draught. Obviously the carriage was one which had survived the previous night's crash. Within an hour the train's speed reduced to a crawl as we passed the wrecked train, with carriages piled up and strewn alongside the track and adjoining field, and the locomotive on its side still emitting clouds of steam like a stricken dragon. They had certainly done a thorough job. Shortly afterwards I saw flames shooting skywards from a whole host of fires a short distance away and, peering through the darkness, I realized that they were emanating from two separate villages. That was indeed the terrible price that was to be paid for the recent attack and the usual punishment dispensed by the SS.

With several hours journey ahead of me my thoughts constantly turned to my mother. I wondered how and where she was and prayed that she had not suffered greater hardship as a result of my arrest. I had no idea what I was going to find when I arrived in Warsaw, assuming I did get there without encountering trouble. It was devastating not to have had any news whatsoever for a year and a half. I felt Hania was more likely to have come through that time unscathed, for if anything had happened to her it would assuredly not have been in connection with my arrest. I decided that my first port of call would by my mother's flat at Saska Kepa.

The train pulled in to Warsaw Central at 7.30 on a cloudless Sunday morning. Thankfully the main hall and stairways were free of leather-coated Gestapo and I made my way outside to catch a tram along the route I must have taken a million times in the past.

Traffic was sparse at this early hour, there were no roving street patrols in sight and it was a beautiful day. Saska Kepa looked fresh and inviting and so conveniently separated from the city itself by the Vistula River, thus giving one the impression of being in a different world. A few minutes' walk brought me to the road where my mother had her flat – before turning into it I made sure I had not been followed and, reaching No. 18, I entered and rang the doorbell of flat No 1. It was opened by a strange lady who eyed me for a moment before saying, 'You wouldn't be Tom by any chance, would you?'

'Yes, I am,' I replied, whereupon she disappeared inside for a moment. There followed an excited babble of voices and my mother emerged to greet me with tears of happiness.

Later, my mother explained the events that followed my disappearance in March of 1942. When I had failed to return home after the 9 o'clock curfew, she immediately telephoned around friends asking if they knew what had happened to me. Due to a lapse in communication she did not know Hania's telephone number and was therefore unable to ask her – that had to be left to someone else. Hania then promptly got in touch with my mother and told her about my proposed visit to Mrs Markowska, she of course herself not having an inkling about any trouble. A sudden disappearance usually meant one thing – arrest by the Gestapo. For her own good my mother then had to disappear herself in case of a visit by the Gestapo, but she was obliged to wait until the morning to do so. It was an unenviable experience, knowing that a visit could happen at any time during the night, but she was unable to leave the house because of the curfew.

In the event she spent three weeks with friends in a different part of the town and when it seemed that immediate danger was over, returned home. As far as was known by watchful neighbours, the Gestapo never called during her absence. Again, her luck held, but she still had no idea where I was until the arrival of that first *bedarfschein* (request for comforts) from Montelupich six weeks after my disappearance.

Nothing now remained of the escape network in Warsaw. Most of its principle members had been caught with the exception of Mrs Markowska, its leader, others having scattered into hiding, including George Newton, George Weeks and John Grant. Kathleen Smith also 'disappeared' for a time and was forced to keep a low profile, not daring to communicate with anyone connected with the organization, but was lucky enough not to have been arrested. The effects of the disaster reverberated beyond Warsaw, where tentacles of the organization stretched out into the provinces, but to what extent I had no idea. Including myself, two others had been freed, Ignatowicz and Bormanova, one of the women in our group. Dr Dabrowski, who was released six weeks after our incarceration in Montelupich jail was in no way connected with the organization, having visited the ailing Ignatowicz in a professional capacity. I did not know whether Ignatowicz and Mrs Bormanova were in any way involved.

Chapter Thirteen

In the meanwhile, life in Warsaw had become increasingly hazardous. The tragedy of the Jewish ghetto, about which we had only heard rumour in Montelupich, had ended in its total destruction and is well recorded in the history of the Second World War. I was able to see for myself the remains of what must have been one of the worst tragedies of that war.

With their fortunes dwindling on all battle fronts, the Nazis, like a wounded and demented animal, turned all their venom onto the civilian population in a desperate effort to crush any sign of rebellion. The killing of a German was avenged by the execution of dozens of hostages in the city squares and even on a beach by the river at Saska Kepa. I very nearly got caught up in this particular episode, only avoiding trouble by darting down an alleyway as soon as I detected signs of some 'unusual activity' on the part of two armed SS men. In fact, there were a lot more of them about, appearing from almost nowhere, but I gradually made my way in what seemed to be a safe direction and hid inside a small shop on Francuska Street (French Street), at the same time warning the owner what was happening. A deathly quiet seemed to descend on the area as though everyone sensed impending danger. In fact, word of anything like this spread like wildfire, warning people to keep away. Presently the sound of a volley echoed through the air, followed by another hush. 'For them it's all over,' whispered the shopkeeper's wife with tears welling in her eyes.

Twenty-five people were gunned down on the beach on that occasion, just a few hundred yards from my mother's flat. Mass raids by the security forces were also becoming more frequent in which entire blocks were surrounded, followed by house-to-house searches, which sometimes lasted for two or more hours. Even going about one's daily business became a hazardous occupation, with trams being stopped and searched (buses had long since ceased to operate), and one walked the streets with an eye in the back of one's head.

With this background, the need to be in possession of a valid identity card and good certificate of employment, even if it were a bogus one, became more important than ever. Helpful employers often issued employees with these documents with a very impressive job description, such as 'work vital to the Wehrmacht', which was probably anything but true, but could mean the difference between becoming another hostage and being allowed to go free. The Gestapo could not possibly check out everyone's credentials and if one could get away with it, so well and good, but in the last resort, you were on your own.

Once again, the procurement of an identity card became vital. This meant that discreet enquiries had to be made through friends who knew someone in the right department in the town hall. Presently a message came through for me to report to a certain individual, taking a photograph of myself with me. He may have been someone important in the department, but if his manner exuded a certain confidence, his appearance was of the oddest for the times, dressed in an immaculate white summer suit with white shirt and silk tie, and sporting a cream Panama hat, an ensemble far better suited to the South of France in peacetime. I waited for an hour whilst he breezed in and out of the office, creating the right impression in order to hide his true activity from the Germans working therein. One relied on people like him all the time. He finally emerged with the vital document with the words 'It was a little difficult but we managed it'. Questions were never asked.

At this time I was still acutely worried at the possibility of being tailed by Gustav's men, and went out of my way to avoid contact with friends I least wished to implicate.

I telephoned Hania and said that a meeting would be unwise, in what was a rather stilted conversation as the line could also very well have been tapped. The reality was that with her Jewish background I could not take any chances – she had in the meantime moved away from the centre of town to a distant suburb and still worked in an office somewhere. In the event, my motive for staying away was, in all probability, misinterpreted, and eventually, when other events intervened, we drifted apart. There was much I was grateful for, however, not least her valuable contributions to those eagerly awaited packages that I received in prison. In the end, she emigrated to Israel when hostilities ceased.

My suspicions increased when I ran into an SS man I knew well by sight in Krakow – he was waiting at a tram stop in the city and I had to do a quick about turn in order to avoid a direct confrontation. His name was Sarger. Seeing him raised the fear that the Krakow Gestapo might be casting their net again and I decided that my best bet was to clear out of Warsaw as soon as possible. My mother, who had been fretting about my safety ever since my return, was in full agreement with my plan. Luck played a part too. I badly needed to earn some money and by chance I was offered work by a friend, who though unaware of my true identity, suggested I join him in a bridge-building project in the Tarnow district. I said that I was prepared to do anything, so long as it took me away from Warsaw.

In this sort of arrangement formalities were easily overcome regarding registration, as there was always some sort of work available. What I did not know was that the project was one of vast size and entailed the building of a railway viaduct. Obviously the viaduct itself fitted in to some grand overall plan, the extent of which seemed to have been somewhat misjudged.

Nevertheless, when my friend Karwowski and I set out one Sunday on the journey to Tarnow, I had no clear idea what my role would be. At any rate, when we arrived at our destination a BMW car awaited with four German civil engineers in it. I was obliged to sit on top of one of them and hoped that he would have the most uncomfortable ride of his life – I was probably right because of the appalling road conditions we subsequently encountered. We eventually got out of the car in a desolate sandy area and trudged half a mile or more to the site, leaving the Germans to continue their journey.

Climbing an escarpment we reached a pleasant hamlet shrouded by trees where Karwowski went into a cottage and deposited his luggage. He explained that regrettably, as all the cottages were already occupied by 'management', he would show me to my digs. We emerged at the other end of this nice place, out into a bleak landscape, and made for a hut which stood close to the edge of the escarpment so that it was exposed to the four winds. We had an uninterrupted view of the countryside and, in the immediate foreground, a picture of the vast project, as yet in its early stages of construction. As we entered the hut a young man rose from a bunk to greet us. His name was Jan and he was the foreman. Karwowski said that I would be working under Jan who would explain everything that I needed to know about the job, and left.

As he was the sole occupant of the hut I had the pick of several empty, tiered bunks. Echoing my previous experience he advised me to opt for a top bunk because of the fleas – he was expecting the place to fill up quite soon, so why not let the others take the brunt of the fleas' attention?

We trudged around the site for an hour or so with Jan enthusiastically explaining what was happening, before leading me to one of two pile drivers perched on rails on the edge of a deep trench. My job would be assisting him operate one of them. The other pile driver was in the process of working a parallel trench, but was operated by a different company. There were more of these trenches to be excavated and shored up, and I tried to imagine what the end result of our labours would be. Where we stood, we were in a depression some 30ft below the surrounding terrain. The edge of the escarpment, where our hut was, rose at one end of the depression, while a quarter of a mile away a matching embankment was being built up with the aid of railway tipper wagons running on a narrow-gauge track. The trenches were excavated to a depth of about 10ft and the edges were reinforced with heavy planking to prevent them from caving in. The planks, with sharpened ends, were driven into the sandy subsoil by the pile drivers, which was where we came into the picture. The trenches would eventually be filled with tons of concrete and form bases for the vertical supports intended to carry the bridge. With things going badly for the Germans now, especially their steady withdrawal from Soviet territory, I could not see a hope in hell of it being of any use to them, let alone being completed in time.

The two pile drivers and the narrow-gauge railway were the only mechanical components in the entire construction. There were no mechanical diggers or excavators – all that was done by scores of conscripted country lads, some of them no more than boys, clad in some kind of basic uniform and brought on site each morning by army trucks. Characteristically they all worked barefoot, as country folk always had done in that part of the world.

Now, however, it was Sunday and the site was deserted (the Germans were obviously not pushing the work forward with great urgency) but the next day would see the place alive with activity.

The word 'amenity' had not been heard of here and amounted to practically nothing. Apart from a rickety 'single cylinder' closet situated some distance away, the only water supply came from a standpipe Jan had sunk at the base of the escarpment. Worst of all was the problem of obtaining any food. Evidently Jan had managed to persuade a woman from a distant village to call every other day to prepare some soup on the stove which stood in a corner of the hut, but that didn't last, and nothing would persuade the women from 'management' to oblige. All we were left with was a meagre supply of bread. It was the same story I had encountered back in 1940 all over again. A week or two later we repaired to that distant village one Sunday in order to persuade the same woman, this time for a larger remuneration, to call again, bring some bread and cook her soup, which she grudgingly did briefly, after which we were on our own again.

I spent the first few days with Jan learning how to operate our pile driver – when I became proficient enough he left me alone, along with three or four lads, to carry on the work. It was tedious work but not without its problems, for moving the giant machine along the rails in order to drive each pile into the ground required great care, the edge of the trench being so unstable that on two occasions the whole thing very nearly toppled to the bottom of the ditch. However, the machine itself was an ingenious piece of German engineering, the only trouble being that it was not up to the job. Whilst our rivals at the next trench hammered away steadily on their old steam-driven contraption, we began to suffer regular breakdowns. Ours worked roughly on the principle of a diesel engine, but the piston rings and cushioning pad/ring kept breaking up. So whilst we awaited the arrival of spare parts I turned to helping Jan in whatever else needed doing.

All in all it turned out to be very hard graft and, with the blazing hot sun beating down relentlessly and nowhere to shelter, I found it hard to bear. At the end of each day we were too worn out to move anywhere and spent most of the time resting on our bunks, beating off the flies and mosquitoes.

About a mile away to the south-east of the site, the barren terrain ended with a lush green forest stretching away into the distance. Rumour had it that it was alive with partisans and that the Germans never dared venture into it. Forests here were truly forests in every sense of the word, being extensive and in parts dense, and it was easy to get lost. It was therefore necessary to use the sun as a guide, if possible, and at best, having found a footpath, to stick to it until some form of habitation was reached. One night, almost to our cost, we found that the rumour was a reality. Slumbering peacefully in our bunks we were startled by the sound of gunfire which quickly escalated into a pitched battle with bullets whining through the air in alarming proximity to our hut. We dived for cover underneath our bunks as several bullets cracked through the woodwork. It lasted for about ten minutes before gradually diminishing and finally ceasing altogether.

Our first sight in the early morning was that of a detachment of troops slowly moving forward, combing the open country as they approached the dense line of trees, although they went no further.

Sheer starvation at the end of my fifth week finally made me decide to leave the place. Perhaps Jan had a greater motivation to remain and pursue his work, civil engineering being his profession, but this was not for me. Added to that I simply did not wish to assist the Germans in their project any longer. Jan, at any rate, was understanding about it.

And so on the Friday I decided that I might as well go out with a bang. The force of the hammer when it struck was governed by a hand-held throttle control at the end of a long cable. It was exactly as a throttle control on the handlebar of an old motorcycle or lawnmower. So with judicious adjustment of the small lever, it was possible to allow the hammerhead to strike either with extreme 'gentleness' or with great strength, as the job required. It was at the upper end of the scale when the damage usually occurred. And so, at an opportune moment, I set the throttle at maximum power and watched the thundering ton of metal slowly disintegrate in a shower of red-hot shards. Appropriately, I made the right noises and gestures to fit the occasion, as everyone on the site stood and stared in awe. Presently a German inspector turned up to view the damage and made equally nasty noises, mostly aimed in my direction. But I had a good alibi: the machine had always given us trouble and he knew it.

I did not intend to await repercussions and, saying goodbye to Jan, hitched a lift on the back of an army truck to Tarnow. At the station the ticket clerk demanded to see my travel permit so I told him I hadn't one and was only going home for the weekend. No, he needed to see my travel permit first and, fearful of attracting the attention of two or three Security Police drifting about the place, I demanded that he gave me a ticket. I got it. The timing was right for just as some of the police were busy rummaging through another man's cases, the train drew into the station. I reached Warsaw without trouble.

Still in possession of an excellent work permit which was valid for a few more weeks, but without work, I soon remedied this when I commenced work for a repair garage at the far end of town. However, in my absence, my mother had had a shock when a young woman called at her flat and introduced herself as an employee of the post office. She handed Mother a letter which she said had been intercepted by a postal worker at the sorting office as it was addressed to the Gestapo Headquarters on Aleja Shucha. Its handwritten contents were entirely compromising, revealing Mother's true identity and her involvement with British prisoners of war. Significantly, there was no mention of me at all, which indicated that whoever had written it must have had a personal grudge against her. Sadly this was not an uncommon facet of the war and many similar letters had been intercepted during the days of occupation. There was nothing we could do but thank those stalwarts for their vigilance. On the other hand, the Resistance movement had its own way of dealing with the perpetrators.

For a time I was faced with a difficult and potentially hazardous journey to and from work at the garage, and I was happy when my old friend Jurek and his mother suggested I stayed with them for as long as was necessary. This reduced my journey by half but the centre of town was no safe haven either. Of course, nowhere was safe and we lived on a knife edge from one day to the next. By this time at least I felt safe from any kind of surveillance, if indeed there ever was any. That, I will never know.

We survived the winter of 1943/44 with the shortage of both food and fuel worsening steadily. I remember being desperately hungry every single day and the thought of enjoying a square meal was for ever gnawing at my innards.

It was around this time that I came face to face with a 'ghost' from the past: Tadek Stanczyk. I remembered him as a fresh-faced youngster, one of the group of arbeiters on the first floor in Montelupich. He had a happy-go-lucky disposition and was no doubt seen as a harmless individual by his jailors. That, combined with his command of German, meant that he was seconded to the sick bay where he performed the duties of assistant to the medic in charge. Apart from Vladek Czajka, he was the only other prisoner allowed out under escort to obtain medical supplies for use in the sickbay. Somehow, with the connivance of the young Ukrainian guard, who it will be remembered had also been helpful to Kazek and myself, he had managed to pursue a clandestine affair with Maria from the laundry. As fellow arbeiters, we had had an inkling of this affair, but having left Montelupich I never thought I would see him again. And here we were standing in the same queue waiting for a tram in a busy Warsaw street! I had to look twice to be sure it was him. He was dressed in the khaki uniform of the Todt Organisation and appeared thin and haggard. When our eyes met he looked startled and left the queue, making his way to the entrance of a block of flats. I followed him and we began talking only when there was no one within earshot. Expressing surprise I asked what he was doing in uniform. He was obviously frightened and embarrassed, and spoke in rapid tones. Begging me not to look surprised and act normally, he explained that he and Maria had been married secretly in Montelupich by a fellow inmate priest; when Maria was freed, it was more than he could bear. He escaped whilst out on a routine purchasing trip and was now being sought by the Gestapo. He then realized that the best place he could hide would be in the ranks of the Todt Organisation and volunteered to join up. He hoped he would be sent to work in the port of Stettin, or any other port from which there was a possibility of escape aboard a Swedish ship. I wished him luck and we parted.

The Todt Organisation was made up of volunteers and conscripts from all countries which were under Nazi occupation, and were put to work on road construction, transport, handling supplies, and so forth. As the Germans were desperately in need of extra manpower, all comers were welcome to join – unbeknown to them, men like Tadek Stanczyk, who were wanted by the Gestapo, and indeed many others, joined up with the express idea of escaping either to the Allied lines or by sea to a neutral country, primarily Sweden.

Chapter Fourteen

The spring of 1944 dawned with a sensation of menace and foreboding. Although now in full retreat from the grinding might of the Soviet Army, the Nazis still found the strength and wherewithal to hold down a population on the verge of open rebellion. One sensed it constantly now. Everyone knew it and willed it to happen. It showed in the behaviour of the Germans too. Soon, the explosion was bound to happen. But life had to go on and sometimes, amazingly, people's behaviour seemed so much at variance with the prevailing menacing undercurrent. Human nature seemed to dictate the necessity to carry on in as normal a way as possible, as the following episode illustrates.

In June, news of the Allied landings in France was a wonderful tonic, for it spelt the beginning of the end for the Germans. And yet – not that we knew – so much blood and suffering had yet to be endured before the end came. Having missed previous chances of escape I now began to think seriously about making a bid for freedom, only this time there would be no constraints in making me do so. Furthermore, as I imagined, it should be an easier proposition than escaping from Montelupich! But I would need to get away from Warsaw, which I visualized would become a death trap once the Russians came within firing distance of the city. Exact news of the fighting was hard to come by from German sources, consequently we relied on BBC news bulletins more than ever, as well as rumours passed on by word of mouth from people fleeing from the battle front. Added to that, units of Hungarians in the service of the Germans began to appear in the streets of Warsaw heading in a westerly direction, which was a positive indication of an army in retreat. Naively, as it transpired, my plan was to make my way towards the Russian lines and get through to them at the first opportune moment. As they were now our allies, I could not envisage a problem once I was on the other side. But I would need a base somewhere east of Warsaw as a starting point – and that was a problem which had to be solved. Then, by one of those strange coincidences, my mother sent me a message to call at a certain house in town and see some people who had a proposition which might, coincidentally, be helpful in the fulfilment of my plan.

A meeting was duly arranged over the telephone and when I met Mrs Kondratowicz, I found her 'proposition' quite bizarre. It transpired that both her daughters had been learning English (clandestinely) and needed to practise their conversation to further their knowledge of the language. Kathleen Smith had been approached but had turned down the offer in my favour. Discretions observed, no questions were asked regarding my identity, although people usually drew their own conclusions, whatever they were. It was at this point, when I began searching for a suitable excuse for declining the job (for which I would be paid), that she explained where these 'lessons' were to take place. It would be at their country residence and farm near Minsk Mazowiecki, about 40 miles east of Warsaw, in the last two weeks of June. My problem of a 'base' thus appeared to be solved and I accepted the job at once.

Well before the appointed time I obtained two weeks' leave with my employer, as well as a covering letter to this effect, in case I was stopped for questioning at any time. Although the conversion of mainly civilian cars and trucks from petrol to butane gas was not exactly work of vital importance, it was made to sound in the letter so by my helpful boss.

When the day of my departure finally dawned, the farewells seemed sad and final. Thankfully, Mother stood up to it very well, somehow managing to avoid a flood of tears, and I sensed that in her heart of hearts she knew that I stood a better chance of survival, and possibly every chance of succeeding in my plan, than remaining in Warsaw. Of my friends, only Jurek and his mother knew, and wished me luck. I was never to see them again.

I left Warsaw by train on a beautiful Sunday morning, not even marred by the presence of the ubiquitous Gestapo, arriving at Minsk Mazowiecki an hour later. Here, as was usual, a long line of horse-drawn cabs and breaks awaited the arrival of their owners, visiting guests and others plying for hire, like rural taxis. I walked along the row calling out the name of the Kondratowicz estate until one of the drivers responded with a 'Ho' and raised his arm in recognition. The drive to Rudzienko was all too short, as I revelled in the leisurely journey through the peaceful countryside with the morning sun beating down and the world at rest. Had it not been for two truckloads of gendarmes racing in the opposite direction in a cloud of dust, disturbing this vision of tranquillity, I might have been back in more peaceful times. Still, I wondered what awaited me at Rudzienko, how I should cope with my two charges and how my plan to break through to the Russians would develop. That next and all-important step would, in fact, hardly be up to me at all, for much larger events had a nasty way of taking over and controlling one's destiny, regardless. At least fate, or luck, had presented me with the initial step in my plan – my arrival at Rudzienko.

Here, I was surprised to find a large gathering of people, apart from Mr and Mrs Kondratowicz, the two daughters, Jadwiga, the older one, and Irena, and son Zbigniew. There were two almost identical maiden aunts, an attractive blonde, Danuta – Zbigniew's alleged girl-friend, Mietek, the resident bailiff and finally Jurek Berezowski, who was also there as a guest, to make up the party. Introductions were formal and ritualistic, but once dispensed with the atmosphere became congenial and relaxed.

Curiously, by a chance in a million, I had met Jurek Berezowski before the war and we had known each other quite well for a time. He knew very well who

I was but accepted my adopted name, Kopystynski, without expressing surprise. However, for the benefit of the others, we merely commented that we had met before and left it at that. Nevertheless, at the earliest opportunity, I told him my full story which he understood and promised reverently to keep to himself. As young teenagers we had always got on very well and I was glad to find we continued to do so.

The Kondratowicz estate was a large one. At the front of the single-storey manor house a large patio was graced with serpentine steps on either side, leading down to the drive, which encircled a huge flower bed, studded with a variety of colourful plants. At the rear, a yard contained a woodshed, cold storage and other ancillary outbuildings. The whole property was thickly ringed by trees giving it a feeling of security and relative isolation. Beyond the ring of trees stretched golden wheat fields for miles, the sheer expanse broken up here and there by woods and forests. But immediately at the rear and outside that ring of trees was the kitchen garden, and beyond an orchard and soft fruit plantations, cowsheds and stables for fourteen workhorses. Yet further afield were several breeding ponds sporting scores of fat carp. On the lighter side, there was a hard court for tennis concealed within the adjacent woodland. All in all, it was an idyllic setting. Not since before the war had I experienced such pleasure and abundance of food.

I took my job as 'tutor' seriously and laid down a ground rule that for two hours each day after lunch, Jadwiga, Irena and I were to spend that time reading and conversing in English. There was an English textbook and for reading exercise I chose a suitable book from their extensive library. Other than that I tried my level best to keep the conversation going during the day but soon found that it was an uphill struggle, for although Jadwiga, who was twenty-three, took it seriously, Irena, a lively and impish sixteen year old, found every excuse under the sun why she should not attend these sessions, the prevailing holiday atmosphere hardly lending itself to too many disciplines anyway. But I struggled on in order to justify my presence there.

As bailiff, Mietek spent most days away on horseback doing his rounds of the extensive property, usually returning dusty and dog-tired in time for the evening meal. At twenty-five, he was tall and erect in stature with rather an aloof manner. Zbigniew Kondratowicz, of the same age, quick witted and life and soul of the party, also spent much of the time attending to matters concerning the running of the estate, often with Mietek, but now and again disappearing somewhere on his motorcycle, to where no one knew, but one guessed to some clandestine activity in the area. His mount was his pride and joy, of German make and painted in the drab grey of all German army transport, its acquirement remaining a deep secret, and at the end of the day invariably carefully hidden in a barn. He was no one's fool.

Under the circumstances, the three girls often pursued their own interests whilst Jurek and I spent much time in each other's company, in leisurely rambles or singular idleness. He was an amiable and easygoing character with a good sense of humour, which suited me well. However, whenever the party was complete there was a lot of fun to be had and as carefree as one would wish, often lasting well into the evening. I sometimes told myself that it was all a dream, a dream which had to end soon. We were indeed making hay whilst the sun still shone.

On the third day of my visit, it was decided to have a game of tennis rather late in the evening, as the sun was setting. We all had a go, sharing the two or three available racquets between us, however, as it grew darker we became conscious of brilliant flashes which lit up the eastern sky, the significance of which did not register with us at the time. Bitten by the tennis bug we continued our attempts at playing in the dark and again observed these nocturnal illuminations, although this time to the accompaniment of distant rumbles. As the rumbling grew louder we soon realized its significance. It heralded the end of our tennis, end of our fun and the end of sanity itself. Everything changed in an instant. With the approach of what can be described as a gigantic tidal wave, it was time for decisions. The Kondratowicz family became locked in serious discussion, knowing full well that very soon their lives there would disappear, possibly for ever. By the same token, my days as a 'tutor' were also at an end.

The following morning a party of German officers arrived in two cars and proceeded to inspect the place, commandeering the farmyard with all its outbuildings, sheds and barns. In the afternoon the entire estate buzzed with the sound of motors as truckload after truckload of troops arrived, filling every inch of space. It transpired they were a maintenance and repair unit; they promptly started to unload their gear and were soon hard at work. At least they left us alone in the manor house. We were surprised to note how calm and relaxed they were, considering they were on the retreat. Although they behaved well and did not interfere with us, we nevertheless decided that the situation called for caution, and kept out of their way as much as possible. However, when we did come into contact with them, common courtesies were usually observed on both sides. Amongst them was a group of Russians, former prisoners of war who worked with the unit, and it was with them that we found conversation interesting. Still wearing their Russian uniforms, they seemed to keep to themselves and, curiously, the Germans didn't seem to mind us talking to them. With one exception they were straightforward and uncomplicated young men. The senior of them, a typical tall blonde and articulate Russian, when asked why they went along with the Germans, replied that it was because they all detested the Communist regime in Russia. They weren't keen to discuss politics and before long produced a balalaika, and broke into a soft lilting chorus in which we willingly joined.

The unit's departure several days later left an eerie vacuum, with the obvious conclusion that the Russians would not be long in arriving. If only it had been that simple.

Zbigniew, in the meantime, had repaired to the nearby village of Rudzienko (from which the estate bore its name) and returned in a state of excitement with the news that a Russian spearhead unit had arrived there. He noted that one of the tanks was under the command of a woman officer. They had exuded confidence and bravura, explaining that they intended to make a break-through to Warsaw, whereupon they took off in a cloud of dust. All this seemed to confirm our thoughts, but swarms of refugees who suddenly began to descend on Rudzienko had a different story to tell. The main retreating German force was still intact and approaching Rudzienko. As though to bear this out a formation of Russian aeroplanes suddenly appeared and began dive-bombing a target about 2 miles away. (Much later, a Russian communiqué stated that a spearhead consisting of tanks had penetrated German lines and had raced on towards Warsaw, only to be destroyed within striking distance of the city.)

Presently there was a sound of sporadic gunfire coupled with the grinding noise of German tanks proceeding along the main road a quarter of a mile or so away. The four of us grew restive, wishing we had had a gun or two with which we could hit the Germans. We were thus engaged in a bout of wishful thinking when Jurek announced that he knew exactly where he could find one – a machine gun no less! Following him, we rushed over to a barn where he proceeded to scrabble around frantically in the straw and fished out a beautiful Kalashnikov automatic rifle. Unfortunately there was no ammunition but Jurek knew where to find that too. Our clamour to know where was answered by a matter of fact 'Oh, in the duck pond.' He was goaded into removing his shoes then, wading into the muddy water, he stood there looking thoroughly sheepish, sloshing about, announcing every now and again, 'I think it's here, no – it must be just over there', stooping down each time to fumble in the mud with his bare hands. But his efforts finally met with success and he produced two metal boxes full of ammunition. He had spotted the Russians disposing of the cache on the day of their departure.

We had no idea whether the ammunition was any good after its soaking, nevertheless we began making 'strategic plans' as to how we should use the gun to best effect. I suggested that we make our way to the main road and lie in wait for oncoming trucks and cars, as the ditches on either side provided good cover. The plan was generally agreed upon but a few practice shots were necessary before we left. We were already making tracks in the direction of the highway when someone noticed that the all-important firing pin was missing. Retracing our steps in disgust we hurled the useless object and the boxes of ammunition into the duck pond when at that precise moment a staff car with four SS officers dressed in full battle gear roared into the yard, and within minutes the place swarmed with troops armed to the teeth and obviously in a high state of agitation. Fortunately they ignored us, but I hated to think what would have happened had they caught us brandishing a machine gun a matter of seconds earlier.

Now there was complete uproar as droves of frightened refugees poured in mingling with the harassed troops scurrying around as tanks rolled in, smashing down saplings and bushes and churning up the beautiful lawn with its flower beds. At the same time the officers took over the manor house occupying two of the largest rooms at the back, from where they would apparently direct the battle, which seemed imminent.

Leaving their decision to quit Rudzienko until the last minute possible, the Kondratowicz family hastily packed a small amount of luggage and prepared to depart in a pick-up truck which awaited them in the yard at the rear of the house. Zbigniew, their son, felt duty bound to remain and take care of the estate for as long as possible. Jurek, Mietek and I opted to stay, my own reasons for so doing already having been explained, and I was glad of their company. Calmly, Mr Kondratowicz put it to us that if any of us harboured any doubts about staying on we would be welcome to travel with them, hopefully to Warsaw, but if we were to remain, then with Mietek's guidance as bailiff, we should try and keep the farm going for as long as possible. In the circumstances, reliance on help from the farm hands was uncertain, as they would naturally be more concerned with the safety of their families. The harvest would have to wait, but the thirty head of cattle as well as the fourteen horses had to be fed and taken care of. He said that he was not prepared to wait for the Russians because as a landowner he knew what they would do to him and the family, and whether they were our allies or not, they could not be trusted. Mrs Kondratowicz thanked me for my tutorial efforts and paid me the agreed amount of 300 Zlotys in spite of the fact that my time had been cut short, adding another 100 Zlotys in case I needed it.

The two maiden aunts, so quiet and unobtrusive that they had hardly been noticed in all the turmoil, had also elected to stay, adding an additional responsibility for their safety on Zbigniew. To give him credit he showed great concern and consideration in ensuring that they came to no harm in the frantic days that followed.

In the meantime, many of the refugees had packed the cellars in an effort to escape the worst of the impending bombardment. In the evening, whilst Zbigniew concerned himself with helping the refugees with all their problems, the rest of us attended to the cattle and the horses, returning to the manor after dark.

That same evening, whilst the Germans were still busily digging in and preparing for battle, we heard a rumour that the long-awaited uprising in Warsaw had begun. Events were now moving fast and although we dearly wanted to know how it was going for the brave citizens of Warsaw, more news was impossible to come by.

An eerie lull lasted for two days, contrary to our expectations, and, taking advantage of the silence, some of us ventured onto the terrace for a 'breather'. Then, high up in the darkening sky above, we noticed the shadow of a large four-engined bomber travelling on a steady course in the direction of Warsaw. The distant beam of a searchlight shot skyward, frantically trying to seek out its quarry. It searched in vain, but others soon joined in weaving their long tentacles hither and thither, until finally caught in the centre of their web, the bomber presented a perfect target. We watched in awe as a constant barrage of anti-aircraft fire followed it until it was hit. With one engine on fire it continued on its unwavering course until we lost sight of it altogether. Somewhere behind me a woman prayed aloud for the safety of the airmen, whilst another, seeing the burning plane, burst into tears.

(History records that during the Warsaw uprising of 1944, attempts were made by the RAF to drop supplies of arms to the beleaguered Resistance fighters in the city. Flying Halifax and Liberator bombers, the crews on these missions consisted of Britons, Poles and New Zealanders.)

In spite of our own problems, that episode created a deep impression on all who saw it. It gave one hope that maybe after all there was someone out there on our side.

We continued tending to the animals first thing in the morning and in the evening, and gained the unexpected help of one loyal farm hand. During the day, however, we did our best to keep out of sight of the SS troops. They were obviously edgy and our presence in the farmyard looked decidedly unwelcome. In the end we were told to stay away. Next, our precious supply of food was stolen from the cold cellar, leaving us with only an emergency supply hidden in the manor house. Even that was sniffed out by the Germans when by chance I ran into six of them heading for the closet where it was kept. I saw red at that and placed myself between them and the door to the closet. For one moment they hesitated and I immediately began an inane conversation with them which completely put them off. One became somewhat belligerent but the rest prevailed upon him and eventually they slunk away looking rather shamefaced. I couldn't believe my luck. It was for nothing, however, because a day later that supply had gone as well. Worse still, we sneaked into the stables and cowshed to feed the animals only to find them empty. It was inevitable that it would happen sooner or later. We later found that the Germans were driving every head of cattle as well as horses before them in droves, thus depriving entire farming communities of their source of livelihood at a stroke.

Zbigniew confided in us that he had 40 litres of vodka stashed away beneath the cellar floor, which he said he would guard with his life. 'You'd be surprised what you can do with a bottle or two of the stuff, especially in times like these,' he added wisely. Prophetically his words proved to be only too true.

With their tanks well dug in on the outer perimeter of our sheltered enclave, the Germans set up a barrage in the direction of the Russian lines, with a corresponding response. Russian shells whizzed overhead, falling mostly to the rear of the manor house. Rather than return to the cellars we decided to remain in our rooms and trust to the protection of the solid walls of the building. The only drawback to this was that we were in direct line of fire should a shell find its way through a window, but this seemed preferable to the packed cellars with their frightened refugees and whimpering children. The battle continued well into the night with an occasional shell exploding in front of the house, the rest still falling somewhere to the rear. As darkness fell the shelling ceased allowing a modicum of rest and, drawing the wooden shutters, we fell into a deep sleep.

The second day saw no change, with the battle starting up at eight in the morning and following a definite pattern throughout the day. Whoever started first, the shelling would go on for about fifteen minutes followed by a pause of about ten. Then the other side would respond with a barrage of similar duration, and so on. It all seemed to go like clockwork and the tension drained our sensibilities. A few more shells exploded on what was left of the lawn, the rest still mercifully flying over the roof. We occasionally descended into the cellars to see if there was anything we could do to help, otherwise staying within the confines of the two upstairs rooms, and when the battle died down again, it was time for bed. I was lucky in finding a stack of pre-war magazines in the bedside cabinet and by the light of a candle, transported myself to a world now long gone. It was marvellous therapy for nerves in tatters.

On the third day of the battle we were faced with a new and totally unexpected menace. The word went round that we should keep out of sight because a detachment of *Feldgendarmerie* were on the prowl around the manor house. They then surrounded the house, ordering all men out and to gather in the yard at the back. We stood no chance. They had already rounded up all the farm hands, who stood there in a line with fear written on their faces. It was a desperate moment, especially as none of us had any illusion as to what might follow, with the realization that they were not going to allow any of the menfolk fall into the hands of the Russians.

In the meantime, Zbigniew, somehow having eluded the *Feldgendarmes*, immediately made his way to the commanding officer who was poring over his battle maps at the time, and explained that as owner of the estate it was his responsibility for maintaining it in good working order and he needed at least three extra hands to do so. He mentioned Jurek, Mietek and myself as the three indispensable hands. But the German was in no mood to listen and only allowed Zbigniew to remain.

Formed into two columns we were marched for several miles across country under armed guard, avoiding all habitation, eventually reaching a hamlet where we were driven into a barn and locked up. There we languished for the rest of the day and night, almost suffocating from the heat, the pungent smell of hay and sheer overcrowding. It seemed to be the end of the line, for barns full of hay were a natural choice for incineration, costing the Germans not a single bullet. The three of us managed to find a space at the far end, by a wall, and began testing the strength of the planking. It was firm and solid and our efforts at dislodging one met with no success. Others did likewise with equal lack of success. They had certainly picked the right place for the job and there was no escape. Even if there had been, we would be surrounded and anyone attempting to escape would be picked off like a fly, but mercifully nothing happened and when the day dawned we counted our blessings.

The barn doors were flung open and we were ordered out, formed into a column and marched for a mile or two along a rough, sandy road to a spot where it descended steeply to an ancient river bed, rising up at the far bank. The scene here was one of furious activity, for in the course of construction was a high trestle bridge which, when completed, was intended for the use of the retreating Germans, whose transport vehicles would otherwise sink into the soft sand below. The labour force consisted of village lads, under the eagle eye of a vile SS sergeant whose only means of communication seemed to be in the highest pitch of decibels. His shrill invective reverberated around the ravine, striking fear into the hearts of the boys. With the exception of this vocal exhibition, it all brought back memories of my previous bridge-building days near Tarnow, on a small scale.

The Sergeant obviously in charge of road works then gave one of our guards instructions that we should be put to work, which in effect meant filling in potholes at the approaches to the bridge. As there were no tools of any kind whatsoever, we were obliged to use our bare hands. So under the watchful eyes of our two guards, we scratched around picking up handfuls of sand. This process merely served to replace one set of potholes with another and meant that we would still be there to the present day, long after the Germans had gone! We drew our guards' attention to the stupidity of it, but they waved their arms in futile gesture. The sight of so many men running about with handfuls of sand was utterly ridiculous – had it not been for the underlying seriousness of the situation it could even have been hilarious.

We had barely returned to the wretched barn when a guard called out for three volunteers. For what purpose we had not the slightest idea, but in an instant the three of us stepped forward. Jurek, Mietek and I had agreed to explore every possibility of escape and this, for all we knew, could be a chance not to be missed. However, we made one stipulation, that all three of us would escape, or none at all.

It transpired that a herd of cows had been driven into an adjacent meadow and in order to ensure that none got away, we were placed at various points to prevent that from happening. Our 'watch' was to last from about eight in the evening till one in the morning, our place thereafter being taken by others. Every ten minutes or so we were told to call out 'All's well', or in case of problems give some appropriate warning. Two armed guards patrolled the entire meadow perimeter keeping an eye on us as well as the cows.

On the face of it, it looked as though this was the best chance we might ever have to make a run for it, therefore it was all the more galling that we had not had the opportunity to formulate a plan of action. From where I stood I could just about see my two companions, but as night fell we were unable to see one another, which prevented any form of signal communication. Earlier on, I was able to make a quick survey of the land, noticing a clump of trees and bushes about a hundred yards away in an adjoining meadow, which would provide good immediate cover, with a large open expanse beyond.

As the minutes ticked by, the guard patrolling my sector appeared regularly like a ghost in the night, we hooted our signals as ordered and the docile cows presented no problems, not even attempting to make a break for it, as cows are inclined to do. With mounting frustration I wondered how to communicate with my friends in order that we make a coordinated escape, but there was no way in which it could be done, and I began to wish that we had never made the 'pact'.

I had no idea of the time and suddenly realized that the other two were no longer calling the prearranged signal. I waited and listened in vain. The silence was deafening. My immediate thought was that the sods had gone without me and I felt cheated. However, the guard loomed out of the darkness again to announce that my watch had ended and led me back to the barn. In the darkness I stumbled onto Jurek and Mietek who were amazed to see me, for they too were sure that I had done a bunk, leaving them behind and were on the point of doing so themselves when their guard turned up. Thoroughly peeved over the missed opportunity we all turned in for what remained of the night.

The second day of our road-repairing efforts followed the same futile pattern, except that we were left with only one guard, which again presented a tempting opportunity, but to overpower him, considering our overwhelming number, again needed concerted agreement and action. It was very unlikely that all fifty of us would have escaped anyway. Many would have been caught with the inevitable result.

The only excitement that day was provided by a low-flying Russian reconnaissance aircraft and we were ordered to take cover, although there was nowhere to hide, but it went on its way slowly and at a low level.

By now we were desperately hungry, not having had any food at all for three days, and tempers began to fray.

The following day the general topic of conversation was all about food. Normally placid and aloof, Mietek took such a disliking to our oafish guard that he stood directly behind him and mimicked his every word and gesture with devastating results, as we fell about laughing, which only angered the guard. At least that single topic of conversation – food – seemed to weld us all together and helped pass the time. In the end general agreement was reached that representations should be made to the Germans. We could but try. Eventually, by a process of eeny-meeny-miney-mo and the question as to who could speak the best German, both Jurek and Mietek announced that without doubt I was the one for the job. Furthermore, it was obvious that the only German in authority we could turn to was the vile SS Sergeant. Our guard raised no objection and duly took me to him. After Montelupich this was child's play so I stood in front of the glowering little man and made out what I thought was a pretty convincing case, presented in my best quasi-military vocabulary. His first reaction was to erupt into a torrent of invective, but then, having run out of steam, he suddenly became rational and with the promise of seeing what he could do, turned on his heel and stalked off. My return was awaited with eager anticipation and I had to repeat everything word for word, but the Sergeant's final comment brought groans of disappointment.

The general opinion now was that we were to be worked like slaves until we dropped dead from starvation, and we presented a very bedraggled bunch on our return to the barn that evening. Barely had we staggered into the farmyard when there was a warning shout for everyone to take cover. As we dived for cover a Russian aircraft, possibly the same one we had seen the previous day, appeared overhead and released a load of small bombs. As the screaming missiles approached, it looked as if it would be the end for many of us cowering in the yard, but miraculously the bombs were carried forward by the momentum of the plane's speed and missed the yard, setting up a series of small explosions in a nearby copse. Later we were allowed to remain in the yard for a time and mingled with several Germans who were billeted in the farmhouse. They were Bavarians and seemed to treat us as human beings, which was a pleasant change from the usual run of things. Nevertheless it didn't prevent one of them from telling me that the Reich now had a new weapon with which they were going to wipe out Britain. He was referring to the V2 rockets and although I took it with a pinch of salt, I remember feeling rather less than dismissive of the news. There's no animal more dangerous than a cornered tiger, the saying goes, and yet I prayed that it was just German propaganda.

After we had been herded back onto the barn, the topic of food reared its head again engendering a general feeling of hopelessness and despondency. But we were in for a surprise, for the barn doors were opened and a guard called for three volunteers, adding that we were all going to get some food. Three of us were quick to respond. Led by two guards we proceeded to a farm cottage about half a mile away where they unceremoniously barged in and demanded that the farmer and his wife prepare food for fifty men. The poor souls stood completely speechless, then the farmer, spreading his hands in a gesture of dismay, said that they had no food. The guards became aggressive and demanded that some food be prepared, adding that there were hungry people here who had not eaten for days.

This was an awful situation for, desperately hungry though we were, we never expected to have it acquired in this fashion. In fact, it made us feel like thieves, but there was nothing now that we could do. There was little the farmer and his wife could do, either, but comply. Later we did manage to explain to them our predicament and express our apologies. Whilst the farmer and his wife retired in order to prepare something, one of the guards returned to the barn to fetch a party of twenty-five men.

An hour later an enormous platter was carried in with the whole carcass of a freshly cooked calf; when it was placed on the table we began to slice chunks off it and eat it with our fingers. I took one mouthful and had had enough. I simply felt that I could not go along with this notion of Nazi inhumanity. No doubt it was all done on the orders of that vile little Sergeant. And so, as the first group had partaken of the meal and been escorted back to the barn, it was the turn of the last of our contingent to repeat the journey. I went hungry.

Surprises are said to come in pairs and, that being so, some of us at least were in for another one.

Having completed our road repairs we were marched down to the bottom of the ravine to await a reallocation of work. It was obvious that the completion of the bridge was running behind schedule and that some of us would be thrown in to hasten the work along. Whilst the Sergeant and his minions were busily engaged in sorting things out, a dispatch rider on a motorcycle appeared suddenly, pulled up and handed the Sergeant a message. He studied it for a moment and then began calling out some names. Amongst them were those of Jurek, Mietek and myself. He then announced that all those mentioned were free to leave, adding, 'Go on, get going.' Unable to take in the significance of his words, no one moved. It was but a brief moment, however, and we did not need to be told twice what to do. Somewhat dazed by this turn of events, the lucky eight whose names had been called stepped forward and, waving goodbye to the rest, wasted no time in putting as much distance between ourselves and the Sergeant as possible, not stopping until we felt it safe to do so. We concluded that only Zbigniew could have performed this miracle, as all eight of us came from Rudzienko, whilst the remaining group were men from other villages and hamlets. Other than Jurek, Mietek and myself, our five companions were old Rudzienko farm hands, which partly explained our good fortune, but the key question as to how Zbigniew had pulled it off, we discovered later. Certainly from my point of view, a return to Rudzienko along with the others seemed the only thing to do and was a more attractive proposition than taking to the forests, there to await the Russians for an unknown period of time. At any rate, the three of us were agreed on that point. How to get through to the 'other side' was the big question.

We proceeded cautiously, trying to avoid German troops and especially the SS, however we came across a detachment resting in the forest before we realized it, but they showed no interest in us and later, crossing a wheat field, we passed a battery of light anti-aircraft guns manned by youthful soldiers. So well concealed were they that we only spotted them at the last minute, but they too gave us no trouble.

We reached Rudzienko two hours later, approaching it with care, and at this point parting company with the five farm hands who made a beeline for their respective cottages. At first sight everything seemed peaceful, with no sign of Germans anywhere, and we wondered if they had in fact already withdrawn from the estate, but as we drew nearer, a heavily laden farm cart emerged with Zbigniew and the two aunts perched on top of it. Greetings were warm but brief. Zbigniew breathlessly explained that the position at Rudzienko had become untenable and he had no option but to seek a safer haven for himself and his two aunts. We could stay if we wished, but he advised us to go along with them as they were heading for the Illowiecki estate which was evidently still in relative safety. We agreed to go with them.

The heavily laden cart made excruciatingly slow progress along the deeply rutted road, and it wasn't long after we had left left Rudzienko that an artillery barrage promptly started up behind us. The Germans were hanging on to Rudzienko like grim death and the general situation seemed utterly confused.

When at last we were safely clear of Rudzienko, Zbigniew told us all about the story of our release. As guests of the family he felt completely responsible for our safety, as he did indeed for the safety of his farm hands who had served the family so well. With that in mind, he pleaded with the senior German officer to have us released on the grounds that we were indispensable farm workers. When that failed to move the German, he went again, armed with two bottles of vodka. In due course, when the alcohol began to have the desired effect, Zbigniew cunningly persuaded him to write a letter authorizing our release, which he did. The rest can be put down to the German Army's efficiency in carrying out the order of an inebriated commander.

So it was the precious supply of vodka which did the trick after all, nevertheless it showed the sort of man that Zbigniew was – in all probability his selfless act had saved our lives. I found the dedicated care with which he looked after the two elderly maiden aunts touching, displaying a responsibility almost beyond his years.

To save the horses having to haul the extra load, the four of us walked alongside the cart with Zbigniew holding the reins and urging the horses along whenever the cart got bogged down in the sand.

(Very much later, I heard that the remaining group of men with whom we had worked were force-marched for many days, eventually being murdered.)

Already exhausted after our return to Rudzienko, we began to feel as though our legs were separate entities, but there was no time to lose and we kept moving on slowly until we finally reached the Illowiecki estate just before midday. Here we were warmly greeted by Illowiecki and his wife, who invited us to make ourselves at home. Not dissimilar to Rudzienko in its setting, the place exuded an air of peace and cosy domesticity. It was hard to believe that they had hardly seen a German in months.

We made a beeline for the ablutions having not had so much as a cupful of water, let alone seen a bar of soap, for a week. When I think of it, we must have made unwelcome company!

Presently, over a genteel cup of tea served by a maid in the comfortably furnished lounge, the Illowieckis listened with sympathetic understanding to our harrowing experiences at Rudzienko.

I wondered whether we had been transported to a world where the meaning of war was an unheard-of phenomenon. They, too, like the Kondratowicz family, had come here for the summer months, along with their two small daughters, and had the same responsibilities of running a farm of considerable size. The estate consisted of a hamlet where the farm workers lived, while the Illowiecki household, a solid, whitewashed building built on the lines of an English chalet, stood comfortably encircled by a thick green belt of trees and bushes, beyond which stretched vast acres of gently undulating wheat fields. Unlike Rudzienko, where the harvest had been cut short by the fighting, countless rows of neatly stacked stooks testified to the unruffled order of life which had still prevailed here. A mile away, where the golden wheatfields ended, there rose a solid green wall of forest which continued in an unbroken line from one end of the horizon to the other.

At dinner that evening we sat at a table laid out with gleaming silver-plated cutlery, napkins neatly folded alongside each place setting, and two baskets full with bread rolls in the middle. When the maid had finished lighting the candles she announced in a well-trained routine: 'Dinner is ready, ma'am,' addressing herself to the lady of the house. Although badly out of training for this kind of ceremony, we loved every minute of it and felt like civilized human beings once more. There was none of the brash jollity of Rudzienko here. Everything appeared to function in a quiet, well-organized manner. Now due to the sudden overcrowding, sleeping arrangements had to be suitably prepared, Jurek and I sharing one room and Zbigniew and Mietek another.

In times like these it was true to say that we lived from one hour to the next, and the following morning saw a completely changing scenario. Streams of bedraggled and exhausted refugees began pouring into the village, spilling over into the grounds of the manor. This was followed by the familiar grinding sound of tanks which dispersed around the outer perimeter of the estate, digging in hull down in the concealment of the thick belt of foliage. They were facing an enemy a mile away concealed on the edge of the forest beyond the golden wheatfields. Strangely, although we could hear all these ominous sounds, we did not actually see a single German. Apart from that, the picture was taking on a startling similarity to the one at Rudzienko.

The four of us conferred over the situation. Zbigniew was adamant in his resolve and promise to see to the welfare of his two aunts first and foremost. Because of this he would forego any plan of attempting to get through to the Russians. However, he would help the three of us in any way he could, as well as acting as lookout, should the *Feldgendarmerie* put in an appearance. So this left Jurek, Mietek and I, this time absolutely determined that the next attempt at getting through to the Russians would be successful. At that moment someone was heard to shout, 'Quick, hide, the Germans are coming!' We sprinted for cover, diving into the bushes and waited with pounding hearts. But it was a false alarm.

In the meantime the Illowiecki family were preparing themselves for a rapid departure should their position become untenable, and a horse-drawn wagon stood by in readiness.

From our Rudzienko experience we noted that having moved to new positions it took both sides about twenty-four hours before resuming battle. The day passed relatively uneventfully and as the evening approached, everything was once again set for dinner. The local priest, a friend of the family, sat at the head of the table and engaged the family in serious discussion. The mood was sombre indeed. Within minutes, however, there was a tremendous barrage which shook the house to its foundations. The Germans had started first and when they stopped, ten minutes later, it was the turn of the Russians to respond.

It was our turn to be on the receiving end of a ferocious barrage and it was as if the world was coming to an end. Rudzienko had been bad enough, but this was worse. Everyone endured it stoically for a time, but in the end it was the priest who spoke, directing his words to the Illowieckis. 'I think the time has now arrived for you to leave, dear friends. For your sake and that of your children, I beg you not to delay. Go now.'

With these words the Illowiecki's rose from the table, gathered their two little daughters and left. Everyone else dispersed hurriedly, each seeking out a refuge, preferably at the front of the house, and prayed that the thick walls were sufficient protection from a direct hit.

We all ducked instinctively when there was the ominous whine of an approaching shell which mercifully passed overhead, missing the roof by inches and exploding in the village. Other shells exploded much closer to the German positions. When it grew dark, all shelling ceased. The three of us repaired upstairs to the children's nursery and dragged some mattresses onto the floor, soon falling into a deep sleep.

The Russians started their bombardment promptly at eight the following morning. It lasted ten minutes, followed by a break of five minutes, starting again for a further ten. It was a set pattern, but more intense than it had been at Rudzienko, and it was obvious that they were stepping up the pressure.

We emerged warily from the house in order to see how we might make our way to the Russian lines. In all the noise and nerve-jangling racket not a living soul was to be seen. Concealed on the edge of the thicket overlooking the wheat fields, we took stock of the situation and made our plan. The main German force seemed to be concentrated to our right whereas the sector to our left appeared to be undefended. We decided that with a good deal of luck, we could make our way, hopefully, to the middle of the field and hide in any of the hundreds of stooks dotting it. Whether we would be observed by the Germans was a chance we were prepared to take, but we felt that it was a case of now or never. Satisfied with our findings, one of us was dispatched to find Zbigniew in order to tell him of our intention. Zbigniew suggested that he would find us some food later in the day if one of us would risk coming back to fetch it. We had already made a thorough search of the house and found that every scrap of food had vanished, but we agreed that one of us would run the gauntlet at twelve sharp and Zbigniew would be waiting at the back of the house with anything he could find.

We then waited for the five-minute lull before striking out into the field. Instead of crawling, we walked, heading boldly towards the Russian lines. The temptation to keep going all the way, once we had reached the approximate halfway mark, was great, but we decided not to push our luck too far. By this time the Russians had opened up again, so that we found ourselves under a blanket of screaming shells, which proved to be more than our nerves could stand, and we dived into the stooks, Jurek and Mietek into one and I into another a few yards away. We lay there laughing and joking somewhat hysterically, although we could not see each other, wondering how long we could survive there without food, if needs be. Our banter was suddenly cut short when several shells exploded a matter of yards from us, sending metal fragments tearing through the haycocks, missing us by inches. Then followed the usual five-minute lull, but when the shelling resumed we found that we were being constantly straddled with exploding shells and were gripped with a terrible fear. We wondered if the Russians had spotted us and mistaken us for Germans, for there seemed to be nothing worth targeting in that vast field. With nerves at breaking point we were ready to leave our hideouts and bolt for safer territory. Anywhere seemed better than this. Then, no doubt having satisfied themselves that they were unnecessarily expending valuable shells on a non-existent enemy, they thankfully switched their attention to more distant targets, so that only the occasional shell landed near us. When the shelling was at its worst, we called out to each other every so often just to ensure that we were still alive and uninjured.

The inane backchat and morale-boosting banter between us resumed again and, as midday approached, we had to decide which of us would run the wretched gauntlet, as had been agreed with Zbigniew. We were still feeling the hunger pangs from our experience at the hands of the Germans, a hunger that had not been satisfied ever since our arrival at the Illowiecki household. However, the decision was quickly made, by a majority verdict of two to one, that I should be the one to go. The two laughed loudly, adding that the decision was based on my superior knowledge of German.

I waited for the next lull before emerging from my stook and started to walk. As I passed by my two invisible friends I threatened to eat all the food I got myself, to which they raised a sardonic cheer. I now had five minutes in which to reach my goal, until the next barrage commenced, knowing full well of the impossibility. But in the brief lull I marvelled at the apparently peaceful scene. Not a sound was to be heard and with the exception of the solitary figure of a man crossing a distant field, no other sign of life was evident. I was halfway across when the shelling started again and I fell flat on the ground. I continued in fits and starts, eventually reaching the verdant estate perimeter. Emerging from the thicket I approached the house from the front, then cautiously made my way around to the back. True to form, Zbigniew was there and as he saw me he waved frantically, shouting a warning that the *Feldgendarmerie* were about and to get out immediately. He also managed to tell me before I beat a hasty retreat into the thicket that there was no food. I lay on the ground quite still, wondering what to do next. I waited for the next lull – that eerie silence when one could hear a pin drop – and began to retrace my steps back across the field. Presently shells started to shriek overhead again and I realized that I had lost my bearings. This was no place to linger, so I began crawling on all fours calling out 'Where the hell are you?' – for all the world bleating like a lost sheep.

Eventually I heard their reply, 'We're here.'

'Where's HERE?' I yelled. When an arm appeared out of a stook and waved, I knew I was on the right track, but the sad news about the food situation drew groans from my companions.

And so our confident resolve that we would stick it out in the field for two days took a severe knock. Of course there was no knowing how long the

Germans would hold out in their present positions – if Rudzienko was anything to go by it could be several days. (In fact, they held Rudzienko for about two weeks). Now the prospect of trying to continue towards the Russian lines seemed far less appealing, as we saw it, for two reasons: they were still about half a mile away; and when all was said and done, the stooks offered precious little cover and could easily be picked off by a German marksman. If we did succeed in crossing the wheat field to the other side, we would run straight into the target area of the German heavy guns. Then there was every likelihood that even the Russians might mistake us for infiltrators and shoot us. We were thoroughly dispirited and it was eventually the lack of food which swayed the issue in favour of a return to the estate. And so at about 4.00 p.m., we waited for a break in the bombardment and started retracing our steps. As we did so, a German 88mm gun opened up about 5 yards from us. So well was it camouflaged that we had not noticed it and never anticipated that they would position a gun in such a forward position. But there they were and it undoubtedly explained the reason for all our miseries. Whether the Russians did eventually knock it out, we didn't stay around to find out.

We were amazed to find the house still intact and empty, in fact just as we had left it early that morning. The dining-room table was there with the gleaming cutlery gracing the table, and the pathetic crumbs of our last meal still on the plates. All that now seemed to have happened in a different lifetime. Locking all entrances, we foraged around in the hope of finding some abandoned food, again to no avail.

By now the Russians had intensified their bombardment, saturating the area in a desperate effort to dislodge the Germans, to the point where we feared the building was bound to be hit, so we darted outside and tumbled into a cold cellar at the back of the house. Here we found Zbigniew, his aunts and several other souls cowering in the semi-darkness. With shells exploding all around us and the cellar affording even less protection from a direct hit than the house, being in effect an earth dugout with a soft covering of soil which constituted the roof, we rushed back to the house and remained in the living room which was geographically furthest away from the line of fire. Here at least there were three thicknesses of wall to protect us. Mietek peered out of a front window, froze and yelled, 'Gendarmes, quick, hide.' We tore upstairs, frantically searching for somewhere to hide and in the children's nursery discovered a small door which led into the loft. The loft was the last place to hide from flying shells but at that moment there was no option, and whilst there was no sign of the gendarmes, we devised a cunning method of concealing the little door with a cupboard. First, having found a length of cord which we tied around the cupboard, we placed it in front of the door at an angle, allowing sufficient room for us to slide behind it and into the loft. Once inside the loft a pull on the cord then positioned the cupboard snugly up against the loft door, completely concealing it. This worked extremely well and we stayed there for as long as our nerves held out, before deciding to make a dash for the cellar again. Without a doubt we were now in such a state of nervous tension that our actions were becoming irrational, but at least we had the choice to decide for ourselves where to hide and found that infinitely better than sitting numbly in a corner in a state of stupor.

Our decision to hide in the cellar at that moment was providential, for there was a terrific explosion so close that it dislodged clumps of earth from the cellar roof. Alarmed, we looked outside to see a gaping hole in the nursery wall. However, we later found that instead of wreaking havoc inside the house, the shell had passed through all the walls and exploded in the front garden.

With the approach of evening the ferocity of the Russian bombardment was such that it renewed our hopes of an imminent German withdrawal but, cowering in that dark little cellar, we were soon to be treated to an unusual and unexpected experience. The rickety cellar door suddenly opened and three SS officers burst in, complete with collapsible table and camp stools and, after a cursory glance around all those present, set up the table and began poring over their battle maps. They muttered amongst themselves and were obviously extremely tired men. Each in turn took a catnap and eventually one of them left. The cellar door was left open, however, and every now and again a runner appeared to report the state of the battle. From him, we gleaned the trouble they were in. With increasing frequency his reports told of mounting casualties. Later, a soldier appeared with a pair of binoculars draped around his neck and was questioned as to their ownership. 'They were the Lieutenant's, sir,' answered the soldier. The officer merely grunted at that. We watched fascinated at all this, as shell after shell exploded even closer to our cellar, smothering us in debris and dust. Although it numbed our brains, the officers appeared immune to it, only ducking and swearing whenever there was a really close one. Some of the women in the cellar prayed silently with eyes glazed in a fixed stare, as we now waited for the one accurately aimed shell that would end everything.

By now the strain of responsibility began to show on the Commanding Officer and when a runner tumbled down the steps to report that tanks numbers 5 and 6 had run out of ammunition, and requested orders, he rose from his stool and flew into a rage. 'So tanks five and six have run out of ammunition! What do you expect me to do, soldier? Do you think I have an ammunition factory in my pocket?' And with that he struck the young soldier a blow across the face.

Instinct told us that this was the right time to get out of the cellar and the three of us left at short intervals, virtually having to brush past the Germans in the process, but they took no notice of us. With no ammunition left, there was only one thing to do – withdraw. On the other hand we thought it prudent to leave the cellar before the departing Germans decided to toss a grenade into our midst as a farewell gesture. We ran like the devil into the house, locking and bolting the doors and securing the window shutters.

We then drew all the curtains tightly and, lighting the candles from the dining-room table, settled down in the comfort of the living room. It seemed like heaven in comparison to the highly charged and claustrophobic atmosphere of the cellar. Why others hadn't used it as a shelter remained a mystery. We went upstairs later in order to fetch some mattresses which we dragged down to the living room, noting that the damage inflicted by that single shell wasn't serious. Having dragged the mattresses downstairs, we laid them out side by side and fell upon them, physically and mentally drained. However, a good sign was that the banter began to return and to my great pleasure I found a stack of pre-war magazines, just as I had done at Rudzienko and, placing a candle close by me, I began to read them with relish – such wonderful therapy, old magazines. 'I don't know how you can do it, lying there reading magazines with all that racket going on outside,' muttered Jurek from beneath his blanket.

Sleep was out of the question. Having extinguished our candles we lay in the dark muttering occasionally until around midnight we noticed an easing of the relentless bombardment, as, mingling with the sound of the heavier guns, came the sharp staccato rattle of machine-gun fire. It was a welcome sound for it meant the Russians were staging a final assault on the German positions and were now getting close. That was all we needed to send us into a deep sleep and we were out like a light.

Chapter Fifteen

I awoke on the following morning with a start which seemed to indicate that something unusual had happened. The silence was overwhelming. In the semi-darkness I saw Jurek squinting through the shutters, through which the early morning sun threw narrow shafts of light.

'Anything going on out there?' asked Mietek from under his blanket.

'Can't see a soul and it's dead quiet,' Jurek replied.

'Well, if you would only shut up we could try and listen,' said Mietek with a chuckle.

We decided to investigate and, unbolting the front door, opened it ajar. A bleary eyed individual sauntered by and we asked him what was going on. 'The Russians are here,' he replied in a flat voice, without stopping. We stepped outside into brilliant sunshine and made for the cellar to see if all was well with those who had stayed there through that memorable night. As we approached it Zbigniew emerged to confirm the news about the Russians and that thankfully all in the cellar had survived. He then went on to tell us about the last moments before the Germans retreated from the village. When the two officers left the cellar everyone thought they had seen the last of them, but soon afterwards two other officers appeared and drew their revolvers. Zbigniew was convinced at that point that they were all going to be shot, but the Germans demanded that he handed over his wristwatch, which he said he almost did with pleasure, and they went away.

We then went in search of the Russians and eventually found them scrumping apples in the orchard. There were four of them, all mere boys with rifles as tall as they were, but they took little notice of us. When we bade them a good morning in Russian they responded, then casually asked if we knew where the Germans were. We told them that the Germans had left the village during the night, but couldn't say exactly where they were. They went on to explain that they were part of an advance party, but as they were more absorbed with finding something to eat we left them to it. The poor devils looked utterly exhausted and bemused.

Remarkably, none of the civilian population had been killed – considering the violence of the attack this was a near miracle. How many casualties the Germans had sustained we never found out, but reports from the village had it that two deserters were found hiding in a barn.

We were now left with the strange feeling of being in a vacuum. But at least we had succeeded in our aim, even if for the time being we were punch drunk, bemused and worn out physically. Having weathered that particular storm, it was time to gather one's wits and plan our next move. Thoughts only ventured as far as immediate plans of safety and expediency. The prudent thing to do was to get out of the area in case the Germans, in turn, set their sights on this village. Together with Zbigniew, we had a discussion and decided that we would all make tracks for Rudzienko which we reckoned should already be in Russian hands. As his aunts elected to remain where they were, Zbigniew was free to do what he felt was now of greatest importance – find out how the estate has survived.

As far as my own position was concerned, I knew I had to be patient a little longer and wait for the dust of battle to settle before contemplating approaching someone in authority who could be of any help. So for the present I was happy to join the others in their trek to Rudzienko, especially as we had established a splendid rapport and I now felt that, in my hopefully exalted position as a 'British ally', if there was anything I could do to help, I would do so. As there was no need to conceal my identity any longer I told Zbigniew and Mietek the truth; Jurek of course already knew. The news caused great surprise and it was in an optimistic mood that we set out on our journey back, crossing the wheat field where we had suffered agonies the previous day. Upon reaching the edge of the forest which rose in front of us like a thick and forbidding green wall, and where the Russians had laid concealed with their artillery, a Russian emerged from the trees and, waving us on, frantically shouted at us to get out of the way as they were just about to open fire. We hadn't even noticed their presence and were walking unawares in front of their gun barrels which seemed to be pointing at us, mere yards away.

We ran like scalded cats and noticed some of the Russians looking at us, grinning broadly, as well they might.

Much later we joined up with another party from Rudzienko village, who told us that further progress was pointless because the Germans were still holding out there. They took us to a cottage where we rested and spent the night with eighteen of us crammed on the floor of one room. Food was so desperately short that our breakfast consisted of a mouthful of bread swallowed down with a cupful of well water. We were so hungry that we began to get stomach pains.

All of us then decided to press on and find out how things were for ourselves. The one or two Russians we met on the way had no idea what was happening at Rudzienko and eventually we came across a sergeant who advised us against going any further as a battle was raging there at that very moment, but didn't think the Germans would be there for much longer. Nevertheless we continued on our way, albeit cautiously, until, standing on higher ground, we came within sight of the village and estate itself.

It felt curious to be able to stand on the sidelines and witness a battle raging before our very eyes. Columns of smoke rose from cottages which had received a direct hit, and when the German guns fell silent, Russian troops began advancing across a field in swarms, in a final onslaught. Rudzienko was finally free. The Sergeant appeared again and told us it was now safe to carry on.

The place was littered with Russian and German dead, as well as scores of horses and cattle, the latter reminding me of toy farmyard animals which had fallen over. The sight of so many dead animals was more upsetting than anything.

We parted company with the others from the village and made for the estate, where Zbigniew was faced with a new problem, one uniquely associated with the old Soviet attitude to landowners, as the Poles had bitterly experienced in the earlier part of the war. True, they were now supposedly on the same side as the Poles – and the British, as well as the United States of America – and had been signatories to this and that agreement, but the fact still remained that they were, for very good reasons, deeply distrusted by the Poles. It now all depended on whether they might have changed their attitude. At any rate, Zbigniew had no intention of being arrested on the spot for being a 'blood-sucking capitalist'. We discussed what best to do without endangering Zbigniew and I suggested that I could take a chance myself. I could but try. I reasoned that if I flaunted the 'British ally' angle sufficiently I might get somewhere with the Russians. All Zbigniew wanted was to be able to inspect his property and find out what state it was in. The three of them waited whilst I marched boldly up to the rear entrance where a soldier stood guard. With a great show of confidence I explained that I was British and wished to inspect the house as it was my property. 'No, it's not allowed,' (*Nyet, nyelzya*) was his curt reply. I repeated my request more forcefully, side-stepping him and making for the door. He became aggressive, pointing his rifle at me and swearing volubly. I backed off and Zbigniew, realizing the futility of it, said that he would try again later when things had had time to settle down and the Russians were less jumpy.

Zbigniew then took us to a friend's cottage in the village where everyone took part in serious discussion about the future. We stayed the night, sleeping in a barn. I remember thinking what a crazy idea it was to have made out that Rudzienko estate was my property, because it was I who could have been arrested and not Zbigniew. The fact that I was British – not that I could have proved it – might have made matters worse, and my mind boggled at the thought. Soviet doctrine at that time was of the extreme kind which did not tolerate property ownership on that scale, and anyone so connected was considered to be an outright enemy of society, destined for 'elimination', which meant banishment to Siberia for hard labour. It mattered not one jot what nationality one professed to be, the result would have been the same. In the event, all our worst fears were confirmed.

The following morning Zbigniew was determined to try and gain access to the house himself and duly set out to do so. On his return, he told us that the guards were more cooperative and allowed him in, where he was confronted by an officer who, already drunk as a lord, threatened to shoot him if he didn't disclose the whereabouts of the store of vodka which Zbigniew had hidden in the cellar. Whether the officer had actual knowledge of it or whether he was bluffing was anyone's guess, but Zbigniew came away from that visit thoroughly disgusted and disenchanted.

(Zbigniew was in fact arrested later and sent to Siberia along with many other Poles, but was eventually released and returned to Warsaw after the cessation of hostilities.)

In spite of the uncertainty of the situation, Zbigniew decided to remain in Rudzienko, the rest of us now having to make up our minds whether to stay or leave. There was much to be done in Rudzienko, what with the crops which were already beginning to rot in the fields, as well as the re-establishment of the farm to its former state – provided, of course, there was no drastic change to its ownership. Both Jurek and I had our ties in Warsaw and now, bearing in mind that the capital could quickly fall to the Russians, my anxiety for my mother's safety began to override all other considerations. Mietek on the other hand appeared to be a free agent and didn't mind where he went, so when Jurek and I said that we had made up our mind to make our way back to Warsaw, he readily agreed to join us. We had not an ounce of luggage to carry between us and lived and slept in the clothes we stood up in.

Thus we left Rudzienko in a buoyant and optimistic mood, expecting to reach Warsaw within days. We gave the Russians three weeks at the most in which to capture the city. To us, it was all a foregone conclusion. We trudged across fields and through woodlands in a westerly direction all that morning, but by the afternoon ran into the rear of Russian troop positions. This was disconcerting and wherever we tried, further progress seemed impossible. We quickly realized that the Russian advance was far slower than we had anticipated. At one point we blissfully sauntered past a rocket launcher concealed on the other side of some bushes just as that frightening device let loose with all barrels. We later asked an officer if there was any news of Warsaw, but he couldn't tell us anything. None of the Russians we asked subsequently knew anything about it. Eventually we were advised against proceeding any further by an efficient-looking sergeant who pointed to a copse about a hundred yards away and said that the Germans were still holding out there.

Retracing our steps we later knocked on a cottage door and asked if we could purchase some food. To our surprise we were presented with a large enamel bowl full of pigs trotters in aspic. When we had devoured it, the little old lady appeared with another one, but as hungry as we still were, we simply hadn't the heart to deprive her of it and, pressing some money into her hand, thanked her for her kindness and went on our way.

Later we came across a village which teemed with Russian soldiery as well as refugees, the latter, like ourselves, were stranded with nowhere to go. Most of them congregated in and around the church where we found the priest and a helper distributing bread. We were grateful to receive a chunk each and were told that had we arrived sooner we could have had some soup as well, but there was none left. The place buzzed to the sound of chatter, with everyone recounting their experiences of the past few turbulent days, some expressing optimism for the future, others shaking their heads in gloom and desperation. But talk that the Russians were evidently not expecting to advance on Warsaw in the near future interested and indeed worried us most. That evening a Russian mobile cinema arrived and set up in a barn, to which soldiers as well as civilians alike thronged. A newsreel was followed by a feature film about the heroic deeds of a fighter pilot.

After spending an uncomfortable night in a barn, we left the village and decided to try our luck once again, but ran into the Russian forward positions. We spoke to an officer telling him of our plan to reach Warsaw, but he shook his head doubtfully, saying that it 'would be some time yet'. This was bad news and required a complete rethink of our plans. Obviously we had to prepare ourselves for a difficult time which could last many weeks or even months. A return to the village was unthinkable and we began to consider either returning to Rudzienko or making our way to the nearest town, which was Siedlce. In the event we opted for Siedlce, thinking that work and shelter would be more readily available to tide us over, even through the winter months if necessary.

With the complete lack of signposting and proper roads, it was easy to get lost. When we did reach a highway, the military traffic heading in both directions was heavy and in a hurry. With Siedlce 20 miles distant we flagged down a truck carrying empty ammunition containers, which appeared to be heading in the right direction. It obligingly slowed down sufficiently for us to clamber aboard and then took off at breakneck speed. The containers had obviously been hurled onto it willy-nilly and, perched on top of this unstable load, we clung on for grim death. As the vehicle took a sharp right-angled bend on a bumpy dirt track leading into a forest, without slowing, Jurek yelled a warning to duck. We did so instinctively and with mere inches to spare passed beneath a wire stretched across the track. Why it was there at all was not the point, but we had missed being garrotted by a very narrow margin. Eventually the truck slowed down with the driver shouting that he was turning off again, at which point we felt glad to be parting company. However, just as we were preparing to jump, the truck accelerated again, each of us landing in the dirt in a sorry heap, one by one. There was nothing for it but to continue on foot.

Later on we were overtaken by a farm cart driven rapidly by two young men, and, running after it, leapt aboard. The two men were in a highly agitated state and told us that in some areas the Russians were not only carrying out mass arrests of civilian population, but were rounding up able-bodied young men, in the style of press gangs, and impressing them into the ranks of the Soviet Army. They said that the Russians were obviously 'up to their old tricks again' and should things get any worse, they would both think seriously of taking to the forests as they had done under the Germans.

We wished them luck and, jumping off the wagon, continued walking until we reached the outskirts of Siedlce by early evening. By now we were deeply disturbed by our latest encounter and in low spirits. We approached a row of cottages, neat and inviting, and somehow untouched by the fighting. Although it was still early evening, there was need for rest and some food. We stopped to talk to a man tending his vegetable garden but he regretted being unable to help us with the offer of shelter for the night and suggested we try nearer the town. As we talked a Russian officer approached us, demanding to see our identity cards. We produced them explaining that they were issued by the German authorities and, having examined them, he returned them to us without comment. Although we were used to this kind of routine with the Germans, we would much rather not have attracted the attention of the Russians at this stage, or indeed at all. He sauntered off and we continued our chat with the man. Presently the officer returned, this time in the company of an armed soldier. He once again demanded our identity cards and when we handed them to him, they promptly disappeared into his pocket and we were told to follow him.

To all intents and purposes it looked like we were being arrested, and we were immediately gripped with the fear of being press-ganged into the Soviet Army. At this point the best thing to do was to explain about my nationality and hope for the best. So in my best fractured Russian I explained that I was a British '*Vojenno plenny*' (prisoner of war) who had escaped from the Germans, and my two Polish colleagues had helped me to do so. Animatedly, I said how wonderful it was that the British and Russians were allies fighting the Nazis in a common cause for freedom and democracy. But the more I spoke, the less he seemed to listen and I soon realized I would have had a better reaction from a brick wall. In the end I gave up and Jurek and Mietek grimaced painfully. Nevertheless, the prisoner-of-war story would, I reckoned, sound more plausible than a badly related interpretation of the true and involved facts. I could only pray that the British connection would somehow save the day for the three of us and needed to push it as much as I could.

In the meantime, we were taken to a collection of cottages, led through a barrier and told to wait, guarded by a soldier. We waited for ages before both Jurek and Mietek were told to enter one of the cottages. It was now dark and when they re-emerged it was my turn to go inside. The room I entered was in semi-darkness, with a solitary oil lamp throwing deep shadows on the walls like black silhouettes. I was perfunctorily greeted by a general of middle age and as bald as a coot. He eyed me through tired, red-rimmed eyes set in a pale, haggard face. I was offered a chair. Sitting at a table at the other end of the room a corpulent red-faced woman in army uniform sat in front of a typewriter. The General started by asking routine questions about my age, address, parents' names, father's occupation, and others (one's father's occupation always seemed to be important in any Soviet questionnaire). I then explained that I was British and that my father was employed in the British consulate in Warsaw before the war, why it was necessary for me to have adopted a Polish name, and how my mother and I were trapped in Warsaw when it became occupied by the Germans. I explained that my sole aim was to return to the city in order to find my mother and then travel to England, where my father now lived. I told a deliberate lie about father's occupation, hoping it would carry more weight, rather than attempt to explain the meaning of the word 'businessman', which I thought could be misconstrued into something sinister, and in those days usually was.

As my Russian wasn't up to explaining all this, I spoke in Polish, and although he listened impassively, he appeared to understand what I said. The typist must have understood as well since she hardly stopped typing. Although not unfriendly in manner, the General's inscrutability left me with a feeling of unease. Without doubt we were in the hands of the 'Security Service', probably the notorious NKVD or KGB.

The three of us were then escorted some distance away to a barn and unceremoniously ordered to get down onto the floor. When we protested a guard threatened us with his rifle butt. We stumbled about in the pitch darkness tripping over reclining bodies which grunted at the intrusion and eventually found a wretchedly hard corner in which to lie down. As we lay there wondering what was going to happen to us, a constant undertone of voices outside told us that we were being well guarded.

Poor Jurek and Mietek were in the depths of despair and failed to understand why, as a Briton, I should be so badly treated, whilst themselves not expecting any favours from the Russians. The fact remained that I had no proof of my true identity whatsoever, and in no way could the Russians corroborate it. I could only hope for the proverbial miracle, especially as the Russians never took kindly to foreigners being at large on their territory. Our position looked anything but rosy and if I was to be seen as a suspicious character, then by implication so would my friends be. Those days were still light years away from 'glasnost' and the downfall of the communist regime.

The three of us were roused at daybreak and led to a water pump for a wash – only then did we realize how heavily guarded we had been, for the barn was ringed with armed soldiers who were in an aggressive mood. We were then immediately taken to the cottage where we had been questioned the previous evening and told to wait outside. Presently, in the company of two unarmed guards, we climbed aboard a military truck and were taken to a new location about 15 miles away. Here everything changed dramatically. We had arrived at a camp, with tents erected in neat rows in an orchard, and, driving through a wide gate, pulled up by a terracotta villa where we were promptly ushered into a large tent by a genial major.

'Ah, so you are the Englishman,' he said. We chatted and I explained briefly how I came to be there in this part of the world; he ended by praising the British for being good allies.

Later a batman, seconded to see to our every need, brought towels and soap, and presently some tasty, hot food. We hardly knew what had hit us. Upon retiring to our tent that night, the batman dutifully tucked us up in our camp beds, as though we were his children.

'You're such a good ally, Tom. If this is how it's going to be from now on, I think we'll stick with you all the way,' chuckled Jurek.

The following morning we were interviewed by the friendly Major, each in turn, which meant repeating our entire story all over again, but at least he was human and appeared to enjoy having a chat as well. But when asked when we would be free to go on our way, he became evasive. Whereas I could see their reasons for wanting to detain me, I cherished the hope that my two friends would be allowed to go free.

We basked in this relaxing environment for about two days, but when we decided to take a stroll around the camp, were promptly and politely requested to remain by our tent. Nonetheless, we were full of hope and I could almost see myself being sent to England at any moment, my plan to reach Warsaw now doomed. But we had not reckoned on the unpredictability of Russian behaviour. When a sergeant appeared out of the blue and told us we were to be moved elsewhere, we protested and I demanded to see the Major for an explanation. When the Sergeant said there was 'no need' I stormed past him and made for the Major's quarters in an effort to track him down, with the Sergeant hot on my heels in a virtual state of panic. But the smiling Major had disappeared into thin air. For us, the 'elsewhere' turned out to be a chicken run at the back of a barn.

'Here you are, comrades, make yourselves comfortable. You will be staying with us soldiers now,' said the Sergeant benignly. And so we found ourselves pitchforked into a chicken run with a layer of straw to sleep on and open to the four winds save for a corrugated tin roof.

For the next four days we ate and slept with the half dozen or so soldiers, who came and went as their turn of duty demanded. Fortunately the weather held otherwise we would have been a sorry and soggy bunch. The soldiers were a simple, unsophisticated lot with a down-to-earth philosophy and no overt political views. We ate their huge helpings of '*kasza*' and dark-brown bread twice daily until it began to ooze out of our ears. Gone were officers' rations and perks, such as soap and tipped cigarettes. I managed to sneak away on two occasions in search of the Major and, having found him, enquired at the sudden change in our treatment, but he offered neither apology nor explanation, merely saying that everything would soon be sorted out and we should not worry. They had their favourite expressions such as 'zavtra' (tomorrow) and '*skoro budie*t' (will soon be), which had the same timeless meaning as 'manana'. With nothing else to do, we allowed our imagination to run riot, dreaming up the notion of being allowed to travel to England, away from all this misery and persecution.

Sadly for Jurek and Mietek it only remained a dream, as on the fifth day a sergeant appeared and read out their names from a slip of paper. We felt instinctively that this could signify the parting of our ways and, shaking hands, wished each other luck. I last saw them as they clambered aboard a truck for the start of a journey into the unknown. After all our adventures and tribulations together, I felt much saddened and lonely. (Both were pressed into the Polish division of the Red Army and survived the rest of the war.)

I had not long to dwell on my misery when another sergeant appeared, this time in full marching kit, sub-machine gun slung across his chest, and told me to follow him. At the same time he was busily stuffing a large buff envelope into his pocket, which I gathered contained a set of directions. Our journey was on foot and we trudged along deserted dirt roads and footpaths for miles on end. More than anything, I was curious as to our ultimate destination and as he seemed a decent sort, asked the question.

'I'm afraid I'm not supposed to tell you,' he said.

'Do you mean to say that you don't know where we're going?'

'Yes I do,' he began, but I interrupted him.

'Well, what does it say on the envelope you have in your pocket?' I asked.

He fished it out of his pocket and began to read it out loud and then, realizing his mistake, quickly stuffed it back in again with the words '*Da nietu, da nietu*' (Oh no, oh no), clearly embarrassed at having fallen for such a simple trick – not before I had noted every word, though. And I certainly did not find them reassuring, for they read:

TO THE COMMANDING OFFICER
No. 1 COUNTER INTELLIGENCE HEADQUARTERS
WORSACH

I had no idea where Worsach was so decided it could only be a hamlet or village of otherwise little significance.

Later we flagged down an army truck and saved ourselves many miles of hard slog, eventually jumping off at a crossroads. After a further hard slog we sat down by the roadside for a rest, the Sergeant somewhat carelessly, I thought, placing his gun between us. Suddenly, the temptation to do something desperate gripped me. It would be all very well grabbing hold of the gun before threatening him with it, not knowing where the safety catch was – I would have to find that out first somehow. But it would have to be in a subtle way so as not to arouse his suspicion. I had no clear idea what I should do. As we sat there watching scores of rooks cavorting about in the adjoining field, I suggested that he take a pot shot at the noisy creatures. I would then see where the safety catch was. At first he declined, but when I challenged him to hit one he had second thoughts and, with a glance up and down the road to ensure no one was in sight, he settled down and took careful aim. He had fallen for my little ruse again and I watched him transfixed, wondering whether I had the nerve to do what I had intended. It seemed a shame to harm him since he was a decent chap and I realised that once done, I would be pursued relentlessly to the bitter end as a fugitive. I could be ruining any chance of freedom for good. However, he sat up suddenly and said, 'No, I had better not.' Then, standing up, he said we ought to be on our way.

We spent the night in a farm cottage where the farmer and his wife were distinctly unfriendly and my efforts at conversing with them were frustrated by the Sergeant. In the end, however, I managed to do so, apologizing for our intrusion and explaining who I was. From then on their attitude completely changed.

By mid-morning our long trek had taken us to a hamlet which had been commandeered by the military and buzzed with activity. Here the Sergeant showed me to a cottage, assuring me that there was someone who understood English, and disappeared into the one next door to report our arrival. I said 'Good morning' to an officer sitting at a table.

'*Ach, ja, guten morgen*,' he replied, grimacing.

'Not so,' I hastened to correct him. '"*Guten morgen*" is German, but "Good Morning" is English – and I am English.'

At that he rose from his chair with a pained expression, throwing his arms into the air. 'English or German – what difference does it make? They're all Saxons.'

He continued to mutter something disagreeable to a comrade who had just entered the room and I was glad when it was time for us to go on our way again. So much for his idea of a 'good ally'.

Worsach was difficult to find but we eventually reached it within the hour. No. 1 Counter Intelligence HQ consisted of a collection of cottages where I was handed over to the care of a Major Levkov. After completing certain formalities the Major explained that I would be taken to a cottage where I would be made as comfortable as possible. He was polite but, as I discovered, like so many Soviets in a position of authority, completely bland and devoid of any animation whatsoever, which was disconcerting. When I posed the key question of why was I being held in the first place, he replied that, pending clarification of certain matters, it was for my own good that they do so. That too turned out to be a stock, official answer, repeated on subsequent occasions. Together with a sad-faced little lieutenant, we clambered into a jeep. On the way I noticed that a large section of the village was surrounded by a high barbed-wire fence. We soon arrived at a spacious, oblong village green flanked by rows of neat-looking cottages. We pulled up outside one of them and I was shown inside. As we did so we were met by two Russian soldiers and two scruffy looking individuals. I stared at the two for a moment and said, 'Are you two British?'

'I'll say we are!' replied one grinning broadly.

'So am I,' I replied, and we shook hands. My new companions were Bob Easterbrook, a sergeant in the Royal Army Service Corps who hailed from Bristol, and Private Len Mann of the Queen's Westminster Rifles, who's home town was Shiplake Cross, near Henley-on-Thames; we soon got down to exchanging experiences. Both of them had been taken prisoner in France in 1940 and eventually transported to prisoner-of-war camps which had been set up in German-occupied Poland, from whence they had escaped. For many months they had been taken care of and sheltered by courageous Poles, Len managing to survive near Warsaw until the arrival of the Russians. When that happened he emerged from hiding but later changed his mind when he realized that they were arresting Poles whose allegiance had been to the Polish government-in-exile in London, the government which was recognized by Britain, America and other governments of the day. It seemed that Soviet Russia only paid lip service to that agreement, having ideas of their own. Frightened by this turn of events he retreated once again into hiding, but was found out, arrested, interrogated and accused of being a British spy. He next found himself here in Worsach.

Whereas Len was easygoing by nature, Bob Easterbrook was very different. A resourceful individual, his free and restless spirit got him to Gdansk, after his escape, before he moved on to the Warsaw area, where he joined up with a group of partisans leading a rough and ready existence, constantly on the move in the concealment of thick forests. As most of this was done on horseback he became an expert rider. They had many a skirmish with the Germans and when the Russians arrived on the scene the partisans immediately offered their services to fight alongside them. Instead, they were disarmed and held captive, and Bob was also brought to Worsach. Since then they had been kept under constant guard and were forbidden to have contact with the villagers. They were livid with this treatment and had complained bitterly to both the Lieutenant and Major Levkov, but to no avail.

Their experiences seemed to support the rumours that the Russians were bent on eliminating resistance groups and individuals alike who where non-communist, right from the outset. It all had a familiar ring about it.

Already at this early stage Polish people were being denied information from Western sources. For example, when it became known that Mr Churchill was to broadcast an important speech on the radio regarding the future of Poland and other eastern European countries, it created an enormous amount of interest to the population at large. A specially printed bulletin was also to appear the following day, but nothing happened and subsequently never did, as the Russians had imposed a total blackout. Instead, only a bulletin of a speech delivered by Stalin was published in full, several days later.

In this overtly hostile atmosphere the three of us felt decidedly uncomfortable, firstly, having been forced to intrude upon the farmer and his modest household, and secondly, we were not even allowed to speak to them. But in spite of the guards' efforts, we eventually managed to do so, much to their discomfiture. We had a roughly made-up bunk in our room, large enough to sleep the three of us, a cupboard and a chair. The two guards who remained with us day and night shared whatever space there was in the room, sleeping on the floor or sitting propped up in a corner. Like all Russian troops, they uncomplainingly put up with any amount of discomfort and deprivation.

Bob, whose sole attire amounted to the pair of ragged trousers was by far the worst off in that respect compared to Len and I. Fortunately he was a tough character and the exceptionally clement weather helped him to survive another month before he was given a pair of boots, and that only after repeated representations to the Lieutenant. We noted that the boots were of American manufacture. We were issued with a large quantity of army issue bread every other day, lard, tea, sugar, cans of American tinned meat, and occasionally soap as well as good-quality Russian cigarettes and a coarse tobacco called *machorka*, although 'tobacco' would be a misnomer, which took expert handling when 'rolling your own', usually in scraps of the newspaper *Pravda*.

So there was no shortage of food in the early days and we could not even cope with the ridiculous amounts of bread which were given to us, and found we couldn't even give it away to the farmer and his wife, who baked their own, which they preferred anyway. In the end it was used to fatten up the chickens.

It was a good thing that the three of us got on well considering the confines of our living space and the fact that we were three individuals with very different characters. Our day revolved around discussions concerning our plight – especially what the Russians intended to do with us – playing endless games of 'Battleships' and annoying the guards by threatening to walk out on them. With his restless spirit Bob found it very difficult indeed and discovered baiting the guards at every opportunity to be an entertaining diversion. The guards were unused to such rebellious behaviour and actually put up with it remarkably well, generally adopting a conciliatory tone, but occasionally showing signs of irritation when pushed too far by his taunts.

As in most situations of captivity one's hopes rose and fell easily with each passing day, our worst drawback being that none of us had any means of identification and Bob was convinced that our ultimate destination would be in the salt mines of Siberia. The bland, noncommittal utterings of both the Major and Lieutenant only served to fuel Bob's wrath, leading to a series of awkward confrontations, the result of which were a relaxation of the rules by allowing us to go for short walks around the farmstead under guard. So within our own camp there emerged two opposing points of view, with Bob wanting to 'rattle their cage' constantly, and I, thinking I knew the Russians better, advocating a more 'diplomatic' stance, with Len somewhere in the middle of the argument.

Every so often we had a change of guards which meant having to get used to their ways. Whenever we were landed with a disagreeable one, we soon let it be known and he was soon replaced. We noticed, however, that the friendly ones didn't survive for very long either, although certainly not because of us. In the end we got a tall, lanky soldier, who survived the longest and who we called Baldy because of his shaven (red) head. He was a conscientious lad who tried hard to please his superiors as well as us at the same time.

In the meantime life in the village was gradually changing for the worse, the first portent being the appointment of a Commissar whose job it became to ensure that crops which had remained dormant in the fields due to the fighting were swiftly harvested. Also, a fine of 2,000 Zloty was threatened for any household which failed to deliver a statutory amount of 5 tons of potatoes. This appeared to be an arbitrary figure and way beyond the physical resources of most farmers to implement. The ravages of war in terms of manpower and tools for the job were never even considered, causing anguish and distress in the community.

Next came the roving militiamen, armed with rifles and wearing armbands bearing the hammer and sickle, whose job it was to keep an eye on everything and everybody; they became much feared and hated. They appeared to be recruited from the worst elements of society and were obviously drafted in from other areas to do the job. When our farmer heard of all this he sat down and buried his head in his hands while his wife burst into tears of desperation. It was as though a calamity had befallen the whole community. We immediately offered to help and the change in them had to be seen to be believed. Even our guards were powerless to stop us now and in their own way seemed sympathetic to our cause. Later, when all the farm work was done on time, they expressed their admiration for our public-spirited act!

The work had been tedious and backbreaking, and was carried out at top speed in order to fulfil the quota. When we had finished with our farm, we moved on to the next one. It had been a mad scramble with everyone lending a hand in the best communal spirit, resulting in a clean slate and no fines. To give them credit, some of the troops lent a hand here and there, and finally the village celebrated in the traditional and time-honoured way whereby everyone circulated from household to household downing gallons of home-brewed vodka. But due to the terrible shortage of food, *zakaski* (snacks) were in short supply. The home-brewed vodka was terrible and bore no resemblance to the pure alcohol available in Britain these days. Because of the general situation, however, celebrations were muted and the three of us were forbidden to visit anyone, the guards themselves awkwardly standing aloof from it all.

It was in these final days of summer that the Russians installed a new Polish government in the town of Lublin. Unlike the Polish government-in-exile in London, nothing had been known about this development and Poles now had foisted upon them a communist government, cunningly sneaked in, as it were, through the back door. It was made up of Poles who had spent many years in Russia, some as fugitives from the law in pre-war days who in effect were no longer Polish citizens, some hardly able to communicate in their native tongue. It was a tragic time for Poles witnessing their country and its people gradually being swamped by yet another alien force.

Boredom was our worst enemy. For us, everything returned to normality after the harvest celebrations, if one cared to call them that, and it was boredom which in the end drove us to play a practical joke at the expense of our guards. Or so we thought. Our customary daily walk consisted of covering the farmyard perimeter with its barn, pigsty, cowshed and other sheds, with our guards following on dutifully several paces behind. After a time they became rather slack and, we noted, tended to trail further and further behind us. This was our cue and on the next occasion we hid behind a barn and watched the guards saunter by. Having found our room empty they got hold of the farmer who had no idea where we were. At that point we emerged from our hiding place and went to our own room, assuming an air of having been there all the time. Presently we heard some shots and a lot of noise outside, and became aware that a full-scale hunt was on for the 'escaped Englishmen'. Things were looking serious but we had to bluff it out to the end now. A quarter of an hour later one of our guards appeared with a look in his eye as black as thunder and in a truly melodramatic manner accused us of trickery and insubordination. We answered with an innocent 'What, us?' and realized what we had stirred up when half a dozen soldiers armed to the teeth entered the room and eyed us warily. Later, Major Levkov and his glum sidekick, the little Lieutenant, arrived to find out what the matter was. What started out as a prank now began to escalate to a full-blown confrontation, for rather than admit to our guilt we went on to the offensive, accusing them of treating us like enemy prisoners of war instead of allies, and demanding to know when something would be done regarding our repatriation. The two listened and tried to calm things down but we demanded to see a higher authority. Much to our surprise we were visited by a Colonel and three other officers the following day and to them we voiced our pent-up feelings in no uncertain terms. The Colonel expressed his displeasure at our action and also tried to calm the situation, but in effect told us nothing.

The senior of our two guards was promptly removed and either by design or default, our rations were severely cut, never to be reinstated. The cigarettes, tinned meat which we greatly valued, lard and sugar all went off the menu.

One day a friend of our host farmer called and by chance we were able to talk to him without the guards' knowledge. When he heard that we were British, he told us he had been in the Koval area recently (about 100 kilometres south of Worsach) and had encountered a visiting mission of British Army observers there. Delighted to see them, he managed to approach them, but was promptly arrested and questioned by the Russians. His story rang true and much later on its authenticity was verified, but the Russians had ensured that no one else was able to make contact with them. Encouraged by this news we requested to see the Major, but another officer came to see us instead. When we asked him why we had not been handed over to the visiting British, he became evasive. This so disheartened us that we began to consider seriously an escape with the idea of reaching the British. We argued and discussed the chances at length, but it was obvious from the start that the defection of all three of us was out of the question. So the idea simmered until in mid-September when we were told to prepare for a move of No. 1 Headquarters.

When the day came for the move, the dismantled bunk and everything we had was piled high onto a truck already loaded with military paraphernalia. We therefore started our journey wedged amongst all the junk, along with Baldy and several other young soldiers. Our new travelling companions were the most pathetic bunch of soldiers I had ever set eyes on. They were hardly more than boys, but that apart they looked sad and bewildered, one especially standing out from the rest with his pale and emaciated face. He seemed beyond caring what was happening around him and stared embarrassingly at us, as though we were men from Mars. Presently he begged us for some food, but we were unable to give him anything since all our rations had been crated up and lay somewhere at the bottom of the pile. But he wouldn't take no for an answer and pleaded with us in a sad monotone time after time. I had the distinct impression that the poor lad was slowly going mad. In the end Baldy gave him a stern talking to for behaving in such an unsoldierly manner in front of foreigners, and put a stop to his pleas. It was hard to understand what lay behind the lad's misfortune – if it was simply a lack of food, that made it all the harder to comprehend, for Russian troops were certainly not starved of it.

Our truck joined up with others and we travelled in a convoy for what seemed like hours, eventually arriving at a village the name of which I have not been able to recall. Here we unloaded all our worldly possessions and manhandled them to a house some distance away, with the aid of a soldier. The house which was to be our home for the next few weeks was far more prosperous than the cottage at Worsach and we moved into a pleasant room with its own porch and entrance.

When the owner and his wife came to greet us, they appeared far from happy, until we told them who we were. Then their faces lit up and the wife, Janina, couldn't do enough to make us comfortable. However, it was obvious that the guards viewed this normal friendly expression with concern, displeasure and suspicion, and Janina quickly realized that caution would have to be her watchword.

One never ceased to wonder at the dreadful results of the indoctrination and isolation the Russians had been subjected to since their 1917 revolution, which had alienated them to people outside their own boundaries.

The little Lieutenant and Major Levkov called to see us presently and several days later our new hosts invited us and the two officers to join them in an evening meal. It was a friendly gesture which the three of us readily accepted, but which obviously embarrassed the Russians, although they, not wishing to appear churlish, also accepted – with obvious reluctance. In the event, what could have passed as a pleasant occasion turned out to be a near disaster. Instead of the Major, another officer arrived with the little Lieutenant, but the conversation became stilted without a trace of friendliness on their part and they both rose to leave before the end of the meal, which was intended as a signal for us to leave as well. We could have insisted on staying put but did not wish to cause trouble for our hosts and so, proffering our apologies, we also left. In spite of everything, Janina continued to be friendly and looked in on us occasionally for a chat, ignoring the guards.

Chapter Sixteen

September brought with it a distinctly autumnal air. The long, hot summer days had gone and were replaced by a drop in temperatures as well as frequent showers and sombre overcast skies. Boredom had set in once more and our thoughts again turned to the possibility of escape. Bob was more determined than ever to have a go, yet the problem of all three of us defecting still seemed insoluble. However, our hopes rose when we volunteered to help with a very much overdue beetroot harvest which Janina and her husband had to contend with. Two other women joined our group and after a while we began to formulate some sort of plan based on our observations as we worked in the field.

First of all our two guards stayed close to us for several days, thereafter, leaving his junior comrade behind, Baldy took to disappearing for many hours. Then, in order to test the remaining guard's vigilance, when any of us needed to visit the lavatory some distance away, we spun out the time to see how long it took before he began to stir and check on us. When he did, we told him not to worry. In the end we timed his reaction to about fifteen minutes. This was splendid, but we realized that not all three of us could visit the lavatory at the same time without arousing suspicion. That being so, we started going in pairs at which he protested, but quickly relented with a down-to-earth understanding of the calls of nature.

Now it was necessary to move quickly as the advantage we had gained could quickly evaporate. The truth was that only two of us could be expected to make a getaway, not three. Having decided on that, the next problem was who should go. Whoever was to remain would have the job of stalling the guard for as long as possible, as best he could. We drew straws there and then, the shortest one falling to me as the one to act as stooge. Without stopping to argue the obvious disadvantages of that result, we went ahead with the next step. Having timed everything to perfection it was necessary for the guard to get used to Len and Bob sauntering off to the lavatory together. He didn't question it or their absences of a quarter of an hour, which meant that they could count on a headstart of that length and, with my help, maybe a bit longer. Now we needed outside help and here the obvious choice fell on Janina. An extra amount of food would have to be obtained which our own meagre rations did not allow for. Also, because of the inclement weather, it would be vital for the escapees to wear warmer clothing, which was asking a lot in the circumstances.

I explained all this to Janina during our work in the field, the conversation having to appear casual and mundane. We had all become practised at this sort of thing during the war and Janina never hesitated, promising to help in every way she could.

The idea was for Bob and Len to go and seek out an authoritative British body, preferably a military mission, such as had evidently been visiting the area recently, in order to alert them to our presence and the probability of the detention of many other escaped British POWs by the Russians. It was a very long shot – probably one of the longest ever to be devised.

It was now vital to coordinate our moves with Janina and the only way to communicate was to arrange secret meetings at times which would not arouse suspicion. The pretext of a last visit to the now famous outside lavatory before turning in for the night was a good cover for a clandestine meeting and the guards allowed us the privacy of those visits anyway. But it was the barn next to it which was our rendezvous, timed to within ten minutes of an appointed hour. No novice to clandestine work, Janina had everything prepared and, the evening before the escape, hid the food and warm overcoats inside, by the barn door, for Bob and Len to grab before making their dash.

The next morning we were set for the escape soon after Baldy's customary departure to the village. In the meantime we did our stint in the field as usual, along with Janina and the other helpers, nervously awaiting the given moment for Bob and Len to make their way casually, as usual, to the lavatory. As the two did so, Janina and I exchanged glances, the guard, bored by the whole business, took no notice and I sat back to await the fireworks. After about ten minutes the guard began to enquire about them, but I calmed him by saying that they would be back any minute now. Shortly afterwards he began to get worried and asked again. I managed to reassure him, this time suggesting that they might have gone for a walk. He cursed and said that they had no business to do so. Now visibly torn between going in search and leaving me unguarded, he decided to go and look for them. When he returned he announced that they were not there. When I suggested they might have gone to the house, he rushed there and, finding it empty, returned in a state of blind panic.

'Are you sure they went to the lavatory?' he asked, his voice quivering with fear.

'*Nu da*,' I replied casually, adding, 'So they can't be far away.'

Janina gave a chuckle at that. He hurled his cap to the ground, jumping on it in a rage, then rushed off howling like a thrashed child, 'Where could they have gone, where could they have gone?'

I last caught sight of the poor devil racing in the direction of the village as fast as his legs would carry him.

So far so good, for Bob and Len had in fact gained about half an hour's headstart, which was more than we had bargained for. As for the rest of us, we continued working away in the fields as though nothing had happened. With both guards absent I could have easily absconded as well!

Our guard returned with Baldy and the two of them scoured the area for a full half hour without success.

'How could Bob do this to me, when I practically nursed him in my arms?' he wailed with touching naivety, only attributable to a Russian. As I said, in his own irritating way he certainly did his best to cope with Bob's outbursts and demands, and obviously took the job of 'looking after the Englishmen' very seriously.

It was an uncomfortable evening. I sat by the flickering oil lamp pondering everything that had happened and where it would all lead to. Quite late into the night a well-armed squad arrived with two tracker dogs and a major in charge. They looked as though they meant business and I hoped that Bob and Len would by now be well beyond their reach. They were in no way intimidating, and the officer, having dispatched his men to carry out their search, suggested he and I have a game of chess since we had acquired a set several days ago. When I said that I was a very bad player he promptly offered to teach me the rules and we sat there for two hours until the men finally returned, empty-handed.

The following day was one of frustration and at the same time anticipation, because I knew that sooner or later something had to happen. My greatest concern was for my two companions, whose lack of knowledge of Polish could be a real problem, although they thought not and banked on the goodwill of the people to help them on their way. Once the straws had been drawn there was no argument about it, the die had been cast.

After dark, an officer and two soldiers arrived to tell me that I was to be transferred elsewhere. I said goodbye to Janina and her husband and we left, carrying everything we could manage except the bunk. It was pitch black when we reached the village and found ourselves before a high barbed-wire gate. A soldier fumbled with a padlock in the feeble light of a torch and we passed through, stumbling in a muddy quagmire until we reached a darkened cottage. We climbed up onto a porch and into a room where by the dim light of an oil lamp I saw Bob and Len.

'Christ, so they've brought your here as well,' were Bob's first words. 'We're really in the soup now. The bastards nearly shot us yesterday.'

They both looked thoroughly dejected.

They explained how, after a flying start, they had hitch-hiked their way to a railway station where they boarded a west-bound goods train crammed with refugees. After a sporadic journey the train could travel no further so they were obliged to find shelter for the night in a cottage. To their dismay they were challenged by a Russian patrol early the following morning and arrested. Both strongly suspected their hosts of giving them away, mistaking them for German deserters or stragglers. So it was the language problem which let them down after all. That ended another escape attempt and we now faced life behind a barbed-wire fence eight feet high. They were indeed lucky not to have been shot because they only admitted to their identity much later on.

We slept on the floor that night. Our old bunk arrived the next day and was erected again, filling most of the room, which was in fact a kitchen complete with a kitchen range. Our position looked very bad. The room was a virtual prison, the door to the next room being barred and locked and, worst of all, the only window was boarded up, which meant that we had to exist in virtual darkness. Not a chink of daylight penetrated the boards – such daylight as there was at that time of year did not amount to very much anyway. The sole source of illumination was provided by an ink bottle filled with tallow and wick. Two new guards stayed with us in this tiny space standing in a corner all day and, during the night, sleeping on the porch floor. They appeared to be unarmed but a sub-machine gun was invariably handed to them by patrolling guards during their evening rounds, although when we challenged them about it, they strenuously denied it. For some reason we were not supposed to know about it. It was as well that I had brought along our modest store of bread and soup cubes which we had previously kept in reserve, since we were now virtually deprived of any food whatsoever. Twice weekly a soldier appeared with a sack and dumped a few lumps of dried bread on the floor, which was obviously intended to humiliate us – when we gave him a piece of our mind for doing so, he stopped bringing it altogether. Occasionally we were treated to undrinkble fish soup. Now and again it was merely a bowl full of hot water and nothing else. So with judicious rationing of our soup cubes, together with the *kipiatok* (hot water), we made them last a fortnight. After that, and when the original supply of bread had gone, we faced starvation.

Minor calls of nature were performed anywhere outside the house, as one stood ankle deep in mud, and although there was an outside toilet some distance away for major calls, the guards never let us out of their sight.

There was no doubting that we had cooked our goose and were paying the penalty. We were fairly used to surviving in enclosed spaces by now, but the perpetual darkness and lack of food gradually began to sap our morale. However, we were still lucky to be at the 'luxury' end of a wider and more sinister detention complex. Within a large area surrounded by a tall barbed-wire fence there existed a smaller area, about the size of a football pitch, also fenced off but with watchtowers at each corner. Prisoners incarcerated in the partly subterranean earth dugouts within it must have suffered terrible physical privation. That was where humanity reached rock bottom and it was a sight to make one's flesh creep. Whoever they were and whatever they had done to deserve that sort of treatment, no one would ever know.

We protested to our guards about our treatment and were rewarded with a surprise visit by the sad little Lieutenant who listened to our complaints, but as usual offered no solution or comfort and appeared later wielding copies of *Pravda* for our edification. From them we learned how the Russians were paving the way for the introduction of a new 'democratic' German government, in the same manner as the Polish one. Allied progress in Western Europe or in the Pacific theatre of war hardly warranted a mention. By omission, they were obviously deemed to be of minor importance to the outcome of the war.

By now we were in a pretty grubby and unsavoury condition, and were lucky not to have contracted some skin disease or infestation of lice, but then one day we were taken to an ablution area and allowed the luxury of a sluice down with buckets of hot water, the only one we had enjoyed in months. Nevertheless, with our food supply long gone and with no sign of the reinstatement of normal rations, we had a feeling of isolation from reality and began to retreat into a state of silent despair. All further representations to see the little Lieutenant fell on deaf ears.

Our days of darkness and misery lasted one full month before we began to see daylight again. I suppose I clung to some shred of hope that somehow all would be well one day, although it now looked as though all roads would lead to Siberia – that awful, mystical land of purgatory which over the generations had served as a depository for people like ourselves who were an inconvenience to the system. If I could only survive that, ten years from now I might even see England again. Yes, the Russians had a war to wage and we must have counted for nothing in comparison, but to us at the time it certainly didn't look that way.

It was now late November and winter set in like an unfriendly, clammy blanket. Then one day we were told to spruce ourselves up and tidy our hovel in preparation for an inspection. A high-ranking officer arrived and looked us over. He seemed remarkably humane and informed us that we would soon be sent on our way home. We asked when that would be and he assured us not to worry as it would not be long now. We had heard this story too often to believe it and sank back into our state of semi-stupor. However, even our mummified guards suddenly came to life and actually seemed more friendly.

A week later things really began to happen. Two soldiers arrived carrying an assortment of tools, ripped the boards from the window and, having done so, unlocked the door separating us from the adjoining room. They seemed pleased with their efforts and assured us that we would soon be on our way home. That afternoon we were brought two loaves of bread and a can of *kasza* between us. Two days later we were issued with (Russian) uniforms. 'These are for you to wear,' the man said, smiling. When asked why we should wear them, he replied that it was for our own safety, but added, 'Be ready tomorrow at eight in the morning for departure. You're going home.'

In spite of all these promising signs, we still harboured lingering doubts as to their sincerity. Meanwhile, there we stood, dressed like three good Russian soldiers, complete with fur caps.

The morning of 3 December 1944 dawned cold, grey and absolutely still, with not a breath of wind to disperse the snow-laden sky. We were greeted by Major Levkov who led the way into the world outside where a staff car awaited us. We drove for several miles over deeply rutted roads in silence – the Major never did have much to say for himself, even in the Worsach days – eventually reaching a makeshift airfield. In a hut which served as a control room, we were introduced to a middle-aged lieutenant who we were told would escort us on our journey, though our destination still remained a mystery.

The weather having clamped down and turned foggy, delayed our departure for two hours. However, clearance for take-off was given and we piled into a Dakota, that famous maid of all work. Since it must have been used purely as a load carrier, there were no seats at all. Such refinements as safety harnesses were completely lacking. We flew through an endless blanket of cloud at low altitude, but now and again caught glimpses of fields below and I was suddenly gripped with a terrible feeling of sadness.

We were no longer treading Polish soil, but suspended above it as one is in a dream. I could no longer feel it or touch it or smile and wave goodbye to anyone. My feelings of sadness and hopelessness went to Poland and its people, whose dedication and selflessness to the Allied cause had no equal. At that point in time, Poland's future as a free, westward-looking nation lay in the balance, only to be swallowed up by the Soviet empire within months.

An hour later we landed at an isolated airfield. A horse-drawn farm cart drew up alongside our aircraft carrying a radial engine which was quickly manhandled aboard and lashed to some cabin supports with rope. In my book it should have been resting on baulks of timber, clear of the aluminium deck, but not so. It was slid into position until various components of the massive Pratt and Whitney gradually started to puncture the floor. It was rough and ready and not in the least assuring. When we took off, not wasting any time in this godforsaken emptiness as we jolted across the rough-looking airstrip, I watched with horrified fascination as the deadweight load nestling near us slid back until the ropes became taut, and then slowly sank deeper into the fragile floor. It needed a few more jolts to send the wretched thing hurtling clean through the fuselage, but by then, thankfully, we began to part company with terra firma.

We landed at Minsk within the hour with the weather showing no signs of relenting. Here we were taken to the canteen for a light meal and sat next to pilots who had obviously returned from combat missions, several women amongst them dressed in flying suits. It was a strange experience. Now for the first time our escort told us that our destination was Moscow but, after a long wait, he announced that as the weather report was still unfavourable we would be obliged to spend the night there and continue our journey by train the following day. Eventually a staff car arrived and took us into the centre of Minsk and beyond. The terrible damage inflicted to the city was only too evident. We were struck by the milling crowds of people scurrying about aimlessly like robot ants amongst the desolation. It all looked so terribly depressing and sad. However, as foreigners we were to be treated to better things and pulled up in front of a pleasant villa which showed all the signs of having been hastily renovated. It stood in splendid isolation gleaming like a beacon in a land laid waste. Undoubtedly built for some local potentate in Czarist days, it assuredly served the Germans well and now appeared to be serving as a guest house for foreigners and current Communist Party bigwigs. Inside, the restoration had been faithfully carried out true to the period, with subtle pastel colours on the walls. We were shown to our bedrooms which looked comfortable, but to our consternation we soon found that the WCs failed to work and there was no hot water in the taps. In the end they produced a jug of hot water, whereas we longed for the soothing and civilizing experience of nothing less than a bath. Before the arrival of the hot water, however, Len had already managed to leap into the only bath tub, only to discover a sluggish trickle of rust-coloured water emanating from the 'hot' tap.

Toilet paper was conspicuous by its absence which elicited further howls and urgent cries for bits of *Pravda*. There was a bevy of servants who scurried about in reverential silence seemingly achieving little, all our needs being supervised and seen to by our 'personal escort', the Lieutenant. Later we were taken to the rather grand dining room where a long table was neatly laid out for a party of twelve. There was a bottle of beer alongside each place setting, and the Lieutenant, obviously proud of this display of affluence, ushered us to our seats with great aplomb. It turned out we were to be the only diners that night.

The meal was simple and tasty yet hardly adequate to satisfy our hunger, but we had to count ourselves lucky, especially when we recalled all those gaunt faces amongst the city's ruins. What would they be eating that evening? In all probability nothing. 'This good, no? said the Lieutenant in fractured English. Unfortunately the language barrier prevented any attempts at fluent and meaningful conversation, but we managed to understand each other even if it became somewhat repetitive. In a way he had become a bore, but his patronizing attitude was even less endearing, especially when, all of a sudden, he launched into a fiercely patriotic diatribe and reeled off a string of great Soviet industrial achievements in terms of output, reciting statistics and figures which were obviously intended to impress. Then when he had finished, and after two more swigs of bear, he leaned forward with an intense look in his eye and said, 'When you go home to England, what will you say: Soviet Union is good, good food, good everything?'

We were in no mood to listen to his speeches, but after more swigs of beer he seemed determined to press home his point to the utmost. 'So now what you think of Soviet Union, Soviet Union good place, good country?' By this time we began to wonder whether there was an ulterior motive for his ramblings but to please him we assured him that we would all go home with the fondest memories of the Soviet Union. It was a pity, since his party pieces spoilt what could have been a pleasant evening.

After dinner there ensued a whispered conversation between the Lieutenant and the 'director' of the establishment. The latter announced that they had brought along someone who spoke English. This person turned out to be an extremely nervous, pale young woman who refused to move beyond the door with the result that we stood about wondering what to say. In the end we broke the ice with some banal questions, but there was no conversation as she spoke in monosyllables and in the end we gave up. With that she was promptly spirited away. No doubt they meant well.

With the continuing poor weather, we were now destined for a long train journey to Moscow. We were taken to the railway station by car and confronted with an incredible sight, reminiscent of 1940. Thousands of people thronged the approaches to the station, whole families having camped out with all their worldly belongings, miserable and forlorn, waiting for the train that would take them who knows where, in the vastness of the Soviet Union. In the aftermath of the war there must have been millions on the move throughout Russia, either returning to their shattered homes or seeking a new life and shelter elsewhere. But travel was not made easy because of a shortage of rolling stock, and because travel permits were required for long-distance journeys, and these were difficult to come by.

The all-important piece of paper held by the Lieutenant stating that we were foreigners quickly smoothed our entrance to the station platform, where a Moscow-bound train stood besieged by a frantic crowd. Once on board, the Lieutenant made his way to a compartment full of weary army officers and simply ordered them to leave. Their protestations cut no ice for we were foreigners and had to be afforded the space regardless. Now it was our turn to protest at this high-handed attitude, as the compartment could easily have been shared with some of them, but no, the Lieutenant would not have it and the officers left, complaining volubly. We thought it a mean action, but the Lieutenant seemed pleased with his efforts.

Once under way our progress became exasperatingly slow and I doubt whether we ever exceeded 20 m.p.h. Every so often we would stop at some isolated spot and take on water for the asthmatic locomotive, later to stop again and take aboard a load of wood, since there was no coal, which probably explained the reason for our slow progress. We often slowed down to a crawl because of repairs to the track, this being carried out by gangs of large women swathed to the eyeballs in black shawls to protect them from the bitter cold. I will never know how they ever got to these bleak and inhospitable places to do this grinding work. We passed the desolate remains of dozens of villages and even towns, the latter usually being some distance away, razed to the ground by the war. There was simply nothing left of use to anybody, save piles of rubble and charred timbers.

The only food we had was a meagre supply of bread and sausage which the Lieutenant shared among us, a 'packed lunch' given to him upon our departure from the Minsk guest house. We trundled on through the night and at first light I stood at the window to observe our approach to Moscow. Presently we passed a plain with a distant forest which stretched for at least 2 miles. Instead of being flat, the plain was covered in humps resembling outsize burrows in close proximity to each other and stretching as far as the eye could see. It was a sight which baffled me until I noticed the odd wisp of smoke rising from some of them and then the silhouette of a human being making its way between the hummocks; then another, moving slowly like some primitive creature in a horror story. I suddenly realized that people were actually living out there in their hundreds or even thousands in that desolate wilderness, in earth burrows like moles. That was a sight I shall never forget. Within 15 miles of our destination we passed by trenches which indicated the limit of the German advance into Russia and how very nearly they had succeeded in achieving their goal. The whole journey was so depressing that the arrival to Moscow came as a welcome relief.

We were met at the station by a major who took over from our dour lieutenant. Not sorry to see the last of him, we scrambled into one of those ubiquitous Dodge staff cars and headed into the very heart of the city. We drove in silence, the Major showing complete indifference; my attempts at conversation met with little success. Not a flicker registered on his face and his only response was a monosyllabic grunt.

We had convinced ourselves that our next stop would be at the British embassy and felt on top of the world. It did not matter whether our escort uttered a single word now, as long as we got there. However, we crossed Red Square, passing St Stephen's Basilica with its gleaming golden cupolas, and shortly afterwards the Kremlin, and on leaving the city we began to suspect trouble. My questions about the Basilica were answered with an impatient wave of the hand – indeed the only time the Major spoke was to give the driver instructions. We emerged onto a highway leading out of town and followed it for several miles before veering off onto a rough track which led into a forest. Thick snow covered the ground, the trees looking singularly beautiful draped in pure white, but it all went unappreciated as our anxiety intensified. The driver skilfully steered the car between trees until we approached a collection of timber villas and pulled up. Ushered into one of them, we were immediately struck by an unusual sight, for it was obviously maintained in pristine condition, with several soldiers on duty there looking smart and efficient. We were led into a large room with a row of beds in it, each one sporting blankets neatly stacked in squares; there were piles of towels and sundry cartons with other supplies stacked in a corner. Everything here was clearly marked 'British Red Cross'.

Two individuals, who had been busily playing a game of chess, rose from a bed to greet us. Our two new companions were Cyril Rofe RAF and Charles Hillebrand of the Palestine Pioneer Corps. Cyril had survived a crash landing in Holland, whereas Charles was taken prisoner, I believe, in North Africa and was unhappily in poor health. Both had escaped from a camp in southern Poland and later joined a group of partisans. They had been there for several days but were forbidden to get in touch with the British embassy. It transpired that we were the first batch of British ex-prisoners of war (myself excepted) to arrive at this specially prepared reception centre. But why the secrecy?

There was an unlimited supply of American tinned food, a luxury we noted the Russian soldiers also enjoyed, and for the first time we were warm and comfortable, but at the same time not allowed to set foot outside the villa. These villas, of which there were many dotted around the woodland, were called 'dachas', and were houses used by Muscovites for their summer vacations; every room was numbered, each family being allocated one room. There were no washing facilities inside as one was supposed to wash and shower outside in the summer season.

Public baths were popular in Russia and we were escorted to one of these the following day. Each of us had to obtain a metal tag from an officious woman attendant before being admitted to the changing cubicles and then to the communal washing room, where one sat on long benches and sloshed oneself over with hot water from a bucket. It was obviously an important ritual and a social event in the lives of the people, but the stench of humanity was overpowering. I emerged from this experience not feeling suitably cleansed as the whole place was too grubby for words. But even here we did not leave without a minor altercation between the officious attendant and Bob. It was trivial to start with until others – locals – joined in, and a verbal slanging match ensued with Bob gabbling in an unintelligible mixture of Polish, Russian, German and English until we physically dragged him away shouting at him, 'It'll be Siberia for you if you don't shut up!' At that we all beat a hasty retreat into the freezing cold outside. The invective which followed us on our departure sounded very much like 'Bloody foreigners'.

On our fourth day at the dacha we were told to prepare for departure and word had it that this time it was definitely to the British embassy.

We drove in a state of subdued excitement, back along the road to Moscow and into the city centre, eventually stopping in front of a tall, fine, old building. The sullen Major handed us over to a nervous, young Lieutenant who led us inside and up to a first-floor room. A relic of pre-Revolutionary days, it all looked very sedate and imposing. We waited in what was obviously a conference room, furnished with a long table covered with green baize and flanked with rows of chairs. On the wall hung an outsize map of the British Isles. The Lieutenant hovered around us, nervously enquiring if we had any complaints we wished to tell him about. Not wanting to exacerbate his nervousness we assured the poor man that we had none and that all was well. In fact things could not have been better right now, for presently two British Army officers entered the room and, introducing themselves, shook us by the hand. Then without further ado they said, 'Right, follow us, boys.'

We drove a short distance in two cars, entering the gate to a large building which was the headquarters of the British Military Mission. One of the officers told us that the embassy had only been notified of our existence one hour ago!

We had entered a vastly different world. Welcomed by the other members of the Mission, we had the 'freedom' of the building and were truly able to relax and catch up with the latest news, browse through a stack of daily papers and magazines, and at meal times join in with the others in lively conversation. We were served at the table by a Russian maid and an older manservant, and were warned not to say anything compromising about the Russians in his presence. As one young lieutenant put it, 'You want to mind what you say when he's about. We all do. He pretends not to understand English, but we know damn well he does.' He went on to say how well aware they were that the Russians employed here were spying on them and reporting everything to their masters. I didn't need convincing and it left a nasty taste, but then that was the Russia of those days. I fervently hope that with the changes that took place there in the 1990s and since, those bad old days will never return.

We were free to go out and about in the city but, again, were warned not to stray too far and certainly to avoid standing around in a group, otherwise we would attract the attention of the police. At this point we had not as yet been issued with any sort of identity card or passport, which could make things extremely unpleasant. However, Cyril and Charles elected to go to the Bolshoi one evening and on reflection I wished I had joined them. Instead I found myself a quiet corner in the Mess and wallowed through the pile of magazines in solitary contentment. We still wore the Russian uniforms we had arrived in and felt a lot better when we were taken down to the basement stores and kitted out in battledress, gas mask and tin hat. I swapped my Russian fur hat for a British Army issue arctic sealskin 'tea cosy' and regretted it ever since. As regards the Russian uniform, I still have it, including the leather Sam Browne belt stamped with the letters 'CCCP' and '1942'.

The nerve centre of the Mission was housed in the basement. Here was the Communications and Signals room as well as Photography Department. From here, direct contact was maintained with the War Office in London. By mutual agreement a Russian specialist in radio-communication was attached to the centre in order to monitor incoming and outgoing information. He was a swarthy individual in civilian clothes and as one young signals operator said to me, 'He won't leave us alone, you know, and interferes with every damn thing we do and send. He's just here to spy on us, we know that.'

Each of us had our photograph taken and was issued with a passport in record time. It was mid-December and no time was being wasted in order to get us home for Christmas. Home for Christmas – the best Christmas present I could wish for! Before our departure from this little corner of England, we were each in turn interviewed by a Lieutenant General Hall. For my companions this would have been a routine matter, but as a civilian I had a lot of explaining to do. He listened carefully, occasionally making notes and asking questions. Perhaps he too wondered if I was who I claimed to be, in spite of the detailed information I was able to furnish him with. I was left in no doubt, however, that the Embassy had known of me and as far as I was concerned that was all that mattered.

The following day we were called to a meeting with Admiral Archer, Commander-in-Chief Northern Waters, who in sombre tones informed us that we would be leaving the port of Murmansk in a convoy and 'with a bit of luck' should reach home in time for Christmas. It made us feel good, as though a special effort was being made for our benefit. The journey to Murmansk was to take nearly two days by rail, but it would be afterwards when we would need all the luck, for the prospect of having to face lurking U-boats in those Arctic seas was not a pleasant one. That would be our last hurdle.

We said goodbye to all those at the Mission and they wished us luck, expressing their envy at us going home for Christmas. Then, escorted by an officer, we drove to the railway station which was crowded to bursting. Elbowing our way through, we reached the appropriate platform where a Captain Nairn awaited us. We were to travel with him to Murmansk along with a dozen or so heavy diplomatic bags that were in his care. The five of us shared one compartment, whereas the Captain had one to himself with his bags, next to ours.

And so we left Moscow, heading north, to a new scene of snow-laden skies above and the bleak landscape unfolding itself in a familiar pattern, but this time getting progressively more desolate the further north we travelled. We stopped now and again at nonexistent stations, in the middle of nowhere, and were invariably besieged by hoards of peasants carrying their '*tobolki*' (bundles), clamouring to get aboard the train. It was sheer bedlam. However, the railway guards made certain that our carriage was kept free from the scrabbling masses in no uncertain terms. Again, as foreigners we had every priority and that privilege was strictly observed. Later, when we stopped on two subsequent occasions in an area so desolate and depressing one would never have expected to see a living soul, we were besieged by hoards of ragged and emaciated men who begged us for some food. Their pitiful cries were positively heart-rending and the guards set about beating them off, but they kept coming back pleading, with tears in their eyes. Most of them were dark skinned and of southern European, or Mediterranean appearance and spoke little Russian. Who on earth were they and why were they here in this godforsaken territory? Obviously they were part of the human flotsam thrown up in the aftermath of war, but were they that unworthy of normal human treatment to be left to die from starvation and exposure? Perhaps they had no place in Soviet society.

As dusk descended we stopped yet again at some outlandish spot and picked up more passengers; this time we could hear an argument between the guard and a voice which sounded distinctly English. Surely enough it turned out to be a lieutenant in the Royal Navy who was evidently being denied entry into the carriage. A rating stood by with a loaded sledge which between them they had hauled across an endless plain from the port of Archangel. We threw our weight behind him in an attempt to force the issue, the guard finally giving in when Captain Nairn, speaking in authoritative Russian, demanded that the officer be admitted on the train, explaining that his journey was of vital importance. We shared the extra load between our two compartments and waved goodbye to the rating who started on his lone trek back to base.

Our train was roughly divided into two parts, one part being reserved for military personnel and the other for civilian passengers. It so happened that the carriage next to ours served refreshments – tea only – and the ever-enterprising Bob promptly disappeared to find the entertainment provided by Russian soldiers with their songs and wild dances was very much to his taste. There, also, he found Tamara, one of two girls or hostesses serving 'chai' to the thirsty soldiers. He insisted that I went along to meet her and when I declined his offer he promised to bring her along to meet me. I was too preoccupied with my thoughts, wondering what lay ahead and what should be done when we reached England, and spent most of the time gazing through the corridor window – the last thing on my mind was a Tamara. However, Bob was as good as his word and persuaded her to follow him to our carriage. I was quite taken aback because she was a girl of striking beauty and I wondered what on earth she was doing there. It seemed no place for her to be. Now I was forced into making conversation, doing my best to speak her language; she on the other hand proved to be delightful company, quite natural and animated, and we got on splendidly. However, duty called and she went back to her work with the promise of returning as soon as she could. And return she did, quite content to spend the time chatting and gazing out of the window. Her apparent readiness to seek my company made me suspicious and I awaited the inevitable loaded question, but it never happened and at some stage she paid me the compliment of calling me a 'real gentleman', saying said that I was 'not like the others'. I wast touched by her sentiment and at the same time felt desperately sorry for her, having to do the job she was doing in a land so desolate and devoid of beauty. She stayed until it was time to turn go back to her quarters with a cheerful 'See you tomorrow'. A Russian general, travelling in solitary splendour further down the carriage, emerged from his compartment, took one look out of the window, saw nothing and also turned in for the night.

But my thoughts were about our homecoming. I wondered how I would find England in wartime, what my father and brother, George, were doing at this moment and found that because of the years of separation and silence there was nothing for my imagination to feed on. In fact, there was a complete blank. I knew not whether they were alive or dead, serving in the forces or whatever. And yet the mere fact that I was returning to England was joy itself.

In the early hours of the morning I was woken by Bob tugging at my sleeve. 'Hey, Tom, you know what?' he whispered urgently.

'What?' I replied without moving.

'I've just seen Tamara coming out of the General's compartment, all dressed up in a lovely blue gown.'

'Thanks a lot, Bob,' I replied.

So that's how things were, I thought to myself. I should have known and felt just a slight pang. But I wasn't entirely surprised either. As the French say, 'C'est la guerre' or 'Cest la vie'. And in my befuddled state of mind I forgave her – I had enjoyed her company anyway.

By now the scenery had changed dramatically. In brilliant sunshine, we were passing through the snow-clad hills of Karelia and seemingly balancing precariously on the narrowest of causeways, on either side of which stretched clear, glassy water perfectly reflecting the snowy slopes and blue sky above in a scintillating crystal landscape of breathtaking serenity and beauty. Somewhere, beyond those hills lay, the White Sea. Our railway guard informed us that the Germans had only just left the area and that we were fortunate to be getting through without any trouble. Tamara came to see me again and although our conversation had run dry by now, she didn't seem to mind. I was pleased that she had no ulterior motive in seeking my company and genuinely seemed to enjoy chatting to me.

We all longed for a decent meal, but had no such luck, and divided the bread and tinned meat we had among ourselves. We washed it down with 'tea' obtained from the refreshments car.

As we approached Murmansk the skies turned to lead. It was late afternoon and precious daylight hours were short, somewhere between 1 and 4 o'clock, otherwise one existed in a perpetual twilight, which had a depressing effect. Before we reached our destination, Tamara again came to see me, begging me to write to her and gave me her parents' address somewhere in southern Russia. I said I would, but knew immediately that as a 'foreigner' I would never risk her safety by doing so. Maybe my caution had got the better of me, but I felt that it was better to be safe than sorry. In reality, we were both starved of ordinary human warmth and kindness. She in her strange world of perpetual travel and transient associations knew of none, and I knew inwardly how much I longed for it myself. But there was a long way to go and the war was far from over.

Murmansk station was the end of the line. It stood in solitary bleakness about 2 miles from the town itself, as so many railway stations in Russian were apt to be. No doubt today it has become absorbed into an enlarged metropolis, but then it resembled something out of *Dr Zhivago*. The train disgorged its weary passengers onto the thick snow and the locomotive stood there panting white plumes of smoke in satisfaction, its job well done.

Two Royal Navy ratings with sledges awaited us here to assist in transporting all the diplomatic bags to base. We loaded and secured the bags on to the sledges and struck out across the snowy wastes, using the row of telegraph poles as a guide. I turned around to see if I could catch a last glimpse of Tamara, and there she was looking stunning in a long fur coat and huge fur hat like a model from a fashion picture. She waved and continued to do so until we were swallowed up in the gathering darkness. Goodbye Tamara, I'll never see you again, but good luck!

Following the line of telegraph poles, we eventually reached a road and signs of habitation. At some point we split up and were given directions how to get to the Royal Navy hospital, whilst the ratings with their sledges proceeded to their base. Inside the hospital we were shown to a ward with rows of spotless beds and told to take our pick. A rating commented that we were fortunate as all the beds had been occupied a month before. Here we also met Garth Glasson, a South African who had escaped from a POW camp, but I cannot recall more about him, save that he was a straightforward, tough-looking individual.

There was an animated hubbub of voices as young Royal Navy ratings came and went, but it was their cheerfulness which astounded me. I tried to imagine what it must have been like for them at the height of the war, running the gauntlet of preying U-boats and air attacks in their perilous journeys escorting convoys of ships, carrying war materials and supplies to the Soviet Union. It was something I knew very little about at that particular time.

A handful of them were still recuperating from their ordeal while waiting for a ship to take them on their return journey home; others were there waiting to be reallocated from one ship to another, and so on, their varied cap bands indicating the warships they came from.

In the Mess that evening we enjoyed a meal of corned beef and mash served in lavish helpings, swilled down with hot sweet tea, and when that was over we repaired to the cinema in an adjoining hall to see the 1940 film *Ziegfield Follies*. I found that a great tonic and such pure escapism, something we sorely needed at the time. However, it was the newsreels that thrilled me most of all, especially shots of RAF fighters chasing flying bombs, the V-1s, and tipping them over to destruction with their wing tips. This was an absolute revelation since we hadn't even heard of these devilish devices.

Sleep came with difficulty that night in spite of our fatigue. Thoughts of what lay ahead were always foremost in our minds. Not least we had to steel ourselves for that last hurdle. Then I thought of Garth Glasson whose home was so far distant and how alien the sub-Arctic must have seemed to him. He had such a long voyage ahead of him and the journey to Britain would only be the beginning of it. Charles Hillebrand looked so terribly ill but was bearing it without a murmur of complaint. Would he make it home, wherever it might be? I admired Cyril Rofe, his fellow escapee, who stayed with him, helped him and showed such concern for his welfare at all times. Cyril ended up as landlord of a pub in Sussex. Whereas both Bob and Len would soon be home in Bristol and Henley with their families, I had no inkling of what awaited me at the end of my journey.

The following morning we stood on the quayside at Murmansk harbour and were greeted with a wonderful sight. There in the distance, anchored well off-shore, lay a fleet of ships of the Royal Navy along with some merchant vessels. Among them, two large flat-topped hulls stood out, towering above the rest of the fleet. They were the escort carriers HMS *Campania* and HMS *Nairana*, two sister ships. Along with a number of sailors from the hospital, we were whisked out to sea in a pinnace, making for the aircraft carrier *Campania*.

Taken to a mess deck which was situated well forward, in fact almost at the bow, we realized with faint amusement that if the ship hit a mine, we would be the first to know about it, although it didn't necessarily work that way. We were a mixed bunch, strays so to speak, sharing the Mess with some of the regular ship's crew. Our own little group was accorded freedom of the ship which meant that we could go where we wished, within reason. Before we set sail, we were presented to Rear Admiral Roderick McGrigor, commander of the convoy, a small wiry Scot, in whose hands rested the safety of the ships. Once under way we were obliged to conform to shipboard routine, even joining the queue for the daily tot of rum. Finding it not to my taste, I passed mine on to the next man.

As hammocks were still in use in those days, slinging them proved to be quite a hilarious operation. Slung at about head height it was necessary to hoist oneself into it with the aid of a rope, an art we had yet to acquire. In the meantime, much to the amusement of all, there was many a header, clean over the top of the wretched hammock, with a very hard landing the other side. It was like trying to walk a greasy pole. Correctly slung, they were extremely snug.

As soon as we were out of sight of land, our role as guardians of the convoy came into action when the first Swordfish took off from the flight deck. These faithful biplanes lumbered about the grey skies, often disappearing beyond the horizon altogether. By now the entire convoy, consisting of numerous merchantmen, four destroyers and our two aircraft carriers, was gathered in an impressive armada stretching for 2 miles or so. Our sister ship, the *Nairana*, kept station about a mile astern. These convoys usually proceeded at the speed of the slowest ship so our progress appeared to be painfully slow. In the meantime, the destroyers darted about like watchful sheepdogs, one occasionally speeding off in response to the suspected presence of a prowling U-boat. We were told to expect trouble once we were within striking distance of the Norwegian coast.

The following day, the wind blew to gale force, accompanied by mountainous seas. It was so bad that reconnaissance flights were called off and we hoped that it would equally deter the U-boats from putting to sea as well. Nevertheless, as soon as conditions became more favourable, reconnaissance flights were immediately resumed – this meant that instead of 30ft waves, we had 15ft waves. But my total admiration went to those airmen of the Fleet Air Arm who braved these dreadful conditions, bearing in mind that a ditching in these freezing temperatures meant certain death.

Landing an aircraft on a heaving deck had to be seen to be believed. The timing for touchdown had to be absolutely right otherwise the rebound was liable to send the plane and its crew shooting off at a tangent and possibly into the sea. Luckily this did not happen but I witnessed one incident nearly to my cost, when a Swordfish bounced and slewed across the deck, one wing missing my head by about a foot. It ended up tilted at an alarming angle overhanging the water but with part of its undercarriage trapped in a gallery. With a gale blowing, for a moment it looked like touch and go whether the plane remained there or not, but in a flash the deck was swarming with rescuers, including myself, who hung on to it like grim death until the arrival of a tractor, which hauled it back on deck. Throughout all this, the crew of three seemed perfectly calm.

Patrols and practice flights were also carried out by Grumman Wildcats, the small fighter planes.

The convoy wallowed about laboriously in the high seas – 'The worst I've seen', as one sailor put it. At times the small destroyers disappeared from sight altogether and the *Nairana*, as well as our own *Campania*, presented an incredible sight with their heaving flat tops.

The tannoy system often broadcast topical bits of news when it wasn't used for more serious matters, but a call to action stations with the strident sound of the hooter in the middle of the night was no joke. We tumbled out of our hammocks, scrambled into our clothes, donned life jackets and waited further orders. Evidently the ASDIC had picked up the sound of a submarine and a destroyer was dispatched to find it. Luckily all was well on that occasion.

Later the following evening the tannoy obligingly informed us that we had narrowly missed colliding with the *Nairana*. We paled at the mere thought of it happening, especially in the hours of darkness, but I was not surprised as at times the two ships did seem to travel close to each other during the day, and at night, with a total blackout in operation, and the heavy seas, it could easily have happened.

At last we left the worst behind us and entered safer and calmer waters. Once all the aircraft had been stowed in the hangar, and the crews manning the anti-aircraft guns had been relieved of their constant vigil, we knew we were close to home. Although we had experienced some of the worst weather recorded on these convoys, we were lucky to have come through it without being attacked by the enemy. It was only now that we learned that our destination was Scapa Flow, where many ships of the German Navy had been scuttled after their surrender in 1918. We finally dropped anchor somewhere in the middle, barely within sight of land. I have invariably experienced a feeling of sadness upon leaving a ship and felt much like that now, but we had to say goodbye to the *Campania* and disembarked into a small fleet of tugs which jostled alongside and headed away into the gathering dusk. Where exactly we ended up I cannot recall, but another ferry and three hours later saw us in Thurso. At Thurso, we were directed to a transit ship, the ancient *Duluth Castle*, moored alongside a quay, to await further instruction.

As members of the armed forces, my five companions were quickly told to proceed to various parts of the United Kingdom, Bob and Len having to report to a camp at Wonersh near Guildford in Surrey. There appeared nothing to stop me from walking off the ship as well, as I had had no instructions whatsoever and no one seemed to be particularly interested. I felt sad having to part company with my friends, especially Bob and Len with whom I had shared so many ups and downs, but orders were orders. When I went to see the 'man in charge' and told him of my intention of leaving the ship, he got very stroppy and told me to wait as someone was coming for me. So they did know about me after all. Eventually someone did come and introduced himself as Sergeant Meteyard, of the Intelligence Corps, who said he was instructed to escort me to London. We found our way into the town and looked for somewhere to spend the night, which wasn't easy and we ended up in a most uncomfortable guest house.

I was glad to find my escort pleasant company. We caught the early morning train to Glasgow and from there took the London-bound one, arriving at Euston in the evening. We talked a great deal during the journey south and I had the strong impression that I was to spend some time in a so-called 'patriotic school'. This suggested some sort of establishment for lost souls who, having spent a long time in limbo, needed reintroducing to the ways of normal life. I was quite prepared to go along with that, but was afraid it might be a sanatorium for the mentally unstable. In fact a spell in a sanatorium would not go amiss – how wonderful to be cosseted and fussed over by a bevy of gentle and attentive nurses in some tranquil rural retreat, I mused.

But it was not to be and I had a rude awakening when on arrival at Euston Station we took a bus south to Brixton and walked in the direction of Streatham Hill, turned off into a dimly lit side street and stood before a massive, forbidding wooden door. My heart sank – a plaque alongside it read 'Brixton Prison'.

I looked at the Sergeant with astonishment and said, 'You can't mean I'm going in here?'

'I'm terribly sorry, old chap,' he replied apologetically as he rang the bell; a warder let us in through the small pedestrian entrance. The Sergeant handed him an envelope and then, with genuine sadness in his voice, wished me luck as we shook hands and parted.

I handed in all my earthly possessions at the reception desk, such as they were, before being taken to a cubicle where I changed into prison garb consisting of thick brown flannels (without a belt) and a grey jacket. My protestations went in vain. The warder was only doing his job, no questions asked. His was not to reason why.

The next step was to the baths and with that over I was led to a cell. It was all so familiar – I didn't have to be told what to do. It was well past eight in the evening of 23 December 1944. Utter silence prevailed throughout the prison. Presently another warder appeared bearing a mug of cocoa and a chunk of Christmas pudding on a plate. Hooray, they'd said we'd be home for Christmas!

After the initial shock of it all, I lay down on the bunk and ceased worrying, hoping that with luck, all would be revealed the next day. Nevertheless, I was thoroughly annoyed that Brixton Prison was the only place they could find for me to spend the night, hopefully only one night. With Christmas around the corner they might be easing up and see to me later.

The next morning, I had just had time to finish breakfast and clean out my cell, when a dapper gentleman in a pinstripe suit and briefcase appeared at the cell door. He seemed to be in a state of some agitation and announced that he had come from the Home Office. Then he sat down on my bunk and waded through a sheaf of papers. I lost my temper, accusing everyone of gross inefficiency, at which he became most apologetic, regretting 'that this ever happened'. He left assuring me that my release will take place forthwith. Shortly after his departure a warder came and I was back in the reception office changing into my battledress and being given the statutory half-crown, (about five pounds today) prison money, which was all I had to my name. A helpful warder suggested how I could best get to the city and with that I left Brixton Prison behind me.

My first task was to track down my father. As it was Christmas Eve, with the city at a virtual standstill, war or no war, I knew I had to move fast. He could be anywhere in the whole of Britain for all I knew. But my first port of call had to be the only address I knew, that of his pre-war business associates in London Wall. When I got there the building looked deserted but my knocks on the door brought a response and a caretaker appeared. I asked him if he had known a Mr Firth who used to call here before the war. It was a long shot to say the least, but the caretaker pondered for a moment and suddenly remembered. Yes, he said, he did remember my father, but the last time he called in 1940, he was in the RAF. That was wonderful news and I immediately realized that my search would be made that much easier. The caretaker then added that my father, since leaving this office, had transferred his business and joined forces with a Mr Arnold in at Pall Mall. That name was also familiar to me and now I could hardly believe my luck, although I was yet to find out where in Pall Mall.

At any rate I had now two options: either to pursue the RAF lead, or Pall Mall. Of course, his RAF career was a complete mystery to me and even then he might have been posted abroad. Conserving my money as much as possible, I covered as much territory as I could on foot, and in my travels stopped to consult a policeman about my problem. Fortunately I was in the right area and he suggested a visit to the RAF records office at Ad Astra House, or else call at Mount Pleasant main post office where they would be able to trace Mr Arnold's office address in Pall Mall. My visit to the Post Office soon brought to light the number I needed in Pall Mall – it was No. 1. En route to Pall Mall I went to Ad Astra House but their searches revealed nothing. They suggested that he might well come under another Regional Command, but couldn't say where. RAF personnel came and went as I stood there when suddenly a Polish Air Force officer passing by stopped and said that he had overheard me asking about a Firth – did I mean Flight Lieutenant Firth? I said it could be but as I had just arrived in England I couldn't be sure. When he described him and said that he spoke Polish, I was in no doubt at all that it was my father. Unfortunately my anxious query as to his whereabouts also drew a blank, for the Pole did not know.

Now I was obliged to fall back on the second option and made tracks for Pall Mall. It was also deserted and I didn't hold out much hope, but my persistent banging on the door eventually met with success. A bleary eyed caretaker appeared commenting that I was lucky to have found him there just then, but when I told him what I had come for, he sucked in air and shook his head. I said that I had no time to waste and requested that he opened up the office for me so that I could search for a clue, anything that would tell me something about my father. He declined to do so at first, saying that it would be highly irregular, but in the end he relented.

As soon as he unlocked the door to the first-floor office, I was in and rummaging for all I was worth amongst a pile of papers on a desk, with the poor man muttering how highly irregular it all was. There was not a shred of a clue anywhere so as a last resort I sat down at the desk and decided to look for Mr Arnold's home address in the telephone directory. This, I was told, was also highly irregular, but I dialled the number nevertheless. There was no answer, but the address was Sherehall Road, Hendon and I decided to go there straight away. It was a fortunate move.

It was now early evening and although I had not eaten all day the thought of food hadn't crossed my mind for once, so intent had I been on completing my mission in time for Christmas Day. I took the tube to Hendon and found the house at Sherehall Road empty. In desperation knocked on the door of the next one, wondering if the good folks there could tell me about the Arnolds. They were an elderly couple and said that the Arnolds were away at Middleton-on-Sea in Sussex for Christmas, but when I explained the reason for my visit and who I was, they perked up and said that they had met my father when he was staying with the Arnolds and had remembered hearing mention of me. They invited me in, we had tea and they later suggested I stay over-night, an offer I gratefully accepted. They went on to explain that the people next door to them were related to the Arnolds and might be more helpful, but as it was now getting late, it would be better to see them in the morning. I spent the night in this tiny corner of heaven, or so it seemed to me, with everything so quiet and peaceful that it felt as though life had gone on here unruffled forever.

The last pieces to the jigsaw now began to fall into place the following morning when I rang the neighbours' bell. A lady came to the door and I began to explain that I was searching for my father, Mr Firth, when she interrupted me and said, 'Then you must be Tom Firth. And you say that you've just arrived from Poland?' She let out a shriek of incredulity and called her husband. They stood and stared at me for a moment as if I had returned from the dead. They had of course heard all about me – not only were they related to the Arnolds, but they also came from Poland themselves. In all the excitement of the occasion our conversation became disjointed and confused. They then telephoned some other relations and arranged for them to call in later in the afternoon. In due course, when their visitors arrived, there was more excitement. They too originally came from Poland and wanted to know everything I could tell them about their former homeland. Needless to say, what I had to tell them was anything but a happy story.

Luckily for me, this latest relation seemed to 'know his way about' and spent half an hour on the telephone in another room. When he emerged from it he looked happy and said, 'We have traced your father. He's in Blackpool at No. 2 RAF Officers' Mess on Read's Avenue and I'll telephone him now.'

He got through without a hitch and was soon in animated conversation with Father. Presently he told my father that there was someone here who would like to talk to him and handed me the receiver. I found it extremely difficult to know what to say at that moment and simply said, 'Hello Dad, Tom here.'

'Tom who?'

'Tom, from Warsaw.'

'No, that's George, isn't it?' (meaning my brother).

'No, it's definitely Tom and I've just arrived in England.'

'No, you must be George.'

'No, it's Tom.'

There ensued a short silence followed by some incomprehensible noises at the Blackpool end of the line when my father finally realized that it was no hoax. I was later told by his colleagues in the RAF Mess that they had had to hold him up in order to prevent him from falling over; they also assured me that the fact they were celebrating Christmas in the bar at the time had nothing to do with it.

The question now remained whether I could get to Blackpool in the last few remaining hours of Christmas Day and a telephone call to Euston Station confirmed that it could be done as the last train was due to leave at about half past six. Thanking my friends for all they had done, and without whose efforts all this would never have come about with such speed, and with money for the fare borrowed from them to boot, I raced down to the station.

When I got there it was almost deserted. A fog began to descend and what with the blackout, made it look terribly eerie. The fog persisted during the whole journey until we reached our destination and I was practically the sole occupant of the compartment the whole way.

I began to search eagerly for a glimpse of my father as I strode along the platform and then caught sight of a solitary figure in RAF uniform waiting by the gate. I remember being overcome by a feeling of intense pride upon seeing him in uniform and words simply failed us both at the moment of meeting. We repaired to No. 2 Mess on Read's Avenue, where Father was billeted and, with the Commanding Officer's special dispensation, arranged for me to stay there for a time as well.

After the years of silence and separation there was so much to tell and so many questions to answer, but where to begin? At this point, however, foremost in our minds was the fate of my mother, about whom we knew nothing and were not likely to hear anything until very much later.

In 1940, at the age of fifty-three, my father had little future ahead of him, stranded, so to speak, in England, with his business enterprise in Warsaw finished and no home to go to. It was a devastating experience for him, but with the arrival of large numbers of Polish servicemen from France, there became an acute need for interpreters to act as liaison officers between them and the British. This was a role Father was well able to fulfil and promptly volunteered for the job, becoming a liaison officer between the Polish Air Force and RAF. His job covered a whole spectrum of duties which he very much enjoyed, not least because it entailed flying around to the various RAF stations, wherever there were Poles. In this he was unique, being an Englishman with a knowledge of the Polish language, albeit fairly limited, and he did very well. The Polish airmen were glad to have someone who could communicate with them in their own language. He moved from one station to another, eventually being posted to Blackpool. In the summer of 1945 he went to Germany as part of the Occupying Force, where his perfect knowledge of German served him well, and later returned to England and 'demob'. Prior to us finally meeting up again in 1944, he had been absolutely convinced that he would never see me again as the last news to reach him in 1942 had been a carefully worded message written by my mother, sent through the International Red Cross, implying that I was in serious trouble.

Now I discovered that at the time of my arrival in England my brother George had already been in France, in the Army, for several months. This came as a surprise, because when he and Father arrived in England in August 1939, he had joined Samuel White, a firm of shipbuilders on the Isle of Wight, in order to embark on a career as a naval architect. As part of his studies he was sent to Glasgow University, but with the war in full swing by 1942, he saw little future in his work and, rightly or wrongly, changed course completely by joining the Army. He became a sergeant in the Intelligence Corps and was sent to France soon after D-Day. He was one of only two Britons who were the first to arrive in the town of Béthune after its evacuation by the Germans. They were greeted and fêted in great style by the population and I still have photographs which have immortalized that proud moment. It was there that he met a charming girl, Monique, who was later to become his wife.

Shortly after my arrival we sent him a message as a result of which he was able to come back to England on short leave. We had a wonderful though rather subdued reunion, after which he was posted to Belgium. There, riding a motorcycle, he had a collision with a tank and came off the worse for it, breaking a leg. Later promoted to the rank of captain, and upon his return to England for demobilization, both he and Monique settled in London after their wedding. Tragically, however, the accident in Belgium resulted in an illness from which he was never to recover. He was just thirty-one. Monique and her two tiny children returned to France where they live to this day, in Béthune, not far from the cemetery where George lies buried.

Early in 1945, press coverage which followed in the wake of my arrival soon began to snowball, in consequence of which I was invited to speak about my experiences in Occupied Poland to various interested bodies and societies up and down the country. In the course of these travels I was able to meet a number of notable people of the day and recall a particularly interesting meeting of the European Freedom Movement in Edinburgh. This august body, whose purpose it was to monitor the democratic development of countries emerging from under the Nazi yoke, was well aware of events taking shape in Eastern Europe, and sought evidence from witnesses, which is where I was able to be of some help. However, all their efforts proved fruitless when the Russians gained a complete stranglehold on those countries, turning them into subservient puppet regimes.

I was ill at ease talking to large audiences and really did not particularly enjoy the publicity. But my first serious engagement nearly turned into a fiasco. The then Polish Ministry of Information, a department of the Polish government-in-exile in London, invited me to speak to what was described as 'a few people' who were particularly interested to learn at first hand what had happened in Poland, at a house in Chesham Place, close to Hyde Park. I had met the Polish organizer on several occasions and had no qualms about it. I was staying at the Kenilworth Hotel at the time, all expenses paid, and enjoyed a gentle ramble around the West End before gravitating to that wonder of wonders, the Monsignor cinema, Piccadilly, with its continuous newsreels and cartoons. Finally emerging close on 4 o'clock, I proceeded in the direction given me but without having a clear idea where it was. I walked through Green Park, past Hyde Park Corner and along Halkin Street before, without realising it, I emerged into Chesham Place. When I glanced at my watch it was half past four and, stricken with a sudden panic, I hailed a passing taxi and shouted the destination to the driver. Without batting an eyelid he cruised on for a hundred yards and halted. I had arrived and in my frantic rush slammed the cab door on my hand. The pain was so intense that I hopped up and down the pavement for a time, wringing my hands like a praying mantis. I managed to extract my fare to pay the driver and rushed to the door of the building in intense pain. I had barely laid a finger on it when it was flung open and the Polish organizer caught me by the arm and dragged me in. 'Mr Firth, where have you been?' he wailed, mopping his brow. 'Do you know, there are admirals and generals waiting to hear you ...' his voice trailed off.

'Why didn't you tell me ...?' I hadn't finished when he propelled me through a door and into a large room in which the lights had been dimmed and a blue haze of cigarette smoke hung limply from one end to the other. Through it I was just able to see what he meant, as there certainly appeared to be an intimidating amount of gold braid amongst the audience of about 150. Had he not told me there would only be a few interested people?

Now I almost felt as though I was on trial, although in the event all went well. After it was over several people stopped to talk to me and the last of them was a very shy little Polish lady.

'Tell me, Mr Firth, when you were in Krakow, in Montelupich, did you by any chance come across a Major Klink? He's my cousin, you know, and I have had no news of him at all,' she asked and I had the feeling she was half dreading the answer. Old Josef Klink, military historian, prison handyman and latterly *bademeister*, whose job I took over when he was sent to Auschwitz. How could I forget him? Unprepared for this kind of question I was momentarily struck dumb and admitted to having known him well, but hesitated over the rest. What should I tell her, I wondered. She looked at me wistfully and, guessing the answer, said, 'He went to Auschwitz, didn't he?'

'Yes,' I said.

'Oh,' she murmured, her eyes filling with tears as she slowly walked out of the door.

In February 1945, I was requested to call at one of the departments of Military Intelligence which was located in Devonshire House, Piccadilly. There, in a top floor office, I was met by two army officers and a suave-looking gentleman in a pinstripe suit. After introductions and an exchange of banalities, they wanted to know if there was anything noteworthy or unusual about the Germans they should know about. I thought that one could make a great deal from a question like that but refrained from saying anything provocative. At that stage of the war there seemed to be little point in it and I presumed that it was merely a routine which had to be complied with. I said that it was now several months since I had last seen any Germans and couldn't think of anything revealing to tell them. As they were not interested in Russians, we talked about Poland and at that point the civilian mentioned that he had visited Warsaw shortly before the outbreak of war, and explained how he used to park his car on the embankment by the Vistula and call in one of the riverside bars for a drink. As that happened to be on our doorstep, I remembered seeing his grey Hillman Minx Coupé with GB plates quite often on my way home from school, and wondered who the owner was. And now here he was, over four years later. I described his car in detail, including the number plate and he nearly fell off his chair in amazement. As I said goodbye to them, he sat staring at me, shaking his head in disbelief. Some boys collected locomotive numbers, I happened to remember car registration plates, especially when they were British ones in Poland. It takes all sorts.

In time we found that postal communications with Poland had been resumed. The war had come to an end and everyone was trying to pick up where they had left off nearly five years before, but in countries like Poland that feeling of security no longer existed. Britain had been very lucky indeed to have emerged from the war with all its old institutions and traditions intact, for the Poland that had existed before 1939 had been brutally swept aside. It simply did not exist.

Our first inkling that my mother had survived came through the good offices of a British government emissary who had just visited Poland. Thereafter we were able to write to each other in the normal way and she was fortunate to be still living in the flat at Obroncow, in Saska Kepa. She was employed in the offices of the United Nations Relief Agency in Warsaw when it became established there, and managed to survive the rigours of life in the devastated capital for three years. For various reasons, during that time, she steadfastly declined to leave Poland in spite of my insistence, a situation I eventually had to accept. But as the communist government became progressively more hostile towards foreign agencies such as UNRA and closed it down, she was obliged to seek employment elsewhere. Then, in 1949, the screw began to tighten and a high-level scandal exploded, involving the British Ambassador and the French embassy, which resulted in the withdrawal of certain officials of both embassies and the recall of the British Ambassador himself. This was followed by the arrest of a number of Poles who were allegedly involved in the affair. It was all very obscure, but the signs were unmistakeable.

When I next wrote to Mother I was adamant that she should leave the country immediately. In reply she told me that although she had just secured a job at the American embassy, she agreed that the time had come for her to consider leaving. That was the last letter I was to receive from her. Within days she was arrested. In fact the first I knew of it was when I read a newspaper report of her arrest. She was held incommunicado by the secret police, which meant that no one was allowed access to her at all. It was a shattering experience and our main worry was what it was all about and what charges were being levelled against her. We were in close touch with the Foreign Office at the time but, in spite of representations made to the Polish authorities, gleaned nothing. Eventually brought to trial, which was held in camera, meaning that no one from outside was permitted to attend, she was charged with espionage and sentenced to death.

Much later we discovered that the charge against her was aimed at her work in the press office of UNRA where she collected press cuttings concerning the agency's work in Poland. In fact she was in no way qualified to do much other than the simplest of tasks, yet in the eyes of the new regime, gathering 'information' in itself presented a breach of national security. But at the bottom of it all was their determination to discredit foreigners, especially westerners, a technique practised in Soviet Russia.

Months later there was a retrial and the death sentence was commuted to life imprisonment, subsequently to thirty years and eventually to fifteen, but it took three years to reach that verdict. Afterwards she was transferred to Fordon Prison in the town of Bydgoszcz, west of Warsaw, and was permitted occasional visits by an embassy representative. Life for her as well as for other women prisoners was exceptionally harsh, as most of them were classified as 'political' prisoners and as such were treated as enemies of the state. Many of the prison guards were either former criminals or Ukrainians who had served their former masters, the Germans, in the same capacity and were given a free hand in the way they treated prisoners. Cruelty and torture was rife. For example, female prisoners would be made to stand all day long during deliberately prolonged bouts of interrogation and if they either fainted or begged to sit down they were then offered a stool turned upside down. In some of the worst cases they were suspended from the ceiling by one leg and subjected to the cruellest and most degrading humiliation imaginable. Mother was made to stand for twenty-four hours at one interrogation after which she suffered a fractured ankle following a fall. Having to endure humiliation and insults because of her British nationality was the least hard thing to bear. With this sort of treatment many women unable to endure it any longer died, became permanently injured or went mad. And the rest of the world at large appeared not to know a thing about it.

Then, in 1956, seven years after her incarceration, the Polish government issued a qualified amnesty to certain groups of political prisoner. My mother was amongst the lucky ones to be released. Word of it was quickly relayed to us, the stipulation being that she was to leave the country immediately. Taken care of by the British embassy in Warsaw, within two days she was put on board an RAF transport aircraft and flown to Northolt aerodrome in west London. We were there to meet her on that extremely moving occasion. Considering her nightmare ordeal, she emerged from it both physically and mentally in fair shape, which she put down to an iron constitution and an unflagging belief that one day we would all be reunited. However, as I knew well from my own experiences, once over the initial euphoria, the business of readjustment to a totally different way of life took over. For Mother this must have been difficult and at times painful, but when all was said and done, the mental scars were the ones to remain with her the longest.

By this time I had been in the employ of a large company in south-east England, married Wyn and become the father of two sons, Christopher and David.

I have not been back to Poland since. Except for my memories, I have no ties left there. To have seen Poland dominated by an alien race since 1945 was not the real Poland I would have wanted to see, although the people would not have changed. A Polish friend told me I was wrong to have seen things that way, that I should have gone back, and she was probably right. Since those days Poland has become a free nation and I may yet return to see it and remember.

Epilogue

At the end of the war, Tom's parents became separated. His father worked for many years in public relations with the British Council. This work carried him into his eightieth year and he died at the age of ninety four.

Tom's mother, despite all the ill treatment and privation suffered during her incarceration in the communist prison, emerged as a very balanced and stable personality. She lived out her years peacefully among her family and friends until her death in London in 1981.

Since his early retirement in 1981, Tom took up many of his interests seriously. He enjoys porcelain and china restoration, reading, painting and, having moved to Cornwall in 1987, boating as well. He is also a grandfather.

Sadly, his wife Wyn passed away before the completion of this book.

He is not bitter or angry, but finds it sad that today there is still so much hatred and cruelty evident in the world.

For a time he and his second wife, Gillian, lived in the beautiful city of Bath, but moved back to Cornwall to carry on with their favourite pursuits.